FUNDRAISER A

FUNDRAISER A

MY FIGHT FOR FREEDOM AND JUSTICE

Robert Blagojevich

NIU PRESS / *DeKalb, IL*

NIU Press / DeKalb, IL

Northern Illinois University Press, DeKalb, Illinois 60115

© 2015 by Northern Illinois University Press

All rights reserved

Printed in the United States

24 23 22 21 20 19 18 17 16 15   1 2 3 4 5

978-0-87580-488-0 (cloth)

978-1-60909-174-3 (e-book)

Design by Shaun Allshouse

Cover by Yuni Dorr

Library of Congress Cataloging-in-Publication Data

is available online at http://catalog.loc.gov

Contents

Acknowledgments

I would like to thank the following people for their help and support:

Many thanks to Steve Fiffer, a Guggenheim Fellowship winner, for his editorial assistance and encouragement. You are the best at what you do!

Thank you Linda Manning and the Northern Illinois University Press for believing in my story and giving it a chance to be read.

Michael Ettinger, Cheryl Schroeder, and Robyn Molaro, my "Guardian Angels" thank you for standing with me during the toughest challenge of my life. I didn't have a chance against the full force of the United States government without your legal expertise, determination, fearlessness, and good humor.

Eric Thrailkill, Tom Thrailkill, and Andy Martin, you guys were unconditionally there for me when I needed you. I'll never forget what you did for me.

To my wife Julie and my son Alex for your unwavering belief in me. I love you both!

Foreword

The trial of Illinois Governor Rod Blagojevich and his brother Robert was national news. In Chicago, it was daily headline news. It was the latest in a series of "trials of the century," especially for Illinoisans who were about to see the third of their last four governors go to jail for corruption. I watched the trial at relatively close range because, as a law professor, I was using the trial in my classes and, as a frequent media commentator, I had to distill what happened into manageable sound bites or brief commentary. When Robert told me he was writing this book I was thrilled, not only because of the enticing prospect of getting to know what really happened, but also because of the important social interest served by a close-up look at what many saw as a federal abuse of power in the criminal justice system. The government's prosecution of Robert was in all senses wrongful but, nonetheless, prosecutors tenaciously pursued charges long after it was obvious that Robert was innocent. The arrogance of that use of power is a central theme of this book.

In *Fundraiser A*, we now get the story in dramatic and sometimes riveting fashion from the defendant himself. As Robert told the media after the verdict, "I have lived through the most surreal experience anyone could live through. This has been, from the beginning, a slow bleed both financially, emotionally, and otherwise." After reading Robert's complete story, I found him to be an astute if sometimes flabbergasted observer who still doesn't quite believe this happened to him and his family. The criminal justice system in this country is flawed, and the power given to prosecutors is excessive. There's nothing new in those observations, but to really understand why this happened to Robert is simple: it's the story of over-reaching prosecutorial power and the adversarial system gone bad.

Chicago has certainly seen its share of circus-like trials, but this one promised to be the best, even without any dead bodies. Right from the day the US attorney announced the indictment, he promised a story of corruption that would "make Lincoln roll over in his grave." We all waited for the smoking guns, the stories of drugs, sex, lies, and greed sure to come.

While the governor was talking on tape (forty-five days' worth of tape), his main advisors—John Wyma, Chris Kelly, Bob Greenlee, John Harris, and Alonzo Monk—were talking directly to the government because they had legal problems of their own. Chiefs of staff, advisors, and deputy governors—colleagues who had worked closely with Rod for years—were the witnesses the government intended to use to supplement the tapes. Some would be offered legal immunity in exchange for their testimony against Blagojevich, some would start talking right away to save their own skin, and one would be sent back to the Blagojevich campaign headquarters to spy.

Dropped into this maelstrom and soon to become an important part of this story was Robert Blagojevich, the conservative Republican businessman from Tennessee who, to many observers, always seemed to be an innocent in a den of predators. The governor had asked Robert to raise funds for four months before the 2010 off-year elections. Robert had no political experience, didn't really know anybody in Illinois, didn't have a very good relationship with his brother, and didn't like his brother's "too liberal and fiscally irresponsible" politics, but, nonetheless, said he would do it. Why? This is a question he continues to ask himself. Because Rod needed somebody he could trust? Because he hoped to repair a strained relationship? Because, as a businessman, he knew about money and could keep the accounts? In any event, he left behind his wife, home, and business in Tennessee to come to Chicago to do something he had never done before—fundraise for a politician.

Why Robert agreed to step into a campaign already known to be under investigation is another judgment for the reader to make. Conventional wisdom would mandate treating the governor at a very long arm's length. But this was his brother. And for the next year Robert was at the heart of the biggest corruption case in many years. Now, with this book, we find out all the behind-the-scenes action. As he notes in his trial journal, "As a citizen, I can't believe this is still happening to me, and no one in power cares—unchecked unrestricted power."

Robert Blagojevich was surprisingly naïve about the FBI, the federal prosecutors, and the criminal justice system. He thought he could just sit down with the FBI and clear this whole thing up and be back on his way. Didn't they know that it was just Rod talking and talking? It never crossed his mind that the feds might attempt to use him, to make him flip and testify against his brother. It never occurred to him that maybe he and the governor would plead guilty to something in a "package" deal. It never occurred to him that nobody in the government really cared that he was innocent. This case was too big for that. Luckily, Robert found the right criminal defense lawyer who told him, in no uncertain terms, that this trial is not about "clearing anything up." It's a war, led by "self-righteous, zealot extremists," and, Robert, you're in it.

This is what happens to almost everybody who enters the criminal justice system for the first time—guilty or innocent. The government speaks, and everything changes. The government uses its vast power and unlimited resources, and the defendant bleeds. Financial ruin is almost a certainty. Robert Blagojevich spent over three-quarters of a million dollars on his defense. As he said, while describing the loss of his business and his home, "we were essentially in the process of dismantling thirty years of hard work." He's lucky he had the money.

Most defendants can't make bond like Robert did. Most lose their jobs, possessions, and sometimes their families into the black abyss of seeking justice. Many eventually go to prison—African Americans more than others—where they face so much more than tangible loss. The loss of dignity and freedom, the utter humiliation, the loss of self-respect. Robert was spared that disaster, but he tells us how it was constantly on his mind and how his brother never seemed to think about it.

Robert learned more than he ever wanted to know about the criminal justice system. He learned that more than 95 percent (depending on the jurisdiction) of all defendants plead guilty. Only an infinitesimal 4–5 percent choose to fight back. He was shocked to learn that in no way was it to be a fair fight. The government decides whom to charge and what the charges will be. The prosecutors have the FBI, the DEA, the crime laboratories, and all the resources of the federal government. They have the power of the investigatory subpoena, which usually means that they get to examine and threaten all witnesses, whether or not before a grand jury, and long before the defense even has a chance to talk with them. He learned that the government can take as long as they want to investigate, and that, even if they decide not to prosecute, they can change their mind and keep the case open for a very long time. He learned that, even when a case is dropped, the government doesn't say "you're innocent," and certainly not "we're sorry we did this to your life."

He learned that a jury of peers is a group of people with whom you have little in common, who are placed in judgment of you by a judge who asks most of the questions and then tells them about law they probably can't understand. He learned that, while the Supreme Court was considering whether a "theft of honest services" charge (one of the charges pending in this case) is unconstitutionally vague, the prosecutor can just strike preemptively and file more charges in a superseding indictment so that whatever the Supreme Court ultimately decides, it won't make any difference.

He learned that when something good for the defense showed up in the tapes, his lawyers couldn't use it unless the judge said they could, and the judge was prosecution-minded. People don't realize that the judge who presides over a case—the largest percentage of whom are former prosecutors themselves—effectively decides how the case will progress. Robert tells us of how perturbed he was about many of the judge's rulings, in addition to the judge's habit of usually being forty-five minutes late for the start of court, which Robert estimates cost him $15,000 in attorney time.

One of the biggest surprises to Robert was that the criminal trial is a shell game. Neither side knows what the other is going to do. Are they going to call this particular witness, and, if so, when, to say what, and what will the judge allow on cross-examination? To be fair, the defense plays the same game—not telling the government if the defendant will testify or even if there will be a defense. And Robert watched, often comparing the process to his life in business. If he had gone to business meetings with as little definite information about what would be on the agenda, he would have considered himself woefully unprepared.

Robert's layman's eye gives us a fresh, honest, and forthright perspective on the inner workings of one of the most complex and high-profile criminal cases in recent memory. That's what is so refreshing about this book. I have since met Robert on more than one occasion. He has lectured to my classes. He is an utterly believable but now thoroughly angry citizen who wants nothing more now than to tell America how unfairly he was treated by a system that allows such brutal treatment as a matter of course.

The subtext to the book, of course, is Robert's relationship with his brother. The press tried constantly to use the thinness of their relationship to turn the trial into a long-running soap opera. Were the brothers close? Were they even speaking to each other? Or was this relationship one more casualty of the stupid, wasteful, and useless prosecution against Robert— a broken family relationship. Another example of the adversarial system gone bad.

Leonard L. Cavise
Professor of Law
DePaul College of Law

Prologue
April 14, 2009

This is what it's like to be arraigned by the US government on criminal charges that carry a potential sentence of five to seven years in prison.

You enter the Dirksen Federal Building in downtown Chicago, pass through security, get on the elevator, and exit on the twenty-fifth floor. You run a gauntlet of US marshals, newspaper reporters, and television sketch artists, and then enter a side door into a conference room outside the courtroom.

While you wait to be called to the courtroom, you move to the floor-to-ceiling windows and look to the plaza below. You wish you were one of the people down there going about his "normal" business—because for the last four months nothing in your life has been normal.

You exchange smiles with your lawyers, who are costing you a lot of money. You pace. You look out the window again.

When you are finally called before the judge, you feel dwarfed in a room the size of a high school gymnasium. The seal of the US District Court for the Northern District of Illinois on the wall behind the judge stares down at you, a reminder that this is the home team's court. You are more than aware that your opponent, the US attorney, wins 96 percent of the time.

Your lawyer senses your discomfort and motions for you to take a seat at the defense table. The prosecution's table is closer to the jury box, more evidence of the home field advantage.

While you wait for the proceeding to begin you try to clear your mind. You visualize yourself testifying . . . and doing well. You imagine the jury understanding that you did nothing wrong, that you are collateral damage, an innocent player in the government's attempt to convict yet another governor of the state of Illinois, your brother.

And suddenly, you feel calm and confident. I can survive this, you think to yourself. This is a test of my character and will and faith, and I am going to win because I've done nothing wrong. I'm a businessman from Nashville with no experience in politics who responded to his brother's request for help in raising campaign funds. Total time on the job: four months!

Your character is tested sixty seconds later when your codefendant, your brother, the recently impeached former governor, enters the courtroom. You haven't seen each other in four months, haven't spoken for weeks. Initially, he looks slightly disoriented and lost. But then he switches into campaign mode, shaking hands with spectators as he comes down the aisle. He even tries to shake hands with a prosecutor. She turns her back on him and walks away.

You steel yourself for your reunion as he approaches the defense table. You expect him to extend his hand, give you a hug. You expect that he'll apologize for dragging you into this mess. None of that happens. Instead, he leans over the table and says, "You don't look like a criminal to me."

You don't smile or laugh. This day is not a joke. You look at him without emotion and say, "You look like you need a haircut."

The judge, James B. Zagel of the US District Court for the Northern District of Illinois, enters and you rise. Then you are called to the bench to hear the charges filed against you. You stand there with your attorneys and your brother and his attorneys, and you raise your right hand and are sworn in by the court clerk. Looking at your brother, you wonder what your parents would have thought of this moment, seeing their sons arraigned in federal court together. You know they would have believed in your innocence, but you also know this would have broken their hearts.

The judge's first question surprises you. He asks if you are using drugs. "No," you say. Then he asks if you understand the charges. You say, "Yes," and on your attorney's advice waive the reading of the eighty-page indictment. The judge then asks his final question: how do you plead? You say, "Not guilty," firmly, with conviction, as does your brother.

And that's it. After just a few minutes the proceeding is over. Your day as a newly arraigned defendant, however, is just beginning.

You go to meet your case manager, the same person who interviewed you on the phone a week earlier, requesting all your financial information. You turn in your passport and sign an affidavit attesting that you own no firearms.

The calm and confidence you felt earlier disappears. These proceedings begin to make you feel like a criminal. You fight the feeling. You know you've always tried to do the right thing, have never been convicted of anything. You know you are innocent, but these indignities are wearing you down. They are wearing down your wife and son, too. Your friends. They are decimating the business you built and your bank account. Your health.

Just when you think you can go home and decompress, your case manager hands you a plastic cup. "We need a urine sample," he explains. Telling the judge you weren't taking any drugs is not good enough.

In the men's room, the commode in the corner is surrounded by waist-high mirrors. You can't help but laugh at the absurdity of this. You think back to your twenty-two years of active duty and reserve service in the US Army. You not only had to give your own sample, you administered "piss tests" to the troops from time to time.

As you stand in front of the toilet, a surprise. Your case manager turns his back to give you a moment of privacy. It is the first time during this ordeal that a representative of your government has shown you any humanity. You record the scene. Later, you will call him to thank him for such a small but important gesture.

Next stop: the US marshal's office, where you are to be fingerprinted and photographed. The office is protected by heavy-duty bars not unlike what you'd find in a prison. Hearing the hard clang of the barred door closing behind you is a sobering reality check.

The marshal tells you that he had the "honor of fingerprinting the governor when he came through." You sense he's trying to be nice, but you find it strange that he would consider it an honor to process your brother. You've fallen through the looking glass. You have to visit the offices of the Federal Bureau of Investigation (FBI), a ten-minute drive from the Loop, for further processing. Before leaving the Dirksen Building, your attorney tells you it would be a good idea to stop and speak with the reporters who have gathered in a designated area in the lobby. You're surprised that he doesn't tell you what to say. Knowing you could screw things up, you are apprehensive. You are also worried that your anger over being indicted might get the best of you. Potential jurors will be watching the news. You don't want to come across as a hothead.

You avoid saying anything you'll regret by sticking to basic themes. You say you're prepared to cope with the charges and work through them. You stress that you are an innocent man and look forward to getting your name back.

When a reporter asks about your relationship with your brother, your attorney jumps in and saves you from having to answer. "It's obvious this kind of situation would cause strain on any relationship, but everything is fine between the brothers," he says. Not really, you think.

At the FBI offices on Roosevelt Road, Agent James J. Cicchini escorts you to get your fingerprints and mug shot for the bureau's files. You recognize him as the agent who woke you up at 6:21 a.m. on December 9, 2008. On that morning, as he was presenting you with subpoenas regarding the Friends of Blagojevich campaign, his fellow agents were arresting your brother. He is very polite, but you are in no mood to talk. He is the enemy.

While Agent Cicchini waits for a technician to take your prints and pictures, you can't help overhearing a conversation he has with a female agent. They talk happily about their kids. It reminds you of a conversation a couple of carefree neighbors would have over their backyard fence.

You wonder if they realize how hard it is to hear them talking about normal life. You'd like to tell them you don't want to hear this conversation on the day you have been arraigned, turned in your passport, peed into a cup to prove you aren't on drugs, been fingerprinted, and had your mug shot taken twice. But you don't say anything.

When you are finally home, you take a good look at yourself in the mirror. You realize how much you've aged over the last 126 days. Your face looks tired and worn out. You realize you are one man going up against the full force, weight, and reputation of the US government, of arguably the most powerful US attorney's office in the country. You are fighting Patrick Fitzgerald, the prosecutor who put Scooter Libby away and jailed *New York Times* reporter Judith Miller, and whose assistants put Governor George Ryan away. Patrick Fitzgerald, the man who, on the day your brother was arrested, announced, "Lincoln would roll over in his grave if he knew that the Senate seat vacated by Barack Obama was being auctioned off to the highest bidder."

You shake your head and then ask yourself the same questions you ask every day: how the hell did this happen? When's it gonna all end? And most important: how's it gonna all end?

FUNDRAISER A

CHAPTER ONE

Brother's Keeper

Knowledge of the investigation was widespread when Mr. Blagojevich ran for re-election in 2006, and he still won 50 percent of the vote. Some political experts thought Judy Baar Topinka, then the Republican state treasurer, was weak opposition to Mr. Blagojevich's one-on-one charm. And Mr. Blagojevich spent $27 million, nearly three times what Ms. Topinka spent. (*New York Times*, December 14, 2008)

It began with a phone call. On July 4, 2008, my brother—in the middle of his second term as governor of the fifth largest state in the United States—asked if I would come to his home to discuss something "in person." Although I lived in Nashville, I was spending a portion of the summer in Chicago with my wife Julie so we could be near our twenty-five-year-old son Alex, who lived and worked in the city. I had no idea what Rod wanted to see me about, but I agreed to meet. Soon, he and I and his wife Patti were sitting in the book-lined study of his comfortable home in the Ravenswood neighborhood on Chicago's north side.

It quickly became apparent that this was a business meeting, not a social engagement. Rod wanted my help. He was up for reelection in November 2010. If he chose to run again, he said, he had to have a meaningful campaign war chest to scare off any potential opposition within his own party. He told me he needed someone he could trust to head up his fundraising. That someone was me. Would I be willing to put my own business on hold for the latter half of 2008 and take over the reins of Friends of Blagojevich (FOB)?

Trust was the operative word. It was no secret that throughout most of his tenure, Rod and his administration had been under investigation by the Department of Justice (DOJ). Allegations were swirling that people working on Rod's behalf during his campaign and after the election were playing fast and loose with the rules, perhaps with his knowledge and blessing.

In 2005 Rod's father-in-law, the Chicago alderman Richard Mell, had told the media that Rod's chief fundraiser, Chris Kelly, had traded appointments to state boards and commissions in return for $50,000 in donations to the campaign. Although Mell retracted the accusation under threat of a lawsuit, the damage was done—not just to Rod's image on the eve of his first bid for reelection, but also to the family dynamic.

Two years later Kelly was indicted on tax fraud charges unrelated to Rod. Some said, however, that the prosecution would look favorably upon him if he provided information about the governor's activities. I'll relate the sad story of Chris Kelly in chapter 3.

In 2006 the DOJ had indicted another of Rod's friends, Tony Rezko, on charges of public corruption. Rezko, a major campaign contributor and fundraiser, was alleged to have used his clout with the governor and his connections to Illinois boards and commissions to extort kickbacks from businesses seeking contracts from the state. About a month before Rod approached me, Rezko was convicted on sixteen of the twenty-four charges brought against him. Sentencing was pending, and there was talk that he might cut a deal with the government by implicating Rod in this "pay-for-play" scheming and testify against him.

The media was also on Rod's case. In 2007 the *Chicago Tribune* had called for an amendment to the Illinois Constitution that would allow for the recall of elected officials. Translation? Governor Blagojevich should be booted out of office because of the scandals surrounding his administration and "his reckless financial stewardship, his dictatorial antics, [and] his penchant for creating political enemies."

I was aware of the chatter that the feds had Rod in their sights, but I never thought the stories of his involvement in corrupt activities to be credible. He was my brother, and although he might have been guilty of egotism, narcissism, and any number of other isms, he was not, I believed, a crook. A Blagojevich would not condone or approve of such a breach in ethics or betray his obligation to honorably serve the people of his state.

With this mind-set, I listened to Rod and Patti's pitch to have me take over FOB. The investigations were behind them, they told me. Rod went on to stress that at this point in his political career, I was the only one whom he could rely on to fundraise for him. He believed—rightly so—that I would not do anything inappropriate or illegal.

My initial response was measured. I knew nothing about political fundraising. Moreover, I had established a good life for Julie and myself in Nashville. We had everything we needed and, for the most part, wanted. I was a small business owner, and things were going well enough that I had the spare time to get involved in community activities, including heading the board for YCAP, a program within the YMCA that provided support and programs for at-risk youths in Nashville.

Saying yes might have been easier had I been a fan of Rod's politics and policies. But I wasn't. As a moderate Republican, I found much of his legislative agenda too liberal and fiscally irresponsible. If I'd been registered in Illinois, I might have had a hard time voting for him.

"I'm not sure I want to take this on, but I'm not saying I won't," I told Rod and Patti. "Let me talk to Julie." My wife would be the one most inconvenienced if I said yes. I would be in Chicago while she remained in Nashville continuing to work part-time at Vanderbilt University, where she helped prepare the library's budget. I didn't want anything lost in translation, so I told Rod I wanted him to explain everything to her so she would have the same information I had. He agreed, and we set a date.

I was not indicted for bad judgment. If that in itself were a crime, our prisons would be even more overcrowded than they are today. But it's fair to ask, why, with such a cloud hanging over Rod and his fundraising activities, would I even consider interrupting my life to join such an enterprise?

The short answer is that blood is thicker than water. To understand Rod, to understand me, to understand the relationship between Rod and me and why I eventually decided to help my brother, you must understand the Blagojevich family. I'd also ask that you put yourself in my shoes for a moment and consider what you would do if a sibling in need—even a problematic sibling—asked for your assistance.

Julie, whom I married in 1977, understood that dynamic. "This will give you guys a chance to get close again," she said.

Rod and I had been close as boys and into adulthood. But by the time our mother passed away in January 1999, we had drifted apart. Living in different cities while building our own careers and tending to our own families didn't help, but there were other reasons. We were two very different personalities. Our parents understood this. Both my mother and my father, who died in 1988, had expressed the wish that when they were gone Rod and I would be available to help the other if needed.

Truth be told, it always seemed that Rod needed much more help than I did. Julie, therefore, saw this as an opportunity for me to honor my parents' wish. She also thought that Rod would finally come to appreciate what a capable and accomplished brother he had, one whom he really didn't take the time to get to know. Hey, dating back to Cain and Abel, relationships between brothers have been complicated.

Some family history: growing up on the northwest side of Chicago in the Cragin neighborhood, a lower middle-class area that was in the early stages of racial integration, Rod and I were tied at the hip. When we weren't in school, we ran carefree through the streets with our friends. We played whatever sport was in season, dreaming about playing at the professional level some day.

Neither one of us made it. I played football, basketball, and baseball at Lane Technical College Prep, then went off to the University of Tampa to play baseball. Unfortunately, I blew out my arm. Career over.

Rod started at Lane Tech, but after failing to make the basketball team, he transferred to Foreman High, where he made the team. He excelled in boxing, competing as a middleweight in the Golden Gloves competition. Final career record: six wins, one loss.

Sixteen months older than Rod, I was always the more physically and emotionally mature one. My father told me I was responsible for Rod's well-being and to look out for him when we were outside playing. He knew Rod had a quick temper and might say things that could get him into trouble with the wrong kid if he weren't careful. I had no problem defending my brother when he needed it. In fact I'd eagerly jump in to help him. Sometimes, however, it was hard to intervene when I knew he was the cause of the problem.

We were the sons of loving Serbian parents who sacrificed greatly to ensure their boys had a better life. They asked much of us, but gave even more. They demanded our respect and received it—not just out of deference but because they earned it.

My father Rade, a former officer in the Yugoslav army and a prisoner of war for four years in German prison camps, had fled the newly established regime led by Marshal Tito after World War II. With the help and sponsorship of the Serbian Orthodox Monastery in Libertyville, Illinois, he emigrated to the United States, seeking freedom from communism.

My father never forgot that it was the US Army that liberated him from prison camp and was always grateful to Dwight Eisenhower, allied commander, for his freedom. His gratitude manifested itself years later after he had become a US citizen, when he cast his first presidential vote for Eisenhower. He became a staunch Republican, and Rod and I followed his example when we were old enough to register.

I remained a Republican until I became disenchanted with the party when I was indicted and declared myself an Independent. Rod, on the other hand, did a one-eighty when he decided to get involved in Illinois politics, becoming a Democrat to run for office. His newly found liberalism never sat well with me because he had always been a fan of Republican politicians, particularly Ronald Reagan. When Rod was in college, he headed up Students for Reagan and even had his picture taken with the candidate at an invitation-only luncheon for volunteers.

One hot summer night, while I was in high school, my father invited Rod and me to come visit him at the steel foundry where he was working the night shift to earn a little more money per hour. I've never forgotten the sacrifice he made working in that sweltering, depressing, dirty place to give us a life he never had. As he took us on a tour, with red-hot flames spitting out from the furnaces he had to tend, he told us he could get us jobs working there after graduation, or he would continue to work to pay for our college. The choice was a no-brainer for both of us.

As noted, I went to the University of Tampa, where I earned a three-year ROTC scholarship and then a master's degree from Florida State University. After starting at Tampa because our parents wanted us close together, Rod transferred to Northwestern. He then earned a law degree from Pepperdine University in Malibu, California.

My mother Millie was a first-generation American who worked for the Chicago Transit Authority as a ticket agent. She helped to moderate the Serbian nationalism my father proudly maintained until his death. The daughter of immigrants from what is now Bosnia-Herzegovina, she wanted us to honor our heritage, but made sure we were Americans first. We grew up with a wonderful blend of Old and New World values, trying to live up to our parents' expectations that we be well-educated, honorable Americans of Serbian descent.

"Son, never brag about yourself. Let others do the talking about what you've done," my mother told me when I was young. That's stuck with me and served me well—as a young officer in the Army and in my business career.

I'm not sure if my mother ever had the same conversation with Rod. He was not an outright bragger, but he was far better at self-promotion than I when we were growing up. He was always the charming, affable guy when he needed to be, a young man able to attract the attention he craved.

Rod was the one who sang solos in the Serbian youth orchestra my father forced us to join so we could honor our cultural heritage. I sat playing my tamburitza, a mandolin-like Serbian instrument, my heart pounding for him, hoping he didn't mess up. To my relief, he always did a nice job, and the crowd loved him. He still has a fine singing voice.

Long before the trial, starting when we were kids, I worried about Rod, fearing that he may have been missing something in his personality. He was tormented and restless at times and threw temper tantrums when things didn't fall his way. He was so moody that my mother confessed her worry to me.

When Rod and I were teens, Mom asked me if I could persuade my mentor, my high school history teacher Carl Sambo, to help Rod too. She saw what a great influence Mr. Sambo was having on me, so she invited him over to dinner to see if he could connect with Rod. We had a very pleasant evening, but the desired relationship was never established. Unfortunately my mother never had the wherewithal to have Rod evaluated for what might have been causing his temperamental behavior.

Our occupations fit our personalities. Influenced by my father's military background, I was in ROTC at Tampa. I then selected Eastern European Studies for my master's with the intention of becoming an area specialist in the Army. My five and a half years of active duty were spent primarily as a platoon leader with the responsibility to protect and deploy three Pershing nuclear missiles, and as an aide-de-camp to a one-star brigadier general. When I left the Army to enter the business world in Nashville, I continued for seventeen years in the reserves, retiring as a lieutenant colonel in 2001.

In my first real civilian job, I worked as a financial planner, helping small business owners with their investment and estate planning needs. Then the largest Nashville-based bank recruited me to be a part of the sales team for their newly formed trust company. Eventually I became the president of the investment and brokerage arm of the bank in addition to being the executive officer responsible for the $3.5 billion trust group.

In the fall of 1997, the bank's board sent me to, of all places, Tampa to become the president and CEO of its subsidiary, Invest Financial Corporation, a nationwide brokerage business. Two years later, the bank was acquired by a much larger regional bank, which then decided to sell Invest Financial. I agreed to stay on and help with the transition. Soon we were acquired by an insurance company, and I had my third boss in less than five years.

All too familiar with the flurry of mergers and acquisitions in the financial services sector, I realized it was a matter of time before my job would be in jeopardy. Wanting to control my own destiny, I began preparing for a smooth transition into small business ownership. When I chanced upon an infomercial by a real estate guru named Carlton Sheets, I was inspired to look into the possibility of buying income-producing apartments.

After reading up on the business, I found a local commercial real estate broker and began buying small apartment complexes in Tampa. Soon I left the corporate world on my terms and moved back to Nashville, where I continued in the real estate world and reestablished myself in the local business community.

Rod chose a very different career path. Long interested in politics, he had been ready to jump into the fray after graduating from Northwestern. My father, however, persuaded him that a law degree would be of great benefit. When Rod returned from Pepperdine, Dad remained involved in charting his future, asking Ed "Fast Eddie" Vrdolyak, a prominent alderman on the south side of Chicago, to talk to Rod about a job.

In the end, it wasn't Alderman Vrdolyak, but rather Alderman Mell, who launched Rod into politics. He took Rod under his wing and then into his family. As I grew my business career, Rod grew his political career. After starting out as a Cook County assistant state's attorney, he was elected to the Illinois state legislature in 1992. Four years later, voters sent him to Congress.

In 2002 Rod was elected governor of Illinois. It's fair to say he was a polarizing figure—loved by the common man and woman, disliked by fellow politicians and much of the press. His supporters pointed to a legislative agenda that included ethics reform, prohibition of discrimination based on sexual preference, free transit passes for seniors, and the All Kids program, which would provide universal, affordable, and comprehensive health care for children. Detractors cited contracts for contributions, fiscal irresponsibility, and inability to work with the Illinois legislature.

Despite the allegations concerning illicit fundraising, Rod was re-elected in 2006. Now here we were two years later, with a third term a real possibility. Would I be a part of the effort?

We had our family dinner to discuss his request at a nice neighborhood restaurant on Lincoln Avenue. Rod and Patti talked with Julie most of the time while I tried to entertain our young nieces Amy and Annie. A couple of days later, I told Rod that Julie had given her blessing. I would take the job with two qualifiers. One, I would not play people for contributions. And two, he and I had to get along and not argue about differences that would likely come up between us . . . as they always did. He agreed.

Now all I had to do was learn everything I could about political fund-raising, keep the pay-for-play sharks at bay, and cross my fingers that the feds had indeed lost interest in taking down yet another Illinois governor.

CHAPTER TWO

Fundraising 101

Illinois has frequently been called the "wild west" of American campaigns based on its largely unregulated campaign finance system. . . . the state has few restrictions on donors that might benefit from some aspect of state government policy including contractors, lobbyists, corporations, unions and industry associations.

This limitless system has nurtured a political climate dominated by "big money" campaign contributions and the problem continues to grow. Rod Blagojevich made history during his six years as governor by collecting 435 individual contributions exceeding $25,000. (http://www.ilcampaign.org)

Two million dollars. That was the figure that Rod expected me to raise by the end of 2008. The election wasn't for another two years, so why the deadline? In May—just as the Rezko trial concluded—the General Assembly had passed legislation restricting campaign contributions between contractors doing business or wishing to do business with the state, and the elected officials in charge of administering their contracts. The governor, lieutenant governor, treasurer, and comptroller could no longer receive donations from businesses with state contracts totaling $50,000 or more.

Known as the "pay to play" ban, the law was aimed directly at Rod, who had been successful in raising large sums from several such businesses. Saying he wanted the reform to be even more encompassing, my brother had threatened to veto the bill.

Some legislators thought Rod was being disingenuous. Some legislators just didn't like him. Some legislators didn't want reform to affect their own fundraising. Whatever their motives, they pledged to override his veto and did so in September.

The legislation was to go into effect on January 1, 2009. Thus the deadline: Rod wanted to raise as much money as possible before the end of year.

I was to start working at FOB on August 1. Raising $2 million in five months seemed like an unrealistic goal to me. In the first seven months of the year, Rod hadn't raised anything near that much. Potential donors were clearly wary with the feds looking over their shoulders and books.

Before I began work, Rod suggested I talk to several people who had helped with or were familiar with his fundraising efforts, notably Bill Quinlan, John Wyma, and Lon Monk. All told me that I would never raise two million. They noted that this was a presidential election year and big donors were more disposed to contribute to the candidate of their choice for that office than a potential candidate for governor two years down the road. This was especially true in Illinois, as Barack Obama was the state's favorite son.

Quinlan, who served as Rod's state legal counsel, was the first person with whom I spoke. My only fundraising experience was in the nonprofit sector—raising money for the Nashville Red Cross and local YMCA—so we discussed the dos and don'ts of political fundraising in Illinois. I had my own idea of how I should behave but had to learn the ground rules.

Quinlan's instruction sharpened my approach with a clear and unequivocal directive to never accept a campaign contribution in exchange for a government action. We had a productive, practical discussion of how to apply this fundamental principle when interacting with potential donors. I never intended to play anyone for a donation, and with Quinlan's instruction, I was able to make a very clear distinction on how to fundraise properly. When I began meeting with people I made it perfectly clear that I had no connection with state government, even though I was Rod's brother.

Quinlan warned me that people would push the ethical envelope and that I should be prepared for it. As it turned out, he was right. I had numerous overtures from potential donors about getting something in return for a contribution. I never wavered, not one time, in my determination to resist the temptation. If you were to listen to all my fundraising calls that the FBI wiretapped, you would know that I properly and ethically conducted myself in every situation.

Quinlan generously offered to help me anytime I felt uncertain about how to deal with a donor. Through the course of the next four months, I called him numerous times to talk about fundraising to make sure I was doing it right. I thought we had a good and comfortable working relationship. He always gave me good advice, and I respected his opinion.

My brother also wanted me to speak with Wyma, who had been his chief of staff in Washington when he was in Congress. Prior to joining Rod, Wyma had worked for then-congressman, now senator Chuck Schumer of New York. Rod felt Wyma had provided some good "inside the beltway" perspective that Rod lacked when coming into office. We'd previously met, and I thought Wyma was a good guy. He had even let Julie and me stay in his Washington condo on a visit when Rod was in Congress. I knew him as a trusted and committed staffer who had moved to Chicago to work for Rod in his first campaign for governor. After Rod was elected, Wyma leveraged his relationship with the governor into a successful lobbying business, representing health care providers and other interest groups in Springfield. (Wyma was also a friend of Rahm Emanuel, who had succeeded Rod as the representative from the fifth Congressional District of Illinois.)

I met with Wyma in July at Caffe DeLuca, a restaurant in Chicago's Bucktown neighborhood. When I asked if he thought I should take the job at FOB, he said he thought I would be a good fit and didn't see my lack of political fundraising experience as a deal breaker. His opinion was important, as I thought he was smart, realistic, and level-headed. He didn't seem to be consumed by ego or an inflated impression of himself, which often comes with financial success. This allowed him to work well with people.

After encouraging me to take the job, he committed to helping me in any way he could. In the ensuing months he played a prominent role in my fundraising activities. Moreover, as we now know, he was the informant who gave the FBI probable cause to get a federal judge to approve wiretaps for my cell phone, campaign phones, and my brother's home phone, as well as bugs in the campaign office.

Lon Monk was also on my "must-talk-to" list. He had been Rod's chief of staff during his first term as governor, and had chaired FOB for Rod's two runs for the office. He was Rod's closest friend, as well as having been his law school roommate and a groomsman in his wedding. He, too, was an Illinois lobbyist using his experience and contacts in the administration to assist his clients working with state government.

Monk, like Wyma, believed that I could help Rod as a trusted, honest fundraiser. He seemed to be a trustworthy guy and I valued his opinion. He was a devoted family man with three kids and a lovely wife.

Nobody with whom I spoke told me that when I formally took responsibility as chairman of FOB, I had to report my appointment to the Illinois Election Commission. Such information wouldn't have prevented me from taking the job, but I would have liked to know that I'd be more in the public eye than I'd expected. I suppose I was naïve not to assume that the political and regulatory establishment would know I was now responsible for fundraising for my brother. At any rate, once I did report my appointment, I felt that the bull's-eye placed on me by anyone investigating fundraising activities for FOB had suddenly grown larger.

Jeanne Arens, whom I was replacing at FOB, had been communicating to Rod and Monk that she was burned out with fundraising and wanted to do something else. Monk had an established relationship with Jeanne that predated me and was tasked to tell her about my new role and responsibilities. This communication of the change was neither timely nor effective and caused problems for me.

When I started going regularly to the FOB office in mid-July to ramp up and be ready to go on August 1, no one had told Jeanne about my new role, so I had to inform her. Needless to say, this created a strain between us initially. Fortunately, Jeanne was professional and agreed to help me until she formally left the payroll in early October.

What a way to start! Prompted by the lack of communication, I had a heated argument with Rod about how poorly this had been handled and the difficult position it put me in. He said he had his reasons for not initially telling Jeanne and I had to understand that he knew more about what was happening there than I. This made no sense to me. His demonstrated ineptitude in this little personnel matter was my first clear indicator of his poor management acumen.

At that time, I thought about leaving even before I started, and in retrospect I should have bailed then. I stayed because I had committed to work for him at least through the end of the year and had submitted the semiannual fundraising D2 report to the election commission. I figured I could deal with the frustrations of working with Rod for four months and then move on.

I quickly became familiar with the fund's balance sheet and noted we had roughly two and a half million dollars on hand. I told Rod that

Monk, Wyma, and Arens thought raising an additional $2 million by year's end was impossible. Rod continued to insist it was doable. I challenged him on his thinking, but accepted the goal. Privately, I set my sights on raising half that amount. I believed I would have made a meaningful contribution to FOB if we finished the year with more than $3 million in the bank. (When Rod was arrested on December 9, we had raised just over $700,000 for the reporting period and had an additional $250,000 in the pipeline.)

In addition to Arens, Chrissy Jacobs, a part-time bookkeeper for the fund, provided excellent counsel during my early weeks on the job. Arens and Jacobs gave me previous donor lists, which I sliced and diced to prepare customized solicitations. Within days, I started making introductory calls to donors, scheduling meetings in early August to discuss fundraising.

I had no problem getting people to take my call. My standard pitch went as follows: "Hello, my name is Rob Blagojevich, not to be confused with Rod the governor. I'm the governor's brother. I'm calling to talk with Mr. So and So about fundraising. May I please speak with him?"

I found it funny that on almost every call I made, the person answering thought I was the governor. In spite of my efforts to avoid the confusion, this happened all the time. In response I would explain to the donor that I was helping Rod fundraise through the end of the year.

My approach was casual and matter-of-fact. I intentionally wanted to avoid any misinterpretation that I was pressuring a prospective donor to either give or hold a fundraising event. I aspired to be professional and businesslike in an effort to reflect well on Rod and, of course, myself. I wanted to make a positive impression to differentiate myself as a straight-up, ethical guy and not some political hack trying to hustle someone out of a donation.

Early on, while I was getting familiar with the fundraising landscape and meeting solely with the people Rod, Monk, and Wyma suggested, I was diligently organizing myself to be an effective fundraiser. I had experience as a cold-calling salesperson in my first job out of the Army, working for a Nashville-based financial planning firm. I made hundreds of cold calls a month, successfully getting appointments with small business owners to discuss financial planning concepts.

In the South I'd learned to deal with people who wanted to hang up merely because they found my ethnic name off-putting. Now the name

Blagojevich turned people off for other reasons, but my experience from those days in Nashville allowed me to handle many who wanted to hang up on me.

As expected, many of the people I contacted said they couldn't contribute because they were focused on the presidential race supporting Obama. I heard more than I cared to hear from former donors that they were tapped out on other races and could not contribute to FOB. I knew if I was going to achieve my personal goal of $1 million, I had to move swiftly to introduce myself to all the key people of influence who in the past had demonstrated they could bundle donations from their political circles. A bundler is someone with access to a universe of people he or she cultivates—friends, business associates, or any other sources willing to contribute to a candidate. The fundraiser then collects all their contributions into one big bundle and gives to the campaign. Only with the help of these people would I have a chance to hit my goal.

These centers of influence became my point of contact to specific donor constituencies—like health care, road builders, ethnic communities, etc. Rod told me Monk and Wyma were the two most important bundlers and I should start with them. In addition, I worked with Milan Petrovich, Dave Stricklen, Doug Scofield, Brian Daley, Paul Rosenfeld, and others. They all introduced me to prospective donors or helped me schedule fundraising events.

In an effort to accelerate my learning curve and flush out donors, I scheduled fundraising meetings at FOB with Rod, Monk, and Wyma. We initially brainstormed to develop lists of people, companies, and interest groups that they thought were likely contributors in a non-gubernatorial election year cycle. I tried to lead the meetings and keep them focused, but it wasn't easy.

I wasn't accustomed to business meetings that were so freewheeling and lacking in focus. Oftentimes Rod would take calls related to state business. This was understandable. More often than not, however, he would just drift off into side conversations with both Monk and Wyma outside the conference room where we worked. Ultimately I learned to be flexible and get as much as possible out of the hour or so we had together.

In our scheduled fundraising meetings, I shared a list of potential donors provided by Arens. Rod, Monk, and Wyma gave me some good insight and background on the past donors and told me whom I was authorized to call. Some of the people on the list were designated to be contacted exclusively by either Rod, Monk, or Wyma—whoever was most likely to advance our fundraising efforts.

I took all the prospective donors from our meetings and consolidated them into a master list that I managed and updated daily. Approximately one hundred names were on the list, each with the person responsible for follow-up, a remarks column to post status, and the target donation for that name. At the bottom of the page I had the totals of the amount targeted and the actual contribution received.

This report was useful for a number of reasons. Most importantly, it organized all the key information I was tracking on to one report. I didn't know any of the key donors and had a lot of catching up to do. The report helped me "look smart" talking with Rod and the other centers of influence on fundraising because it gave me a quick reference to a lot of information. Also it kept us all focused and accountable on tasks that we had committed to in the previous meeting.

I operated on the premise that if you said you would call someone, then it was your job to follow up, and you would be held accountable for what you said you were going to do. I was as tactful and diplomatic as I could be. Because none of the people I depended on to help me fundraise worked directly for me, I had to be careful not to alienate them. They were all independent contractors and could do whatever they wanted.

From the beginning, Wyma told Rod and me that he had held a fundraiser earlier in the year that raised $100,000 and his clients were all done giving to FOB for the year. He said they were now concentrating on the national election. Rod refused to accept his rationale and thought Wyma was using it as an excuse not to help out in our year-end push. Nonetheless he did help me with background information on former donors and identified several people to call who he thought might contribute.

At times during our meetings, Wyma's behavior seemed odd. He often seemed completely unengaged, his mind somewhere else, his eyes gazing into the distance. "He's got a dead man's stare when you look at him," I told Rod. Rod summarily dismissed the observation.

Unknown to us at the time, there was a reason Wyma looked the way he did. During a phone call months after we were indicted, I reminded Rod of what I'd said. With the benefit of hindsight, he conveniently blamed me for not doing something about my perception of Wyma during those meetings.

I was astonished by his lack of accountability. Wyma was his guy, a friend and colleague with whom he had worked for more than ten years. Rod knew him better than most and certainly much better than I. And now suddenly I was the one who should have had a keener insight into Wyma's behavior and know that something was really wrong with him? If we had not been on the phone five hundred miles apart, I probably would have gone to Rod's house and punched him out. This episode was one of many that troubled me about my codefendant brother as we prepared to go to trial.

CHAPTER THREE

Quid Pro Quos

According to the police report Kelly told his girlfriend, "It's my life. Tell them they won, tell them they won."

There was no further discussion quoted and nothing else in the report to indicate who Kelly was talking about when he said "tell them they won." However, it was widely known that Kelly felt intense pressure to flip and take the witness stand against his friend and confidante Rod Blagojevich. The impeached governor has been charged in a racketeering conspiracy and is due to go on trial next June. (http://abc7chicago.com/archive/7137285, November 24, 2009)

The FOB office sat in the same Ravenswood neighborhood where Rod lived, about five miles north of the Loop. This was a new headquarters for the operation (which had previously been on the outskirts of Ukrainian Village), at the intersection of Polonia Triangle. Former finance chair Chris Kelly, who renovated the old factory site, had succeeded in creating a pleasant workspace with comfortable seating in a prairie style design.

The headquarters consisted of a large office for Rod, which looked over the Metra train tracks paralleling Ravenswood Avenue. Two much smaller staff offices lined the hallway. Filling out the floor plan was a big conference room featuring a large flat-screen television and an assembly of large tables pushed together to accommodate at least fifteen people. The room also had a fully functioning sink, refrigerator, coffee maker, and microwave oven. We always had soft drinks and snacks available for any visitors.

As I was only going to be there through the end of the year, I established my workspace at the conference room table facing the sink and refrigerator. I didn't want to disrupt the more permanent staff, who had claim to

the offices. I had direct access to a phone and a good view of the best feature in the room, the television mounted on the back wall. It was my only
company during the many lonely hours I spent by myself calling donors
and scheduling meetings. The television was almost always on, although I
turned it off or muted the volume when on the phone. I surfed all the cable
news channels—CNN, Fox, and MSNBC—but tended to follow mostly
the business news on Fox and CNBC, my favorite stations at the time.

The television was a reliable companion until late October or early
November, when at times I couldn't get a signal. This problem persisted
into December. Even after a visit from a technician, I was unable to get a
reliable signal. As I have had time to think back, it occurs to me that the
timing of the cable problems was suspicious. The FBI probably disrupted
the signal through the television cable with an eavesdropping bug, also
called a spike mic, that they planted in the conference room. This spike
mic and the taps the FBI placed on all the FOB phone lines intercepted
hundreds of conversations they used to allege we conspired to sell Barack
Obama's Senate seat. Needless to say I was oblivious at the time and was
only concerned about getting my cable working.

In retrospect, another, more obvious sign should have troubled me.
In early December I noticed on several occasions an occupied vehicle
parked in front of the FOB office. A woman was seated inside. She was
working on a laptop on the dashboard. My assistant Chrissy Jones found
this suspicious and said she feared someone was spying on us.

I dismissed the idea and reminded Chrissy that we weren't doing anything improper. Our federal government wouldn't indiscriminately spy on
anyone, I reasoned. There was no reason to leap to the conclusion that the
person sitting in that car was a federal agent. Instead I rationalized that
our new FOB "friend" was probably a reporter waiting to corner Rod.

Over the months, as I was meeting new people while fundraising, I
picked up on some other troubling signals—signals I wasn't equipped
to decipher or fully understand at the time. When I heard things about
Rod or past fundraising efforts that concerned me, I compartmental-
ized the comments into the "it's politics" category and moved on. I didn't
consider the rumors credible or let these negative observations distract
me from my purpose of properly and ethically achieving our fundraising
goal by the end of the year.

I will say that I was disturbed by one comment I heard several times
from a lawyer who was a former donor and bundler. He said that the

people he would go to for contributions were hesitant. "They don't want to donate to Rod's legal defense fund," he explained.

We were fundraising for a campaign, not a trial, but I understood what he meant. Rod was on shaky ground, with Rezko already convicted and Kelly indicted. As this lawyer was not in the inner circle and had no personal agenda, I took him at his word. Scary.

Tony Rezko and Chris Kelly play such an important role in this story that they deserve attention on these pages. Rod's fate was tied up with theirs. And my fate was tied up with Rod's. Several people I met, among them a bundler, a lawyer, and a contractor, speculated that had I been Rod's fundraiser from the beginning, there wouldn't have been a perception of corruption surrounding his administration, nor the rumors of a federal investigation that resulted from his association with Rezko and Kelly.

I first met Rezko at Rod's house on November 5, 2002, as we waited to hear the election returns on the night Rod was first elected governor. On that evening Rod told me that Rezko was a successful businessman and had been a very effective fundraiser for a number of politicians, including him. Subsequent to that first encounter, I saw Rezko a handful of times over the years at political events and was struck by his unassuming, low-key demeanor that seemed so out of place in Illinois politics. I was impressed that an immigrant from the Middle East had come to the United States and managed to become a well-respected man in the community, living the American Dream.

As I understood it, Rezko had come to the United States from Syria in the late 1970s and earned undergraduate and master's degrees in civil engineering at the Illinois Institute of Technology. While he worked as a civil engineer, he began buying and developing single family homes, eventually finding the wherewithal to expand into larger, multifamily properties. Along the way, he opened the first Subway sandwich shop in Chicago. In the late 1980s, he and a partner founded Rezmar Corporation, a real estate and restaurant holding company.

Over the years Rezko became politically active, first supporting Harold Washington for mayor, and then backing other local politicians. In time he managed to position Rezmar to develop and rehab more than a thousand apartment units in thirty buildings, using municipal and state money as well as federal tax credits to finance the deals—and taking generous development fees totaling in the millions of dollars. His political fundraising résumé expanded over the years to include his good friend Barack Obama, whom he helped with his election to the US Senate in 2004; Congressman Luis Gutierrez; Illinois Attorney General Lisa Madigan; Lt. Governor Pat Quinn; former Republican governors Jim Edgar and George Ryan; George W. Bush, for whom he cochaired a multimillion dollar fundraiser; and last but not least, my brother.

At first glance Rezko simply appeared to be a successful businessman and a fundraising dynamo for numerous politician of both parties. In actuality he was a man who had gotten in way over his head financially and was trying to keep his failing business afloat by engaging in a number of illegal activities. As noted earlier, he was indicted in October 2006 on federal corruption charges.

While he was facing trial, Rezko wrote a letter to the court stating that the feds were putting pressure on him to say something incriminating about both Rod and Obama, but that he had nothing bad to say about them. By the time I had arrived in August 2008, he had been tried and convicted of those sixteen corruption, fraud, and money-laundering charges.

None of the charges he was convicted of had anything to do with Rod. Indeed, four of the counts on which he was acquitted related to fundraising. I used these facts to distance Rod from Rezko when I talked to possible donors. However, the conviction and Rezko's close association with Rod was a significant impediment for me to overcome. To many, Rod was guilty by association with Rezko. On June 4, 2008, the day of the verdict, the *Tribune* wrote: "a federal jury today convicted developer Antoin 'Tony' Rezko of corruption charges for trading on his clout as a top adviser and fundraiser to Gov. Rod Blagojevich."

The Republicans tried to sully Obama, too. As the *Washington Post* reported: "Within 20 minutes of the verdict's announcement, the Republican National Committee sent an e-mail to reporters under the subject line, 'Rezko: Obama's Longtime Friend and Money Man'" (*Washington Post*, June 4, 2008, http://www.webcitation.org/6WSbW0rfC).

Rod and I discussed the Rezko connection as a potential problem early in my tenure after I told him someone close to the campaign said it was something I should be prepared to address. Rod advised that when the issue came up again, I should point out that Rezko was not convicted on any campaign fundraising charges and that the trial was not a referendum on him (Rod). His answer satisfied me and I pressed on, making more contacts. The

Rezko issue popped up constantly, but I was comfortable talking with donors about it and had no problem distancing Rod from Rezko. No one ever said they wouldn't give because of that; they were never that direct. While I can't say with any certainty that a potential donor passed on contributing to Rod because of Rezko, I do believe a number of my contacts politely gave an excuse to avoid being honest with me.

Rod told me that Kelly introduced him to Rezko. According to Rod, Kelly only knew of Rezko from his reputation as a connected businessman and prolific fundraiser. That description could have been applied to Kelly, a successful roofing contractor, as well.

Sadly, the description "under indictment" applied to Kelly as well as Rezko. In its December 13, 2007, press release, the same DOJ that convicted Rezko and would indict me and Rod announced: "a suburban businessman was indicted today on federal tax fraud charges for allegedly understating his true personal and business income by more than $1.3 million over five years, in part by concealing the use of corporate funds for personal expenses including gambling debts to sports bookmakers" (http://www.webcitation.org/6WSmHlQDv).

In the spring of 2008, I had a conversation with Rod about Kelly's tax problems. He said Kelly admitted to doing a stupid thing by expensing some of his home construction costs through his roofing business to avoid paying income tax on his earnings as a contractor. He told Rod he had made a big mistake and was prepared to take responsibility. The consequence of his mistake was significant. He not only faced three years in federal prison, but would also be separated from his three young daughters and devoted wife Carmen. I felt bad for him when I heard this from Rod.

As I learned all too well when on the hot seat myself, when the DOJ believes it has leverage over an individual in a criminal investigation, it uses it. Fifteen months after the first indictment, Kelly was indicted a second time on an unrelated airport bid-rigging scheme.

Two months later in April 2009, Kelly was indicted a third time, this time alongside Rod, me, and three others. By September of that year, the pressure appeared to be just too much for Kelly, and he took his own life. According to the police report, Kelly told his girlfriend, "Tell them they won," as he lay dying.

I first met Kelly at Rod's swearing-in for governor in January 2003. He was Rod's campaign finance chair and had an official speaking role at the ceremony. Unlike the unassuming Rezko, he presented himself in the Nick Nolte tough guy mold, straight out of the movie *48 Hrs.* with Eddie Murphy. Because we were fellow Republicans surrounded by the Democratic Party establishment of Illinois, we hit it off from the start. I have a soft spot for self-made men and women and was impressed that Kelly, who had grown up in a working-class Irish home, had made it big in business and had such a wonderful family.

Over the years I would see Kelly in various places: at fundraisers, at Rod's house, and at FOB in 2006 when Rod was running for reelection. By that time the political/legal climate surrounding Kelly had soured. I believe he was still involved in fundraising, but on a much reduced level. He stayed in the background.

During the summer of 2006, I was in Chicago as a Blagojevich for Governor volunteer and attended a campaign strategy meeting in the FOB conference room. Rod was hosting all his key state political and fundraising staff to vet policy ideas and issues for the upcoming race. This was an exceptional assembly of people, many of whom would play material roles in Rod's legal drama and mine, too. Among those in attendance were: Doug Scofield, Rod's first deputy governor turned political consultant; Bradley Tusk, deputy governor; John Wyma; Lon Monk; Illinois State Representative Carol Ronan; Doug Sosnick, political consultant and former advisor to Bill Clinton; Louanner Peters, Rod's deputy governor (the first African American woman appointed to that post); Brian Daley, political consultant; Paul Rosenfeld, political consultant; and Kelly.

Kelly sat directly across from Rod at the conference table. For most of the four-hour meeting, he said nothing. He was either reading the newspaper or looking down at a pad of paper. His demeanor was neither friendly nor welcoming. When he did say something, it was brief with dull inflection. When he finished his comments, he'd get back to avoiding eye contact with the people in the room. What I didn't fully realize at the time was how far the IRS and DOJ had progressed in their investigation of Kelly's income tax fraud, business dealings, and fundraising activities. He must have been under enormous pressure, and his behavior was in all likelihood the result. Kelly didn't seem anything like the same confident guy I had met in Springfield four years earlier.

I also learned through Rod that Kelly was an avid and compulsive gambler. One autumn day when I was at Rod's house, Kelly nervously paced the family room while he watched a college football game on the television. I thought he really liked one of the teams. Not so. He had bet a substantial amount on the spread and was sweating it out. I believe $20,000 was in play on various games that day and he lost. Over the years he lost more than he won gambling. His attempt to rob Peter to pay Paul resulted in his IRS woes.

Kelly's name came up occasionally in my fundraising activities, and when it did people freely shared their opinion. They ranged anywhere from "nice guy" to "what a bully." I never saw the bully.

By November 2008, I had added a new line to my fundraising repertoire: "I'm sorry. I'm not Chris Kelly. I can't do that for you." Case in point: my dealings with a prominent contractor in Chicago who had previously contributed to Rod's campaign and served as a bundler. He was an immigrant from eastern Europe and president of a company that was a large commercial builder of office developments, retail centers, and hotels. His company was also a significant road contractor with a good reputation in Illinois.

Rod had introduced me to him in August at the FOB office. I immediately liked him. He had a thick accent, but was articulate and easy to understand. He was another immigrant who had come to America and made something of himself. I believe that was also what attracted him to Rod. Although Rod was American-born, he was the son of a Serbian immigrant who came here after World War II to start a new life. Rod, having been elected governor, was the manifestation of the American Dream for all immigrant families who wanted more for their children.

I arrived early for the fundraiser, which was held at the contractor's company offices on the thirty-fourth floor of a building on Michigan Avenue. I wanted to make sure everything was in order. Equally important, I wanted to collect the donor checks before his attendees arrived. He had arranged for these people to forward their checks to him in advance of the event so we wouldn't have to chase anyone down to collect. This arrangement was refreshing. Usually I had to follow up with potential donors who said they would send a check and never did.

Before Rod arrived, the contractor took me aside. He had collected $65,000 in contributions to FOB from an assortment of engineering firms, contractors, and other construction-related businesses. As he handed me the envelope with the checks, he paused and said that he needed jobs. I thought nothing of it and said, "Everyone needs jobs. It's a hard time for everybody." He then qualified his statement, explaining that in the past he would go to Chris Kelly when he needed help. At that moment I realized perhaps Kelly had done more than just pure fundraising. Maybe he helped donors get business in exchange for contributions. I had no way of knowing that, but I made it clear to the contractor, in the most diplomatic terms, where I stood. "I'm not Chris Kelly and I can't help you with jobs." He was polite and didn't press me further, but I sensed he was surprised by my response.

Later that evening I met the contractor's wife. She was a delightful conversationalist. We talked about many things, but what I remember most is her curiosity about Rod's hair and mine as well. My brother prided himself on a hairstyle that was a cross between Elvis Presley and John F. Kennedy. She thought that for middle-aged men, we both had "good hair." Was it real? I assured her it was and demonstrated by pulling on mine.

Rod and I made it a practice to debrief after every fundraiser, reviewing how we thought it went and how much money was raised. On this night we weren't able to speak immediately because we left in separate cars. Later that night I called him and informed him we had raised $65,000. I also offered some observations about some comments he had made to those at the event.

He had spoken about his strained relationship with Illinois House Speaker Michael Madigan and how he (Rod) wanted a capital bill to jump-start jobs and construction projects in the state. He then swore the group to secrecy and said that he would appoint Lisa Madigan, the Speaker's daughter and current attorney general, to the open Senate seat in order to get a capital bill out of the Speaker. He jokingly said that if someone leaked this plan to the press, he would deny it.

During the phone conversation I told Rod that he should not give Speaker Madigan something for nothing in exchange for a capital bill. I referred to that possibility as "cutting a deal with the devil" and said he "needed to be careful." The context of this conversation was specifically about Rod getting a political deal done for the state.

"Quid pro quo" is a Latin term that literally means "this for that." In legal parlance it is used to indicate that an item or a service has been traded in exchange for something of value. This wasn't a quid pro quo to me but nothing more than political horse trading.

I had no real political insight other than from conversations with Rod and a few others about how he should deal with a skilled and powerful

Speaker like Madigan. I gave him that advice based on my experience in the military and business. Little did I know this conversation would come back to haunt me twice in the future.

The Federal Wiretap Act sets the procedure for court authorization of real-time surveillance of electronic communications. Before a wiretap can commence, a judge must issue a court order. Based on an affidavit submitted by the government, that judge must conclude there is sufficient probable cause to believe that a crime has been, is being, or is about to be committed. A wiretap order initially lasts thirty days and can be extended from the court if more time is needed.

By the time of this post-fundraiser phone conversation with Rod, the FBI had been wiretapping all of our conversations for a month. Probable cause was established thanks to information provided by Wyma. Why would an ally turn informant? We later learned that Wyma himself was under investigation for activities related to the Illinois Health Facilities Planning Board. Sometimes folks facing the full force of the federal government are willing to give up their friends for something in return—a quid pro quo of sorts.

Eavesdropping began on October 22. The government wiretapped us for a total of forty-five days, amassing recordings of thousands of conversations they would use to build their case. No member of Rod's or my legal team believed there was any basis to justify probable cause to wiretap my phone. In the end that opinion didn't matter; we had no say in the decision.

The phone call, during which we discussed the contractor's fundraiser and Speaker Madigan, was one of hundreds of FBI-recorded conversations that the prosecutors cherry-picked to use against me during the trial. They claimed I was conspiring with Rod to get something for him personally in exchange for the vacant Senate seat that he was responsible to fill. During the trial the prosecution aggressively cross-examined me on this particular exchange. I pushed back, clarifying that I was talking to Rod as a caring brother, encouraging him to get a political deal done—not to get something personal for himself.

The conversation came back to bite me a second time during the trial. For some unexplainable reason the government chose to play to the court the recording of my feedback to Rod about the contractor's wife's compliment about our hair. This exchange was played up in the local and national press. The tape actually got a laugh from the courtroom the day it was played. It wasn't damaging but merely a gratuitously nasty act by the prosecution. I didn't think it was funny and didn't laugh.

CHAPTER FOUR

The Congressman's Emissaries

With his full beard, Sikh turban, and heavy accent, Rajindar Bedi could have stepped out of the pages of a Kipling novel. But he was neither a rajah nor servant. Rather, he was a prominent member of Chicago's Indian community and a potential source of contributions to FOB. So it was at the suggestion of Brian Daley, a hard-core campaign worker turned lobbyist, that I arranged to have drinks with the two of them at one of my favorite spots, the Daily Bar and Grill in the city's Lincoln Square neighborhood.

Some background: of the many donor groups that I targeted—health care, contractors, professionals, small business owners, etc.—the one I enjoyed calling on most was Chicago's vast ethnic community. We shared the same experience of bridging ethnic family traditions with American culture. They were going through an adjustment process similar to the one that Rod and I had growing up in our Serbian family. And like my brother and me, many were now enjoying the American Dream thanks to sacrifices made by their parents.

Not only did I relate to this community, I found it open to my fundraising overtures. The ethnic population looked up to Rod as someone who had overcome the same barriers and obstacles they faced. They found hope for their children in his political achievement.

You name the community, I contacted its leaders: Polish, Latino, Korean, Serbian, Ukrainian, Romanian, Somali, Kenyan, and Indian. I genuinely liked most of those I met and did my best to ensure that if they held a fundraiser, Rod would put in the necessary face time to satisfy the attendees. After these events, it was not unusual for Rod and me to have an endearing chuckle about how a certain person we'd met reminded us of our father. We marveled at how the cycle of assimilation was repeating itself all over again.

Daley had some strong, long-standing relationships with many of the leaders in the Indian community and offered to introduce me to them. I met with him at the FOB office shortly after I began my tenure to talk about the best approach. He told me that the Indian community had been supportive of Rod over the years, but that they had cooled toward him because he hadn't appointed many people from their community to Illinois boards or other state positions. They believed the only time he came to them was for fundraising.

Daley also told me that factions existed within the community and I had to be careful not to inadvertently "step into it" while I was among them. Like any other group of people, the Indian community of Chicago was afflicted with petty jealousies. I never fully grasped nor understood the issues that created these tensions, but I did manage to learn enough to avoid any unpleasantness.

The first step in gaining access to the Indians, Daley said, was to introduce me to Bedi, a state employee responsible for attracting foreign companies to do business in Illinois. He had been working for Rod for several years and had contacts deep in the community that would be helpful to me in developing potential fundraising possibilities.

Over drinks, Bedi, a warm and charming middle-aged man, said he was more than willing to help and explained that the lost enthusiasm for Rod wasn't permanent; it just needed some attention and could be rekindled by year-end. He proposed organizing a "steering committee" of community leaders who would meet with Rod to discuss issues important to them. He and Daley both believed that if Rod had a chance to talk to the group about his achievements as governor and specifically about how the Indian community had benefited, they would be more receptive to a fundraiser. After this first step in reestablishing Rod in the community, we would then set a date for an event. Daley and I agreed to this strategy and eventually arranged an October 31 steering committee meeting at the India House in Schaumburg, a suburb northwest of the city.

Bedi, Daley, and I coordinated the event. They called and invited all the leaders in the community such as Babu Patel, a real estate owner and entrepreneur who had been active in supporting Rod in his various runs for public office. A backer of numerous city and statewide

Democratic politicians, he was a sophisticated man who had adapted well to the American way of life. (Eventually, he and I were to have a revealing conversation in November at the campaign office. He wanted to share his concerns with me in person about conversations he overheard at the committee meeting. Our conversation was wiretapped by the FBI and would be played at trial in my defense.)

Raghu Nayak, a prominent Chicago area businessman and owner of numerous outpatient surgery centers, was an equally important member of the steering committee. Daley told me that Nayak had contributed generously to Rod, Barack Obama, and Jesse Jackson Jr. over the years and had a great deal of influence in the community. I had met him once, months earlier, at the campaign office when he came by to see Rod.

On October 28, I met with Bedi at a Starbucks near FOB headquarters to discuss details and to talk about the upcoming steering committee meeting as well as the next steps for the fundraising event, which we had scheduled for December 6. I viewed this as a routine get-together to discuss the attendee list, review logistics, and solicit input from Bedi to sharpen Rod's talking points for his presentation. My hope was to get in and out quickly. By this time I'd been fundraising for almost three months and had my system down. I knew what I needed to hear from Bedi to believe we were on track for a good event.

As we began our meeting, Bedi said he wanted to discuss something else: who was Rod considering appointing to Obama's Senate seat? I was surprised by the question and reminded him that we hadn't even had an election and it was premature to speculate. Despite my rebuff, he went on to tell me that Nayak, a close longtime friend of Reverend Jesse Jackson, wanted to help Rod fundraise. Great. At the same time Nayak wanted to work to get the reverend's son, Congressman Jesse Jackson Jr., appointed as senator. Not so great at all.

In a hushed voice, leaning close to me so no one could hear us, Bedi quietly told me that Nayak would be willing to do some accelerated fundraising on Rod's behalf in exchange for Congressman Jackson's appointment to the Senate seat. He said Nayak would help raise $500,000 by the end of the year. The congressman would raise an additional $1 million for Rod's campaign fund once given the seat.

Shocked at the boldness of this illicit offer, I was reminded of the way in which corrupt political deals are portrayed in the movies. Actually, this overture seemed to be right out of a Showtime network television series that Julie and I had been watching called *Brotherhood*. Of all things, the plot of this show centered around two brothers, one an ambitious state representative and the other a career criminal.

Stay calm, I told myself. On the one hand, I didn't want to alienate Bedi because of the pending fundraiser. On the other hand, I had to politely communicate to him that what he had presented was a nonstarter.

I told him Rod was going through a process in making the Senate appointment, a process that wasn't about money. If he needed to make an appointment, Rod would choose the right person to represent the people of Illinois. I added an FYI: Rod did not trust Congressman Jackson and was not likely to appointment him to anything. This distrust dated back to when Rod first ran for governor. Rod had asked Congressman Jackson for his endorsement while they were both serving in the House of Representatives. Jesse Jr. told Rod he would endorse him, but in the end endorsed Roland Burris, a former Illinois attorney general.

I reminded Bedi that we were supposed to be discussing the steering committee and the fundraiser, not the Senate seat. Still, he persisted and repeated the quid pro quo. I told him a second time that this was not about money, that Rod would "do what was right for the people of Illinois." He finally got the message that nothing was going to come of his proposal, and we focused back on the planning for the steering committee. Bedi never talked to me again about a Jackson appointment.

Where did this approach come from? Bedi gave me the impression that he was representing both Nayak and Congressman Jackson's desire to get the Senate appointment in exchange for campaign funds. I dismissed his overture as a clumsy attempt by an ethnic citizen to be relevant in the American political process. I didn't believe Bedi really understood the gravity of what he had communicated to me as the messenger for Nayak and Congressman Jackson.

Later that afternoon I spoke with Rod. Initially I hesitated to tell him about my conversation with Bedi because of its gross inappropriateness and because I had already dismissed it as misguided. Eventually I did tell him because I believed he needed to be aware of what was being discussed out in the Indian community about the Senate seat. I wanted him to be mindful of this development as he prepared to mingle with leaders of the community at the steering committee meeting in a few days.

Our discussion was brief. I told Rod that I had been approached with representations of accelerated fundraising on his behalf if he appointed

Jackson to the Senate seat, and shared my response that "we haven't even had an election yet." As I had expected, Rod dismissed the proposition. He certainly did not ask me to pursue it or even entertain the notion. We didn't revisit the subject until a month later.

What we didn't know as we talked was that the FBI had begun wiretapping our personal phones and the FOB office. At that time, we later learned, they only had the spike mic bugs in operation in the office. I was speaking to Rod from the conference room where one of two FOB office bugs was placed. They captured only my portion of the conversation on the conference room bug. Unfortunately, they did not hear Rod's response. If they had, they would have heard him dismiss it as outrageous and for me to leave it alone. I did leave it alone. Others, however, did not.

ROD AND I ARRIVED together for the October 31 steering committee meeting in Schaumburg because he was going to give me a lift to Midway Airport later that night. I was flying home to spend election day in Nashville so I could vote. The luncheon, similar to many events I'd organized over the last weeks, was held in a large banquet room at India House.

I worked the room, meeting and introducing myself to the many new and unfamiliar faces. This ethnic group of immigrants seemed no different to me than the Serbian community in which I grew up. They were all anxious to meet and speak with the governor—the guy on television who embodied, for them as for the Serbian community, the potential of the American Dream.

As I mingled comfortably with the attendees, I was flagged down by Nayak, who was standing in the back corner of the hall. I walked over to greet him and express that Rod was grateful for his support over the years and his help with the steering committee.

As I've mentioned, we had previously met. He came to the FOB office in August to talk to Rod about something. At that time, I was struck by how friendly, easygoing, and engaging he was. He said a lot of nice things about Rod and complimented his many good works as governor. Nayak made it clear that he wanted to continue to support Rod. Just a few weeks earlier, Daley had given me a contribution from Nayak to deposit into the FOB campaign fund, and I now expressed my appreciation face to face. On that August day, Nayak was excited about Barack Obama's chances of being elected president. It would be a good thing to have the next president come from Illinois, he said. Rod smiled.

It was a false smile. Nayak didn't know that Rod didn't share the same enthusiasm for Obama. The Democratic governor wanted the Republican senator John McCain to win. Why? I believed Rod harbored a quiet jealousy for Obama because his political successes came too easily, without a resume of achievement. He had come out of nowhere, and now he was running for president of the United States.

The cat was already out of the bag in Illinois—as if it even mattered—that I was a Republican. Rod would often make a playful point about my party affiliation anytime he thought it would get a laugh. He told Nayak he was glad I lived out of state so I couldn't vote against him. Nayak chuckled and said he would still be happy to work with me on a future fundraiser if I needed his help.

As we stood in the back of the banquet hall exchanging pleasantries some months later, Nayak repeated to me what I had already heard from Bedi: he had a twenty-year friendship with Reverend Jackson and his family and would like to see the reverend's son, Congressman Jackson, appointed to the Senate seat if Obama won the presidency. I knew where this conversation was going. Everyone in Illinois wanted to be selected by Rod for the Senate seat, I said with a laugh. I told him, as I had Bedi, that Rod had a selection process in place to help him make the right choice for the people of Illinois. Nayak then took it to the next level and told me he could raise $1 million by year-end, and that once Congressman Jackson was in the Senate, he would raise another $5 million for Rod's campaign fund.

The proposal was still outlandish. And now the dollar amount was out of this world—five times greater than what Bedi had communicated only days before. Again, I said Obama's replacement was not going to be selected in this fashion.

I don't remember exactly how our conversation ended, but we did leave on good terms in spite of what he had proposed to me. He was an influential fundraiser, and I didn't want to jeopardize his potential to legitimately help us, so I was very polite in my rejection. What I do know for sure is that the conversation about the Senate seat ended there. I never discussed his proposal with him again.

I wrote off Nayak's overture as I had Bedi's. They were immigrants living in a foreign country. They didn't really understand our political system and had no sense of how inappropriate and dangerous their proposals were. Because I had grown up in an ethnic community and observed firsthand the lack of political sophistication of many immigrants new to this country, it never occurred to me to think about reporting them to the FBI. They were from a different cultural, political, and social environment in their native country and, I believed, didn't know any better. I gave them both the benefit of the doubt and didn't dwell on it. My job was to ethically fundraise for my brother. I remained focused on that objective and moved on to the next fundraising opportunity.

In retrospect, I should have taken the time to think carefully about who was behind the offer. Doing so would have led me to Congressman Jackson and a very different outcome. I do not believe that Bedi or Nayak would have unilaterally approached me without the instigation and backing of Jackson. During the "discovery" period before our trial when each side shares evidence with the other, we received summaries of FBI interviews with both Bedi and Nayak that would turn out to be most revealing and confirm my suspicions.

Upon reflection, I now look back to October 28 and 31 as the most crucial of days. The course and trajectory of my life changed irrevocably the minute I gave Rod the heads-up about the approach made to me by Bedi. Had I not told him and kept the information to myself, I now believe we would have avoided the most traumatic and disruptive events of our lives. At the time not only was I unaware that the FBI was wiretapping our phones, but I did not know that almost immediately after I spoke to Rod about the overture, he recklessly called some of his staffers to tell them about being approached with a "pay to play deal."

After months of working around Rod, I concluded that he had little professional discipline. He talked openly and freely with his staff and in front of his security detail about his most personal financial shortcomings and sensitive political issues, and he gossiped with them about other politicians. I never got the impression that Rod shared information with specific staff based on their need to know. Rather, he failed to exercise the control necessary to filter information to only the people who needed it to do their job. I never understood this behavior and wrote it off, rationalizing that his openness may have been one reason why he was so successful at getting elected. For many people Rod was fun and amusing to be around because he was so uncensored in his conversation.

Unfortunately, this reckless unfiltered talk can be dangerous when you are the chief executive of the fifth largest state and the FBI is listening. The people closest to Rod, in and around government, tolerated his professional shortcomings because they either had to in order to keep their jobs or were using Rod to their best personal financial advantage.

When the FBI is wiretapping a target's unfiltered stupid talk they have opportunities to connect dots that don't connect in order to make a federal case. This I believe is what happened to Rod. He opened himself up to creative prosecutors with an agenda to bring down a governor they didn't like. I was caught in a situation in which I had no way of knowing the potential danger.

What if I hadn't told Rod about the Jackson approach? I don't believe I would have been prosecuted, nor do I believe he would be in prison today. I try not to dwell on this, but it's not easy. Sometimes you make choices you wish you hadn't that inalterably redefine your life.

Immediately after the steering committee event, Rod gave me a ride to Midway Airport, courtesy of his security detail. We weaved in and out of bumper-to-bumper traffic, racing to get there in time to catch my flight back to Nashville. One of the many perks that comes with being governor is the ability to part the sea of Chicago expressway traffic when you're in a hurry to get someplace by using a combination of a built-in siren and a flashing red light that the state trooper's SUV was equipped with.

This perk came in handy for Rod because from the time we were kids he was always running late, and he didn't change as an adult. I could never understand that about him. He didn't seem to care whom he inconvenienced or how rude it was to the people affected.

The steering committee meeting appeared to achieve its intended objective of energizing the community. I thought Rod did an excellent job of laying out his administration's accomplishments and outlining his future policy objectives. The attendees seemed excited and responded as hoped for when Rod highlighted his efforts to help the Indian community.

From the feedback I received, it looked like we had recaptured enough enthusiasm to get a fundraiser organized. Bedi called me the next day to tell me that Rod had done a great job and that we had secured table sponsorships totaling $65,000 for a fundraiser. I was pleasantly surprised.

Back in Nashville, I checked in with my associates on pending business issues and then called Rod to tell him about the feedback I had received from Bedi. During the conversation, Rod talked about the coming election

and the pressure he was getting from people about the possible Senate vacancy if Obama were elected president. He told me he had people coming
to his home lobbying on behalf of Jesse Jackson Jr.'s being appointed to the
Senate seat. I'm not sure if Rod was amused or put out by this at the time,
but it was soon to become an all-out effort by Jackson and his surrogates
to promote him for the seat. Rod and I laughed about this and I jokingly
said to him that Jackson was "putting the full court press on you, man,
and he's even offering money." I was referring to the offers of money made
to me only a few days earlier, which we had dismissed. Rod brushed over
my comment and moved on to another subject. We didn't discuss Jackson
again in the context of the approach until early December. I would hear
this specific call played in court during our trial.

Upon returning to Chicago, after having spent just enough time to vote
in Nashville, I picked up where I had left off, continuing to call former
donors from the many lists I had compiled. Roland Burris was among
the many men and women with whom I spoke, and among the many
whom the FBI recorded.

As noted above, Burris had sought the Democratic nomination for
governor in 2002. His credentials were impressive. In 1978 he had become the first African American elected to statewide office in Illinois
(as comptroller). Twelve years later he'd been elected the state's attorney
general. His endorsements in 2002 had been impressive, too. In addition to Congressman Jackson, he was supported by then–State Senator
Barack Obama. Nevertheless Rod won the primary with 36.5 percent of
the vote. Burris finished third with 29 percent. (Former Chicago Public
Schools Superintendent Paul Vallas finished second with 34.5 percent.)

I'd only met Burris at an FOB fundraiser held at the Field Museum for
Rod's first reelection bid in 2006. "Hello, Jesse," I said. Oops! I had mis-
taken him for Jesse White, the current Illinois secretary of state. Sensing
I was embarrassed, Burris smiled and corrected me without judgment
or rancor. He then put me at ease by calling me "Rod." Brilliant. I immediately liked him. As we chatted about his political career and Rod's
campaign, I found him friendly and engaging.

That was the only contact I had with Burris until I called him in early
October 2008 to see if he would contribute to FOB. He was now the head
of Burris and Lebed, a consulting firm that focused on public relations,
political strategizing, and lobbying. I began by reminding him about that
awkward moment two years earlier. He remembered and laughed, and I

once again apologized for the mistake. I then told him I was helping Rod fundraise through the end of the year and asked if he would consider holding an event. He said he would be inclined to help, but first wanted to talk to his partner, Fred Lebed. He suggested I call him back after the election.

When next we spoke—two times in early to mid-November, Barack Obama was president-elect and the FBI had initiated its wiretap of Rod, FOB, and me. On November 13, during our second and final phone conversation, Burris told me he had made calls to his contacts about contributing to Rod's campaign, but wasn't having much success. He explained that many of them were tapped out from contributing to local races. Some were concerned about all the negative publicity Rod was getting, he added. In fact, he continued, people in his circle were taking bets on when Rod would be indicted. I was shocked—by the fact that insiders seemed so certain that an indictment was coming and that they would actually wager on it. I guess this shows my naïveté . . . doubly.

Burris went on to tell me that he'd always liked Rod and wanted to help if he could. To actively raise money for Rod at this time, however, created a dilemma for him personally because he was interested in replacing Obama in the Senate. My takeaway was that he truly wanted to help raise money for Rod, but didn't want to be perceived in public as buying the Senate seat in exchange for his fundraising efforts. Unlike Jesse Jr. and his emissaries, I never felt that Burris was trying to do something improper. Just the opposite, really. He was deliberate in wanting to avoid any impropriety. I believed he was sincerely torn between the two goals and didn't want anything to interfere with being considered for the seat.

My response? I can't help with your dilemma, I explained, adding that "a million people of every race, color, creed, and religion are interested in the Senate seat." He seemed to understand where I was coming from; appropriately, he did not press me further. We agreed to stay in touch, but never spoke again. I moved on to other prospects and the planning of the December 6 event in the Indian community.

By this time I had established a comfortable routine of making calls in the morning and meeting with donors and prospects in the afternoon. Typically the fundraisers were evening events, so I had to make sure all the logistical details were properly handled well in advance.

It was my responsibility to coordinate with the event sponsors and make sure that all the little details were taken care of so we had a successful event. These details ranged from where Rod would enter to how the checks would be made out. I also wanted to know how many people would be in attendance and with whom Rod should spend the most time. Once I had the names of all the key donors and knew how much they had contributed, I made sure they each got quality time with the governor. The last thing I wanted was for a generous donor to feel short-changed after an event. I would check in from time to time with the host to make sure he was satisfied that Rod was meeting his expectations.

By the end of November, time was running out for any meaningful fundraising because Thanksgiving and Christmas were approaching. The holidays offered a golden opportunity for potential event hosts to defer a fundraiser until after the new year had begun. This was not good for me because I had a goal to reach before the end of 2008. Because I understood that people don't want to attend a fundraiser when they could be spending their time and money with their family, I never pressured anyone who used that or any other reason not to help.

As November ended, I continued to give Rod periodic fundraising updates either in person or by phone. Since it was crunch time, we spoke at greater length. I'd not only tell him what I had scheduled, but also who had passed on hosting an event.

An example: after putting me off several times, but telling me not to give up on him, a potential host finally agreed to host a fundraiser on December 10, a Wednesday night. When I told Rod about the event date, he hesitated and reminded me it was his birthday. Of course I knew it was his birthday, but I didn't think twice about it because we were racing to hit our goal before the December deadline.

"So what?" I said to Rod. "December 10 is still a work day. You don't work on your birthday?"

Rod was, still is, a devoted father. He said his daughters would be disappointed if he wasn't home to celebrate. Just set another night, he said.

Easy for you to say, I thought. I was angry that he didn't appreciate all the effort required to finally set up this event. This was the only night the sponsor would be able to host an event before the end of the year. Frustrated, I told Rod that if I canceled, I would not only look stupid but that we would have to do the event after January 1. My answer didn't seem to matter and he told me he was fine with postponing it. The goal we were trying to hit didn't seem to matter anymore.

From the beginning of my tenure at FOB, Rod and I had our share of personality and policy clashes, but we managed to get past them.

With this disagreement, my patience grew thinner and thinner. Did I really want to keep working for FOB? Back in July when Rod first asked for my help, he said he needed me through the end of the year but might want me to stay on longer. I had told him I would consider it if my business didn't suffer and most importantly if we got along and enjoyed working together. In early November, he had started taking my temperature on the possibility of staying longer. Each time I was noncommittal. Clashes like the one over the birthday night fundraiser didn't make me want to continue.

While that event was up in the air, the Indian community fundraiser remained on track. Rod had questioned holding the event on a Saturday, but hadn't objected. Then we had learned that December 6 fell during Diwali, the multiday Hindu Festival of Lights celebration. When I asked if attendance would suffer because of this, Bedi and Nayak each assured me there was no conflict with the festival; we would have a good turnout. They expected approximately $50,000 in contributions.

When you fundraise—especially with people you haven't worked with previously—you have to use your best judgment in evaluating their credibility. At some point, you have to trust what folks tell you and hope they deliver. All the people I contacted about fundraising had good track records of delivering, including Bedi and Nayak. All I cared about—Saturday night or not, Diwali or not—was having a good event that would lead me one step closer to my fundraising goal of $1 million.

Unfortunately, as this event approached, I grew concerned about our sponsors' organizational skill and ability to deliver. A few days before the fundraiser, Bedi informed me that not all the invitations had been sent. This was contrary to what he had told me a week earlier.

Trying to remain calm, I asked him how we could overcome this huge shortcoming. Seemingly unperturbed, he asked if someone from FOB could help him with the invitations. I of course said yes.

If strike one was the potential conflict with Diwali and strike two was the ineptitude of the sponsors, strike three was the weather. Snow and sleet that day conspired to freeze over some of the roads, making travel treacherous.

Earlier in the day, Rod and I had coordinated to meet at his home and then ride together with Brian Daley in the state trooper SUV. The event was scheduled to start at seven o'clock in Elmhurst, a Chicago suburb about a forty-five-minute drive from Rod's house.

I arrived at Rod's around 6:00 knowing he would be running late, a continuing point of contention for us from day one. I wanted to be there early to push him to get ready on time. When I got to his home, I discovered he hadn't even showered. Although this was no great surprise, I was still ticked off that I had to wait for him to take a shower. I told him to hurry up, but he nonchalantly dismissed me and said not to worry about the time. As the conversation started to deteriorate, I backed off and called Bedi to tell him we would be late.

My conversation with Bedi didn't go much better. He told me the turnout was light and there was no reason to hurry to get there. The weather was slowing people from arriving on time, he said, but they would eventually show up. I shouldn't worry. Great, I thought. Now Rod would feel justified in showing up late.

Worried by Bedi's assessment of the attendance, I called my assistant Chrissy Jacobs. She had arrived early because we had become concerned during the week about Bedi's ability to get things organized at the banquet hall. Chrissy was there to make sure everything was set up and to give me a reality check on what was happening.

Now, she laughed and told me the banquet hall was as large as a football field and full of empty tables and chairs. She also said hardly any adults had arrived, but a bunch of kids were running around in colorful national costumes. Drawing on past experience at fundraisers, Chrissy took it upon herself to have the staff close off half of the banquet hall with a heavy-duty, ceiling-to-floor curtain so as to hide all the unneeded tables and chairs. She said it would make the place look less empty.

In a subsequent call with Bedi to get an update, I got so frustrated with him that I told him to put Nayak on the phone. I wasn't going to take Rod out there if no one showed up, I said. (Nayak was the primary host for the event and a community leader, and I didn't want to do anything impulsively that would reflect poorly on him if we didn't come.) Nayak also said the weather was slowing people down, but he still expected a good turnout.

When Rod finally came down from getting ready, I told him everything I had learned about the disappointing turnout and related my conversation with Nayak. When I finished, he snapped at me and said my inexperience as a fundraiser was to blame for the poor result, and that I should have known better than to schedule a fundraiser on a Saturday night.

I restrained myself and calmly explained that I trusted the people hosting the event to know what would be best in their community. I also reminded him that he had not objected to the schedule when I had told him all about it weeks earlier. We hadn't even left, and I was already annoyed with him. We finally left his house at 7:15, the time the event was to have started.

As we rode to Elmhurst, I felt a combination of suppressed anger and indifference. I'd had a lifetime of practice in controlling my temper when it came to my brother, but the emotion never advanced to the point of uncaring indifference. This most recent frustrating interaction with him was pushing me to a place I'd never been. As brothers we always seemed to quickly repair any injury our verbal battles may have caused and to move on like nothing had happened. Now after almost four months of working closely with him, I was reaching my limit.

Daley, the Democratic operative who was with us in the SUV, had recently returned from working in Iowa to help get the vote out for Obama. While I intentionally sat mute during the ride, he and Rod were actively engaged in a conversation that I mostly ignored. In an attempt to be polite, when there was a break in their discussion, I asked Daley about his experience working for Obama. He began to tell me about it when Rod abruptly cut us off, rudely admonishing me in front of Daley and the troopers that we were on official business and shouldn't stray on to other topics. I was both amused and angry at his hypocrisy. Talk with Rod was never restricted to "official business." He was the biggest violator imaginable of this situational edict.

Rod quickly resumed whatever conversation he was having with Daley before I could react. My manhood wouldn't allow me to quietly take this public rudeness. No way was I going to let Rod get away with that in front of anyone. As soon as a break in their conversation allowed it, I once again—but louder this time—asked Daley about his experience in Iowa. As I expected, this set Rod off and he said he didn't want to talk about Obama and for me to stop asking Daley about it.

For a moment I felt a little better for having at the very least tweaked him without being insubordinate. Hard as it was, I always viewed myself as an employee first and his brother second. I was, therefore, always respectful of his position in public and never did anything that would reflect poorly on him as governor. This incident was a good example of where I could easily have allowed our relationship to devolve into brotherly pettiness in front of other people.

Rod's blatant disrespect pushed me over the edge and was the straw that broke the camel's back for my continued tenure at FOB. Before we got out of the vehicle to attend the event, I vowed to myself that it was over; I was done working with him. I had reached a point of indifference. I would finish out my commitment to Rod through the end of the year and head back home to Nashville and resume my life. No looking back!

During the speeches of the many community leaders at the event, I stood with Daley in the back of the hall and got a chance to talk with him. I asked him a third time about his Iowa experience. We finally had a good conversation.

After Rod finished his remarks and mingled a little more with the attendees, he told me he was ready to leave. "Not yet," I said. A few minutes earlier I had been approached by the mother of one of the kids scheduled to perform. She told me the governor couldn't leave until he watched the children do their program of national dances. They had prepared this program just for the him. I had assured her Rod would stay. "Why?" Rod asked. He was impatient.

When I explained that he had to stay and watch the program, he glared at me, visibly angry for what I'd told him. He snarled that Daley would never have let this happen if he was in charge. I looked stone-faced at him and told him to turn around and watch the program. Then I walked off. In my view, the governor owed it to the kids to be polite and watch what they had prepared in his honor. We stayed an additional thirty minutes.

We'd started out planning for a $100,000 fundraiser, adjusted the goal down to $50,000, and raised a pitiful $18,000. Bedi and Nayak had grossly miscalculated the potential. Our year-end goal was in jeopardy, and now, so too was my relationship with my brother.

The ride home was uneventful. I was in no mood to talk with Rod and sat quietly while he and Daley chatted. Again, I didn't want to appear antisocial, so I asked Daley about his new baby girl. Otherwise my only interaction was to answer questions directed toward me.

We arrived back at Rod's house around 11:30. It had been a long night. When we got out of the vehicle, Rod and Daley walked off to talk privately in front of Rod's house. I said my good-byes, got into my car, and headed back to my condo.

As I neared home, I got a call from Rod. He said he wanted to make small talk with me until I reached the condo. What was this? Of all the times we were out late doing events, I had never received a call from him. I think he knew I was angry and called to smooth things over. Whatever he might have to say didn't interest me—the evening's developments had finally driven me to indifference and I was ready to move on.

He started out by asking me how far I was from home and said he would stay on the line until I got upstairs to my unit. I told him I was fine and pulling into my garage. I didn't want to talk and just wanted to get off the call. "Hey, look, I'm a big boy. I can deal with this."

He persisted. "You got nothing else to do, so just talk to me."

UNTIL THIS EVENING, I had successfully bitten my tongue many times trying to avoid what was about to happen. I blew up! "Listen to what I have to say," I said abruptly. I made it clear to him that his treatment of me during the evening had "fucking fried me."

What bothered me the most was when I had asked Daley about his work for Obama in Iowa, I said. I didn't like how Rod had rudely told me to only talk about official business. It was hard for me not to react to that, but I had to keep quiet because he was the governor and my brother.

Rod immediately became defensive and responded that he didn't want to talk about anything related to Obama because it was painful for him to see Obama advancing in his career. It could or should have been him, he thought.

I told him he should have told me because I wasn't aware of any issues he had with Obama. Still, he didn't seem to get it, and I sensed he had neither heard what troubled me nor cared, so I emphasized he'd better not treat me the same way again in front of other people. He continued to insist he hadn't done anything wrong. Through the course of the argument we had escalated into trying to outyell the other just like when we were kids.

There was a major failure to communicate between us. He was unable to understand my disappointment. I finally had enough and hung up on him. I went upstairs to my unit where I found Julie waiting up for me.

Seconds after I walked in, Rod called back to tell me he was sorry if he had offended me. He went on to say he didn't think he did what I had accused him of and said I was too sensitive. He then told me he was sorry a second time. I told him I didn't think I was being sensitive and if I was, shame on me. Again trying to end the conversation, I told him we should move on—the argument was over.

Rod wouldn't let go. He continued to tell me how painful it was to hear about Obama. When he said that, I understood how he had felt—

left behind, when only a few short years earlier there was talk about his being a presidential contender.

I told him I didn't realize it was that painful for him and said he should have told me. We wrapped it up with a review of the dismal outcome of the fundraiser and Rod, once again unable to let go, reminded me that there was a lesson in all this for me to trust his instincts about fundraising.

Ugh. I didn't want to restart the argument again and moved on, trying to keep the high ground. Finally we managed to get past our issues and said good night. While this brotherly drama was playing out that night, the FBI was quietly listening, trying to figure out how to use our words against us.

As soon as I got off the phone, Julie asked me what was going on with us. This was the first time I shared with her my many frustrations about working with Rod. I gave her a quick overview of the night's happenings and told her I had crossed the Rubicon, a point of no return in my working relationship with my brother. Three days later, this was moot.

CHAPTER FIVE

Wake Up Call

6:21 a.m. That's what the clock by my bed said when the ringing doorbell woke me up on December 9, 2008. Since I wasn't expecting anyone at that ungodly hour, I tried to go back to sleep. But the ringing persisted.

After a few more minutes, I got up, put on some clothes, and went downstairs to the condominium entrance. Through the glass door of the lobby, two men in trench coats flashed badges. They said they were FBI agents and told me they were serving me with a subpoena demanding that I let them in to the Friends of Blagojevich campaign office.

The subpoena directed that I turn over all documents and information on people whose names were listed. I tried to stay calm. What would happen if I refused to allow access to the campaign office, I asked. The agents told me they would break down the door. This was serious. I told them I would have to finish getting dressed.

I rushed back upstairs to our residence and asked Julie to call our sister-in-law, Patti, while I dressed and tell her what had happened. Patti told Julie in a confused and rattled tone that Rod had just been arrested and that it had something to do with the Cubs and with the Senate seat.

I immediately called Rod's attorney, Bill Quinlan, to find out what was going on and to tell him about the FBI's request to get into the campaign office. He told me to fully cooperate and that he would make some calls to find out what was happening. Quinlan's voice revealed that he was overcome with emotion and shaken by the events as much as we were.

FBI in tow, I drove to the campaign office. There, about a dozen more agents were waiting for us. I led them all to the third-floor office, opened the door, turned off the security alarm, and told them where everything was. I even told them that they could help themselves to the Cokes in the fridge, but that I expected them to pay if they drank any. (Looking back, I have to laugh that I was still able to be a smart-ass in spite of the surreal circumstances.)

This bad day would only get worse. Later that morning, Julie and I sat in front of the television watching local and national news coverage of the arrest of the governor of Illinois. At the obligatory, self-congratulatory press conference, US Attorney for the Northern District of Illinois Patrick Fitzgerald insisted that he and the FBI had stopped a political corruption crime spree spearheaded by Rod. The spree included auctioning off Barack Obama's Senate seat to the highest bidder.

Then he uttered these shocking words: the governor was guilty of "appalling conduct" that "would make Lincoln roll over in his grave" (http://www.webcitation.org/6WShipTtV).

As *Tribune* columnist Eric Zorn would later note, Fitzgerald's anger may have been legitimate, but his remarks were "unethical." Zorn noted that Gloria Toensing, a former DOJ official, soon went to the *Wall Street Journal* to take the US attorney to task: "She argued that Fitzgerald's inflammatory remarks violated the professional guideline that a 'prosecutor shall refrain from making extrajudicial comments that pose a serious and imminent threat of heightening public condemnation of the accused prior to trial'" (*Tribune*, May 27, 2012, http://www.webcitation.org/6WSi8blfZ).

Zorn also correctly reported that, "Blagojevich's defense team cited the over-the-top statements in a motion to have Fitzgerald and his team removed from the case, to which government lawyers successfully replied that 'given the defendant's official position and the serious nature of the allegations, there was little likelihood that the comments would materially affect the public's perception.'"

In announcing Rod's arrest, Fitzgerald also mentioned a party simply known as "Fundraiser A." I knew he was talking about me. As I hadn't been arrested, I wasn't sure how this reference would affect me. Was I next?

The shock of my brother's arrest and the attendant media coverage was overwhelming. Nothing prepared me for the fear and uncertainty that followed. A survival instinct took over, alerting me to come to grips with what had happened and prepare for what might be coming, even though I had no idea what it was.

The US attorney's press conference made no sense to me. It seemed like an altered reality from what I had experienced working with Rod. I felt sadness for my brother, who had been awakened from his sleep and arrested. The whole world seemed to be watching . . . and convicting him without a trial. I wanted to help him but there was little I could do. Later that day Rod, Patti, and the girls came over to our condo, and we talked about what had happened. The conversation is now a blur, but we did try to comfort and reassure each other that this would all work out somehow. It had to be a big mistake. Later, when they were ready to leave, we all huddled outside in the dark and freezing cold, waiting for Rod's state trooper detail to come pick them up. They were unusually tardy. While we stood there, I remember thinking that Rod and Patti reminded me of Tsar Nicholas and Tsarina Alexandra because it seemed to me that everyone had abandoned them.

I knew I needed to focus and start figuring out how to move forward. Should I get a lawyer? I naïvely thought that the vague reference to "Fundraiser A" would not amount to anything significant and would go away. Sheldon "Shelly" Sorosky, a family friend and defense attorney who would eventually represent Rod, disagreed. Anytime you're referred to in a criminal complaint filed by the US government, it's critical to find legal representation, he said.

Since the veiled reference to me as "Fundraiser A" in the criminal complaint concerned Shelly, it therefore concerned me, and therefore, Julie and Alex. A criminal complaint, I quickly learned, is a written statement of facts in which the prosecutor tells the defendant what crime he is charged with, against whom, and when the offense allegedly occurred. Only two people were charged with alleged offenses in the complaint issued the day of Rod's arrest, Rod and his chief-of-staff, John Harris. However, there were references to several other people, only identified as Fundraiser A, B, or C, or Senate Candidate 1, 2, or 3, in the complaint, which raised speculation about who they were and the possibility that they might be charged.

On December 9, *The New York Times* reported: "The criminal complaint filed by the United States attorney's office against Gov. Rod R. Blagojevich of Illinois and his chief of staff, John Harris, is filled with vivid examples of how the two men allegedly conspired to use their positions for personal and professional gain. (It is also filled with direct quotations of profanity-laced speech, so be warned.)"

The complaint is divided into three sections. The first part of the complaint, pages 9 to 41, sets out a series of examples showing how the governor allegedly traded government jobs and contracts for contributions to his campaign fund, the Friends of Blagojevich, over the past five years. One example: on page 34, the governor tells "Individual A" he will hold up giving $8 million in financing to the Children's Memorial Hospital unless he gets a $50,000 contribution from its chief executive officer. "I'm going to do $8 million for them. I want to get [Hospital Executive 1] for 50," Mr. Blagojevich says.

The second part, pages 41 to 54, outlines in graphic detail the various schemes the governor allegedly attempted to get at least one member of the *Chicago Tribune* editorial board, John McCormick, the deputy editor of the editorial page, fired. The firings were to be a quid pro quo for a request from the Tribune Company, which wanted to get state financing for a potential sale of Wrigley Field, which the company owns. The financial assistance to the Tribune, Mr. Harris says on page 48, "is basically a tax mitigation scheme" worth "about $100 million . . . maybe $150 million" to the Tribune Company. On page 44, the complaint alleges that the governor's wife got on a wiretapped telephone call, shouted profanity, and insisted that the financial assistance to the Tribune Company be "held up" unless the writers—who were critical of the governor— were fired.

The third part, pages 54 to 76, is a string of colorful and often profane conversations gleaned from wiretaps in which the governor allegedly discusses with advisors how he can personally benefit from his sole authority to name a successor to President-elect Barack Obama in the United States Senate.

The complaint goes on to say that on that same day, December 4, Blagojevich told a person referred to as Fundraiser A that he was "elevating" Candidate 5 on the Senate list in the hopes that Candidate 5 would provide something "tangible up front." Blagojevich told Fundraiser A to "reach out" to an associate of Candidate 5 and say that Blagojevich was under pressure to appoint somebody else and wanted to know if Candidate 5 would really come up with the money, especially because, in the words of the complaint, Blagojevich "had a prior bad experience with Candidate 5 not keeping his word." (That, of course, suggests that Candidate 5 is probably a well-known political figure in Illinois; no definitive word yet on who that is.) Blagojevich told Fundraiser A to meet personally with the associate of Candidate 5 and, in the words of the complaint, "communicate the 'urgency' of the situation" (http://www.webcitation.org/6WSk6nqNV).

The *National Review* added:

> The dealing seemed very close to a climax—and an explosive political scandal. And then, on the morning of December 5, the *Chicago Tribune* ran a story on its front page reporting that law enforcement had secretly recorded Blagojevich's conversations as part of a criminal investigation. Blagojevich immediately instructed Fundraiser A to "undo" the plan to meet personally with the associate of Candidate Five. Blagojevich instead turned his energy to preparing his legal defense. (http://m.nationalreview.com/articles/226502/blagojevich-case-why-did-fitzgerald-act-now/byron-york)

From the start, the reporting of my alleged role as Fundraiser A was inaccurate. Rod didn't instruct me to "undo" the plan with Candidate 5's associate. I told Rod I wasn't going to meet with that associate, Nayak, because I wasn't sure what Rod wanted me to convey. At this early stage, the criminal complaint was the only clue we had into what might be the DOJ's ultimate finding in a formal indictment that was due within ninety days of the complaint filing. Being cited in the complaint as I was didn't automatically mean I was going to be indicted. But it certainly didn't mean I was off the hook.

My first step was to consult with an attorney and get a professional assessment of my legal exposure. Until I had a better sense of what I might face legally I couldn't relax. (This undefined threat would linger until it became real the following April, when I was indicted and arraigned.)

Shelly gave me the names of several experienced federal criminal defense attorneys. I also received a couple of other attorney referrals from family and friends. As much as I would have preferred to deny it, I was implicated in a national scandal and it wasn't going to change.

I immediately began interviewing lawyers. I knew nothing about how the federal justice system operated and had no frame of reference to prepare for the possibility of being on trial in federal court. This meant I had to make the effort to get educated on the subject as quickly as possible so

I could try to make good decisions. I learned a lot from the attorneys I interviewed—enough, I believed, to arm me with the information necessary to make a more informed hire. This was the most important pre-indictment decision I would make. It had to be right.

Among the attorneys I interviewed was Michael Ettinger. He had been trying cases across the country for thirty years, but concentrated his criminal practice in the Northern District of Illinois where I would be on trial if indicted. We met at 5:30 p.m. on December 17 in suburban Skokie at a restaurant called Chappy's.

Mike, as he instructed me to address him, was on his way home from the office. When we sat down he told me his wife, Maureen, wasn't cooking dinner that evening so he wanted to order dinner. Did I want something? Food was the last thing on my mind. With all that had happened, I had completely lost my appetite and wasn't hungry. "Just coffee," I said.

I gave Mike an overview of what I had been doing as a fundraiser for my brother and told him everything I could remember from the day of my brother's arrest, including the shocking reference to me as "Fundraiser A" in the criminal complaint. Then I cut to the chase: "What qualifies you to represent me?"

The question didn't anger him, but it got his attention. I'm not accustomed to seeing many gray-haired sixty-three-year-olds hardened by the demands of their profession kick into gear. Mike proved the exception. He looked me straight in the eye and proceeded to school me on his qualifications with an intensity and passion that impressed me. He explained that he had been representing defendants for more than thirty years in federal court, knew how the feds operated, stressed he wasn't intimidated by them like many of his colleagues, and convinced me the feds were the bad guys and that he could help me. He also told me he had successfully represented a defendant in the Ryan case. (Former governor George Ryan, Rod's predecessor, was convicted on federal charges and was, at the time we met, in federal prison.)

I showed him the subpoena I received from the FBI. Over the nine days that had passed, I had begun to gather the requested documents. The government wanted them, so—with no experience in these matters—I was ready to hand them over. I also told Mike I had no problem being interviewed by the FBI and DOJ. I knew I had done nothing wrong and was eager to talk to them and clear up any misunderstanding they had about me, "Fundraiser A."

Mike had ordered breakfast for dinner—scrambled eggs, sausage, and hash browns—and was well into his meal. When he looked up, I noticed a small piece of scrambled egg dangling from his lower right lip. Think Peter Falk as Columbo. Was this guy a bumbler or a genius? I didn't know yet.

The man whom I would end up hiring stared at me in disbelief that I would volunteer to go in and "proffer." Proffering, as I later learned, meant to be formally interviewed by the government. At such an interview, one agent asks the questions and another takes notes. The subsequent report summarizing the interview is called a form 302. It can be used against the interviewee (me) in a future prosecution if he or she deviates from the offered 302 during trial—potentially resulting in a perjury charge.

"If I represent you, you're going to plead the Fifth and say nothing to the government," Mike said. His intensity caught me off guard. For my entire life, I had believed that only guilty people pleaded the Fifth.

Mike went on to tell me how the government did not bring cases to seek justice. The government brought cases to win. I should view the prosecution as the enemy. He repeated the theme several times with colorful language and described the DOJ as a group of "self-righteous, zealot extremists" who stopped at nothing to prevail. He destroyed any expectation that I would be treated fairly and honorably in any coming legal battle.

This is tough medicine for a military vet who believes in his government, but Mike spoke to me with a confident, sincere tone that was completely credible. He had energy, passion, and experience. Above all, he struck me as a fearless pit bull who would not be intimidated. He was a fighter whom I would want in the foxhole with me fighting off the federal government.

Mike introduced me to the legal reality that I would inevitably have to live through. I had no role models on whom to pattern my future behavior. I was an army officer, corporate executive, small business owner, community volunteer, husband, and father. These roles I knew how to play. I was not prepared to play the role of codefendant, implicated in a national political scandal involving the alleged sale of a US Senate seat. Who is? And I surely didn't have the experience or knowledge to assess, evaluate, and make good decisions alone. I needed help.

In an attempt to be thorough, I formally met with two other criminal defense lawyers before I actually retained Mike as my counsel. One was a former US attorney in southern Illinois practicing criminal law in a big firm in Chicago. He told me he knew a lot of people in the DOJ and could be helpful in figuring out what was happening with me. Hearing he knew people in the government who might help us was comforting. I thought, incorrectly, that if he got to the right ones he could clear up any misunderstanding about me in the criminal complaint. While I met with him, he had a clerical assistant begin to make copies of some of the subpoenaed documents I had brought with me. The lawyer said he needed a $25,000 retainer to proceed.

I met the second lawyer in Nashville. A friend of my brother-in-law Eric Thrailkill, he specialized in defending drug dealers. As he talked about the plea deals he had cut for his drug clients, I got the impression he rarely went to trial. He was kind enough to read over the complaint while we met and after a quick discussion of the facts related to my case, he read the sentencing guidelines. He said that according to the guidelines, I faced a potential sentence of five to seven years in federal prison if indicted and convicted. I was stunned by what he said. How could that be? What did I do wrong? I didn't intend to break the law. Easy as that I was facing prison time?

Although I hadn't been indicted when we met, this attorney had enough experience reading criminal complaints that he was able to estimate, based on the dollar amounts in question, $1.5 million to $6 million offered by Bedi and Nayak, what the sentencing guidelines dictated a possible sentence might be.

Throughout our meeting he told me how bad he felt for me and made little eye contact, looking down at some papers on his desk. I guess he knew the odds of success were slim, but he never said that to me directly. He was instructive in getting me to understand the harshness of the sentencing guidelines and didn't charge me for his expertise. In a strange way I was grateful to have gotten a cold reality check from him because I needed to know what I was up against.

All this time spent on my legal due diligence was invaluable. I was getting an amateur's look into the world of criminal defense, something I'd never had to think about before. As I learned more, the more concerned I became. I was in real trouble and didn't like what I was hearing. The scope of my problem was almost too big to process. Through this insight, I slowly began to prepare for a new and treacherous phase of my life.

CHAPTER SIX

The Toll

With the shock of my brother's arrest and the realization that I was "Fundraiser A" still fresh, Julie, Alex, and I drove back home to Nashville to spend Christmas 2008 together. I needed to get out of Chicago and return to the security of my home. Never in my life had I felt more insecure about my future and the fate of my family. We had seven hours in the car to talk about everything that had happened.

During our trip I realized I needed something to keep me grounded and alert for the battle that in all likelihood lay ahead. I asked Alex to help me come up with a plan to help me carry on. This may sound a little dramatic, but it was true. The whole world knew about my brother's arrest, including Nashville. A sitting governor doesn't get arrested everyday. And when your last name is Blagojevich, you can't hide like, say, a Ryan or a Walker. I needed a framework to keep me focused on constructive activities that would help me get through the uncertainty of the coming months.

After settling back into our home, Alex and I sat down together to get something down on paper. I was still emotionally rocked by what had happened to my brother and didn't have the clarity of mind to come up with a strategy on my own. I told Alex, who holds a BA in political science and economics from the University of Pennsylvania, that I wanted an outline in the form of a simple business plan. The plan should include no more than five key objectives with supporting, detailed actions that I would commit to carrying out.

The five objectives we soon came up with were simple: the case, business and finances, physical health, psyche, and family. Each of them had several action steps that specified particular tasks to be accomplished every day. They were intended to keep me focused on daily activities that would prepare me as much as possible for the uncertainty. It was as though I was in training for an athletic event.

My simple plan became my training manual for a trial. Thanks to Alex's invaluable help, I was able to lay a foundation that would give me a shot, over time, at getting back some sense of control that I felt had been stolen from me.

One of the reasons for writing this book is to introduce you, the reader, to the world that I was introduced to after Rod's arrest. Whether a defendant is innocent or guilty, he or she is going to pay a high price—not just financially, but physically and emotionally as well. My body, mind, and wallet took huge hits during my eighteen-month ordeal. That's par for the course when you are indicted, whether you win or lose. Sadly, the system doesn't provide for restitution if you do win. And even if it did, there are some things—from sleepless nights, to fractured relationships, to opportunities lost—for which no adequate compensation exists.

THIS WAS MY WORLD beginning on December 9:

My Physical Health

The strain of being part of a criminal action is overwhelming and can destroy you if you allow it. The government, by virtue of its power, has a big advantage over the people they prosecute. They use any means they can to wear you down with threats, press leaks, surprise motions, procedural changes, anything to keep you off balance. If I wasn't physically and mentally healthy, able to stay on top of my case and keep my business viable, I was doomed.

On the day of my brother's arrest, I had immediately lost my appetite. The onset of stress left me with no desire to eat and triggered a pre-indictment diet that resulted in a ten-pound weight loss in two weeks. I also began to feel a pressure in my chest that wouldn't go away and found myself stretching my arms and chest, taking deep breaths, and trying to relieve the anxiety I was feeling. The discomfort was so great I thought I might be having angina or that my blood pressure had spiked to unhealthy levels. I had never had heart problems and figured there was no more likely time to start having them than after my visit by the FBI.

These were real symptoms that I couldn't afford to ignore. I became more aware of my health and tried to be proactive in taking care of myself. First, I got into the routine of eating four to six meals a day whether I was hungry or not. By doing this I was able to reverse the loss and stabilize my weight over time. Second, I exercised five to seven days a week, alternating between running and weight training.

By May of 2010, a year and one half after the arrest and FBI visit, I had regained most of the ten pounds I had lost with muscle and have kept it on to this day. Forcing myself to eat right and exercise every day gave me a psychological edge no matter what happened outside of my control. As long as I ran or worked out and ate well I had a good day. I could do those activities and get the desired, measurable outcomes, unlike what I was experiencing in the unpredictable legal process. When it was time to go to trial, I was healthy and in shape so that I could function at a high level.

I also managed to schedule my annual physical shortly after returning to Nashville. My doctor, Randy Fullerton, listened attentively as I told him about my visit from the FBI, being named in the complaint, the possibility of indictment, and the stress that came from all of it. He knew my medical history and would be able to evaluate my overall health and compare it to my established medical baselines. If something was out of normal range, we would know and, we hoped, be able do something about it.

I went into some detail about the symptoms I was feeling, particularly my lack of appetite and my inability to get a good night's sleep. No matter what I did my mind would not stop racing. When I went to bed I might have managed to fall asleep for a couple of hours, but inevitably woke up between one and two in the morning. My mind was filled with random snapshots of all kinds of images and would not shut down for a full night's rest.

I didn't tell Randy that one night out of desperation I drank way too much Jack Daniels whiskey. My hope was that the alcohol would help me sleep. Eventually I got a good buzz and felt sleepy, but the liquor didn't work as I'd expected. The same pattern emerged as before, waking around 2 a.m.—this time with an added problem, the early signs of a hangover coming on. The negative effects of the alcohol followed me well into the next day. I knew better than to try to drink myself to sleep and paid the price with a splitting headache. I didn't try that again.

Randy put me through the routine battery of diagnostic tests I'd come to expect over the years of getting physicals. Fortunately the test results came back within normal range. My cardiopulmonary vitals were fine as well. Knowing my body wasn't suddenly breaking down was a relief and one less thing to worry about.

After assuring me that I was still in good health, Randy told me he couldn't be much help with my legal issues, but he could help me get a good night's sleep. He prescribed a low-dose sleep aid that had an immediate positive impact on my quality of life. I was able to sleep through the night again and wake up rested and clearheaded. This freed me to focus on other important issues.

My Business and Finances

Like most Americans, I believed in the American Dream. The idea that this country is the land of freedom and opportunity was very real in our home when I was growing up. My parents were a good example and inspiration to me. They taught me that anything was possible in America. If you got an education, applied yourself, worked hard, and saved, you could get ahead and have a chance for a comfortable life. As I aspired to live up to those ideals, I realized how wise my mother and father were.

I am one of the 27 million Americans who owns a small business. The business I own is Blagojevich Properties. It's made up of commercial real estate assets in four states located throughout the Southeast. I am in the rental business, leasing apartment units to individuals and commercial office space to businesses. The daily operation of some of my properties is outsourced to a third party that specializes in apartment/office management. The properties located in Nashville are managed by my trusted business associate and financial advisor for over ten years, Kevin Stinson, with a team of professionals working on-site serving our residents.

My job is to oversee the efficient and profitable operation of the business, making sure we provide a quality product at an affordable cost. The management structure I have in place allows me to focus on the strategic challenges of the business and gives me the flexibility to do other things with my time. When you put your own capital at risk in a small business, it's all up to you to make it work. There is no bailout if I fail. Every morning I wake up eager to meet the day's challenges—first, because I enjoy it, and second, because if I don't get the job done, I have no excuse. It's all up to me with the help of the team that I've assembled to make it work profitably. I would have it no other way.

Continuing to efficiently operate my business in the face of an indictment wasn't easy. The ability to multitask and concentrate on the important issues was even more crucial because I couldn't afford to neglect it. I had a long-established staff meeting every Friday that I convened to talk in person or by conference call and get updates from all my property managers. This system was useful because it kept me engaged in managing the key drivers of the business.

Many times during those meetings I would get interrupted by phone calls from my attorney to discuss something regarding the case. These calls often disrupted the management continuity of my business, redirecting me to deal with a legal issue. When this happened, I had no choice and did the best I could to balance the two and prioritize the most urgent issues first. It wasn't easy and it took some effort to pace myself into a rhythm I could sustain. I needed to quickly assess, weigh, and prioritize the issues according to their urgency, so I wouldn't waste time on unimportant issues. Regrettably, anything related to my case seemed to always take priority when it came up.

I worked just as hard on getting my finances in shape as I did in preparing for trial. This meant that Kevin and I met regularly to develop a plan to prioritize the sale of parts of my business and find a way to borrow from my home to pay my legal fees. We tried to concentrate on the parts of my operation that would least impact the stability and growth of my business. My investment strategy was to buy undervalued properties when they became available. This required I have readily available capital to make a purchase if I found something I liked. This was no longer possible given my legal exposure, and I had to scrap any plans for growth. We were essentially in the process of dismantling thirty years of hard work in order to have the money for my defense.

When the government prosecutes an individual, it has many advantages, one of which is the significant financial burden placed on the defendant who has chosen to go to trial. If I was unable to, the court would have appointed an attorney, paid at a reduced government rate, to defend me. Unlike many defendants I was able to hire an excellent lawyer without asking the court to appoint one. This was no guarantee of victory, but it helped to level the playing field with the government and give me a better chance.

Julie and I both believed in saving for a rainy day. In no way did we expect to be hit with a perfect storm that would put in peril the diligent planning and financial security we'd spent our entire married life building. In addition to the legal battle, this storm included a national financial meltdown in late 2008, an approaching economic recession, and a major fire that destroyed twelve units at one of my properties. We had to financially absorb and manage all these problems if we were to avoid bankruptcy and pay for my defense.

This forced me to recognize what was important and what wasn't. Material things, vacations, your hopes and dreams, all take a backseat. Nothing else mattered except getting through the calamity and surviving. Lining up the fruits of my life's work to sell wasn't easy, but it was necessary in order to persevere and defend myself in court. This is what it means to be prosecuted by the federal government, whether you are innocent or guilty. We knew that if and when we prevailed, there would be no financial restitution.

My Psyche

There are no guarantees in life, and I knew that. Shit happens and you have to adapt to new situations and make the best of them. Like most people I was realistic and prepared to make adjustments to my business or personal life if the unexpected happened. Whether it was job insecurity, a natural disaster, or the loss of my parents and other loved ones, I always managed to adjust and move forward. But the psychological impact and major reevaluation I experienced from an indictment was unexpectedly huge.

My life's work was threatened, my reputation tarnished, my future bleak. I didn't want to lose what I had worked hard to build. This reality forced me to reevaluate my plans, reset my goals, and make the best of it, if I could. My life aspirations and values changed. They took on new form and meaning.

The enormity of my brother's arrest, my indictment, and national media interest in our case was something I had never imagined. I felt like a cork floating aimlessly in a vast ocean. I had no control, didn't know where the next wave would take me. Making sense of what was happening and getting my "head on straight" was a problem. I saw no clear way out.

The thought that I might have to wait for more than a year to go to trial and get a resolution was hard to rationalize. It affected my ability to see past the trial, robbed me of any plans for the future, and left me feeling lost. This uncertainty weighed heavily on me and was compounded by the reality that I was going to trial against a seemingly unbeatable foe, the US government. This was a psychologically daunting challenge that took a lot of effort to work through. The size and scope of the challenge seemed so large and unwieldy that the only way I had a chance to mentally cope with it was to break it down into manageable pieces. By far, of all the tests I faced, this was the biggest.

The plan that Alex and I had drafted was instructive in putting a framework in place to give me something to focus on. Over the course of the crisis, I was able to figure out how to break this big problem into smaller manageable pieces, with each of them prioritized in order of importance and urgency. Hard as it was and simple as it may sound, once I accepted that my new goal was to win in court, everything else was secondary. All other facets of my life had to support it. This single-purposed approach gave me a greater sense that I could still influence things.

Of all the many pieces that I needed to manage, first and foremost, I needed to know my family would be able to get by if the worst happened to me. I wasn't so much concerned about my personal well-being as I was about my wife and son. I knew I would be fine, but I needed to know how they would cope without me.

Julie, Alex, and I sat down together and talked candidly about the possibility of my going to prison. They reassured me that if I was convicted and sentenced to prison, they would manage without me and help each other. Alex said he would move to Nashville to live with his mom until I returned. During our conversation, I told them that if I believed I had done something illegal I would tell them because I could not live with myself if I lied to them. As I had expected, they believed in me and never doubted my honesty. Knowing they would support each other was an important step to allow me to work on other issues. I was slowly eating the whale one bite at a time. I still had many more bites to go.

Another area that needed constant attention was my mental outlook. My mind needed to be centered. Trying to keep a positive attitude was really important if I was to have any chance to cope with what was happening to me. It became a priority and I made the time to work on it any way I could. The strain from knowing the government was prosecuting me was substantial and surprised me in a way I didn't expect. I felt my future had been stolen from me and that I had been placed in a mental black hole I'd never before experienced. I struggled to make sense of it and couldn't. It was almost impossible to be at peace and feel happiness as I once did. The mental drag weighed on me all the time, to the point that I would do almost anything to make it go away.

As often as possible, I tried to be around positive people. After I was indicted, I learned a valuable lesson about whom I should spend time with. A friend I hadn't seen for a while invited me to lunch. He was well intentioned and sincere, but made a real mistake in an awkward attempt to comfort me. He told me how bad he felt for my being prosecuted by Patrick Fitzgerald. He was familiar with Fitzgerald's track record and thought him to be a ruthless prosecutor who never lost.

Listening to him go on about how tough and successful Fitzgerald was, I got the distinct impression he thought I had no chance to win. He meant well, but he made me angry. He failed to understand what it was like for a guy in my situation to hear that it was already over before it started. He, like many other people, just didn't know how to express himself in a way that was helpful.

From that day on, I became very selfish and made a conscientious effort to avoid well-meaning but negative people. They zapped me of my mental energy, which was too precious to squander on anyone or anything that would drain my mind of positive, can-do thoughts. In addition to Julie and Alex, my best friend Andy Martin and my brother-in-law Eric Thrailkill were my go-to guys during this period.

Andy and I have known each other for more than twenty-five years, and he is my best friend. Over that time he had met Rod on several occasions, once in Washington when Rod was sworn in as a congressman. He knew I was a caring brother and wasn't surprised when I told him I was going to help Rod fundraise for a possible third term for governor. Andy had a good understanding of the challenges I had with Rod and knew I was going primarily to honor my parents' request. He also knew that I had hoped I would grow closer to my brother while I helped him.

We've been through a number of life's curveballs together, and I knew I could talk to Andy about almost anything, any time. After Rod's arrest, I'd routinely call Andy and tell him I needed to "lie on his couch," code for coming to his office to drink a little Jack Daniels, smoke a cigar, and talk about my legal problems.

Specifics? How the prosecutors had unjustly indicted me. The strain the indictment placed on me. The difficulty of getting a fair trial. The substantial advantage the government had over a defendant. And the challenges I had to manage with Rod as my codefendant.

Andy always encouraged me to believe in the system, not lose faith, and expect a good outcome. Not until well after the trial did he tell me what he really thought, that his opinion had changed dramatically over the course of the case because he saw firsthand that the government didn't care about getting to the truth. Instead, he concluded that all the feds wanted was the win, no matter who got hurt. Regardless of the stress I felt, Andy and I managed to laugh and rationalize away whatever the problem was that prompted my call. He never failed to lift my spirits and help me get through another day.

My brother-in-law Eric runs the information systems group for a publicly traded health care company headquartered in Nashville. When we arrived back home after Rod's arrest, Eric, his wife Nanci, and their son Davis came over to our home to comfort and support us. We talked extensively about what happened when the FBI visited me and, of course, discussed Rod's arrest. I vividly remember standing in our kitchen talking with them wondering if the FBI had wiretapped our home. Paranoia is another of the unexpected outcomes that one has to manage when one is victimized by governmental eavesdropping.

Eric had been on business in Orlando that day, giving a presentation to a medical group, when he saw news of the arrest of the governor of Illinois flash on a TV screen. He said he had to stop for a minute and process the shock of the broadcast before he faced his audience. He had known Rod from the time I had started dating Julie. He was familiar with Rod's political career and respected him for his achievement, but now feared the worst for him.

Of all the people who stepped up and helped me prepare for trial, Eric made the biggest impact. He is an exceptionally skilled researcher, a very capable guy who worked hard to find law-related information that was relevant to my legal effort. He got so involved with the case that Mike wrote a defense memo appointing him a member of our legal team. As Mike explained to me, this ensured that Eric would have an attorney-client privilege standing like what the lawyers on the case had.

Eric threw himself into learning about all aspects of my defense, even to the extent of creating several charts we entered into evidence at trial.

It's impossible to measure the totality of his contribution other than to say I knew I had his unconditional support on anything I might need. Most often the assistance he gave was given without even being asked for. He seemed to know intuitively what might be useful to me and my legal team.

He and I spent many hours walking together in Edwin Warner Park, a nature preserve near our homes, talking in depth about the allegations made against me in the criminal complaint and indictment. We repeatedly reviewed all aspects of the case in excruciating detail—primarily what I remembered from my four months of fundraising and the content of the conversations from the wiretap recordings.

In time, these talks would prove to be a useful way of testing the reliability of my memory, reinforcing my command of the facts, and building my confidence. I made a practice of asking him if my recollection of the facts was consistent with our previous conversations. Fortunately, each time I asked, he said yes. It didn't register with me then, but I was doing a form of trial preparation that would come in handy when I had to rush to get ready to testify almost a year later. Eric was there for me literally every step of the way, even accompanying me to Chicago for my first arraignment the following April and later attending parts of the trial.

Shortly after I was indicted, Andy told me that he had been working with a management consultant and found it to be very helpful to him and his business. For many months he tried to get me to call the consultant. I resisted—largely for financial reasons. I was looking for ways to cut my monthly household expenses, not add to them. Still, I knew I had further to go on improving my psyche and owed it to myself to go to the consultant at least once to see if I got any value from a session.

My first meeting with Dan Haile was in March 2010, three months before the start of the trial. By that time I had already been through a lot of adjustment and personal change. I had been intensely focused on my case and I was skeptical about how useful it would be to meet with a management consultant at this late stage.

My skepticism was misplaced. We ultimately met nine times, once a week up until I left for trial. I was pleasantly surprised by the breadth and substance of our discussions, which included detailed evaluation of my business and the psychological effect my legal exposure was having on me.

I told Dan that I was troubled most by the fact that I was unable to vision beyond the trial. After much discussion Dan offered a solution, which I later realized had been part of the original plan that Alex had presented me. I'd missed what Alex had written for me all those months ago. "Organize this process into the grand scheme of your life and how you will learn, benefit, and grow from it." Astonishingly, they both came up with the same overarching advice, but from very different perspectives.

Although Alex had wisely prescribed learning from, not fearing the experience, I'd only paid attention when Dan offered the same advice. In doing so, he helped me to become more self-aware, to be mindful of what was going on around me, to live in the moment. This powerful insight further enabled me to meet the uncertain future I faced.

Whatever happened at trial would be part of a continuous learning process that in the end would make me stronger, wiser, better. I'd finally found what I had been seeking for over a year, a mental perspective with the right objective. With the trial approaching, I felt a lot better about how I should approach the next phase of my life.

Dan gave me one other meaningful takeaway. He asked me if I had ever kept a journal. He thought it might be a useful aid during the trial to write down my thoughts in a structured fashion and have them as a record of what I was observing, thinking, and feeling at the time. Again I was initially reluctant to commit to a new project; I thought it would be an added burden. But Dan finally convinced me that I had nothing to lose. If I didn't like writing in a journal, I could always stop.

As it turned out, I wrote in my journal every day we were in court during the ten-week trial. Journaling offered an invaluable retreat during the long days of testimony and procedural delays. After my first day of writing, I never felt an obligation to keep doing it. The process of writing was like therapy to channel my observations, concerns, and fears into a neutral safe place. As long as I wrote, I felt a psychological detachment from what was happening around me in the courtroom. The process helped me to center my mind in the midst of an otherwise overwhelming and all-consuming experience.

Whether it was staying away from negative people, focusing on my plan, or devising solutions with Dan, I still had to get through the next day. Because hearing or reading bad news could send me into a funk, I imposed my own media blackout. I tried to avoid watching any local or national news broadcasts, and unless it was absolutely necessary for my defense, I didn't read the newspaper. Once an avid news junkie, I didn't miss it at all and did better without the media clutter. Corny as it sounds, I even limited my movie viewing to romantic comedies because they temporarily made me happy.

CHAPTER SEVEN

Indicted

After a thorough review of the December 8 criminal complaint in which I ("Fundraiser A") was mentioned thirty-three times, my lawyer Mike Ettinger told me he hadn't read anything that put me in legal jeopardy. Nothing suggested that I was a part of Rod's inner circle, he said. It was clear that I was an outsider who came in for only four months to help his brother fundraise, nothing more. His educated guess? I would not be indicted.

Just to be on the safe side, in the event I was charged with something, I retained Mike as my counsel and paid him his hourly rate to represent me. He suggested we document the key conversations and interactions I had had with people of interest during my tenure at FOB. "While everything is fresh in your mind," he said.

Julie and I prepared memos on the twenty-eight people who were cited in the complaint whom I had spoken to or had worked with on a fundraising. I tried to recall for each one of them as much detail as possible on the substance of our conversation and any follow-up action associated with them. In addition, we provided Mike with a list of seventeen people I'd spoken with, whom I specifically remembered telling that if they made a contribution or hosted a fundraiser they would not receive any favorable government action in return. This we called our "no quid pro quo list." "No" was a word I used with great frequency. I was constantly approached by potential donors with all kinds of requests and expectations of help. Each time, I made it very clear that I could not help them with any favorable governmental action in exchange for a campaign contribution. After having met with me they knew there were no deals. There should never have been a doubt with anyone about where

I stood on this issue; I was consistent. And because of this, I slept well every night—pre-December 9—with a clear conscience.

One of those conversations I documented for Mike occurred in November 2008 when I got a call, out of the clear blue, at the FOB office from a man asking for my help. His name was Barry Aycock, and he told me he was frustrated with Southern Illinois University. He claimed he had completed all his course work, but the university would not process the credit he earned from his dissertation. Without the credit, he said, he could not graduate with his PhD. I had no way of knowing whether this was legitimate or not; I just wanted to help a guy who said he needed help.

One possible reason he may have called FOB was that members of the university's board of trustees are appointed by the governor. As Aycock spoke, I was amused by how misdirected he was in calling FOB for help, instead of someone in the SIU administration. My amusement changed to caution when he offered to make a substantial contribution to FOB in exchange for help in getting his degree processed through the state bureaucracy. At the time, it sounded like an innocent and somewhat awkward attempt at a quid pro quo, so I tried not to overreact. I responded by telling him no political contribution was necessary to take care of something that should be taken care of through the proper channels.

From the outset, Rod and his staff had instructed me not to get involved in state business. Any calls on that subject were to be referred to his chief of staff, John Harris. I told Aycock that all I could do was to forward the requisite documents for his degree to someone who could possibly help him. We had one subsequent conversation when I called him back with my e-mail address. I never heard from him again.

I moved on after that conversation and didn't think much more about it until months later when I learned the FBI had wiretapped the FOB office and my cell phone. That out-of-nowhere call took on greater significance when I put it into context with being wiretapped. I have no proof of this, but knowing what I know about how the government operates, I can't rule out the possibility that they were trying to entrap me with the Aycock request for state help in exchange for a contribution. What seemed like a misguided call could have been something very different.

This is only one example of the many times that I could have easily compromised myself to get a contribution from a donor but didn't. The people wiretapping my conversations and the prosecutors who brought charges against me knew what kind of person I was from listening to these calls. They knew better than anyone how I conducted myself when no one was supposed to be listening. Nonetheless, they seemed to choose to ignore my consistently ethical behavior and ultimately use me as a pawn in their prosecution of my brother.

We spent the next several months suspended in uncertainty waiting for the government to present their indictment.

While we waited, the media contained all kinds of speculation as to what specific charges might be brought against Rod and who the other likely codefendants might be. Some of the speculation centered around my sister-in-law Patti. She was allegedly vulnerable to prosecution because of her business association with Tony Rezko and her active participation in state matters. In October, prior to Rod's arrest, Patti's business records had been subpoenaed by the FBI. Rod dismissed the move, believing the feds just wanted to harass Patti and him. Still, he asked me to get all her records copied and delivered to their attorney. I was concerned for them and agreed to help get it done.

After Rod's arrest, the government released some very unflattering tapes of Patti cursing on a conference call with Rod and some of his political advisors in Washington. She was taped saying, "fuck the Cubs" when they were discussing an issue related to the baseball team owned by the Tribune Company. I have no doubt that the government purposefully released this and other unflattering recordings of Patti to discredit her and Rod publicly in anticipation of the indictment. This fueled the media speculation that Patti might be a codefendant and would be indicted because of her alleged involvement in Rod's alleged schemes. The fallout from the release of these profane snippets was significant enough that Patti's father, Alderman Richard Mell, as well as her sister and brother, all agreed to be interviewed on local news to counter the growing negative public perception of her. As Rod's brother, what struck me most about their interview was that they never said anything good about Rod.

Although Mike believed I would not be indicted, we knew Rod was in big trouble. He was in the process of being the first governor of the state and eighth in US history to be impeached and voted out of office by the state legislature. On January 29 I watched with great sadness Rod's speech to the Illinois State Senate, live on CNN, presenting his argument for retention.

On January 9 the Illinois House had impeached him. Ten days earlier, perhaps sensing that his days in office were numbered, Rod had—by the power still vested in him as governor—appointed Roland Burris to fill Obama's vacant seat in the US Senate. Illinois Secretary of State Jesse White registered the appointment but refused to sign the Senate's certification form. After a review, the Illinois State Supreme Court ruled that only the governor's signature was required. Rod finally got his man appointed and Burris served from January 12, 2009, until November 29, 2010. With the allegations of corruption swirling in the wake of Rod's arrest, the political climate was so toxic for Burris that he was unable to raise the money necessary to mount a credible run for the Senate. A Republican, Mark Kirk, bested the Democrat Alexi Giannoulias in the general election.

In his forty-seven-minute speech to the Illinois Senate, Rod called the impeachment proceedings "an evisceration of the presumption of innocence." He also said: "There was never a conversation where I intended to break the law. How can you throw a governor out of office on a criminal complaint and you haven't been able to show or to prove any criminal activity? I'm appealing to you and your sense of fairness."

The *Washington Post* said, "It was a speech long on passion and short on answers, and it did nothing to help his cause" (*Washington Post*, January 30, 2009). Indeed, after conducting its own hearings and listening to Rod, the Illinois Senate voted 59–0 to remove him from office.

Before the hearings, Rod and I talked several times about an offer made to him to voluntarily step down as governor and take a year's salary as a severance in return. I encouraged him to take it for all the practical reasons that seem obvious when you're facing unemployment. He chose instead to fight it out to the end and left office in disgrace without any transition income. He now had to figure out how he was going to support his family while he waited for trial.

As a family all we could do while waiting for the indictment was to help and support each other as best we could. I spoke with Rod frequently during this time and found him to be strong and prepared to face his unknown future with unwavering resolve and belief in himself. He'd been busy regrouping since leaving office and hired a publicist, Glen Selig, who was able to secure a book deal for Rod to write his autobiography.

Selig also secured a spot for Rod on the NBC reality show, *I'm a Celebrity...Get Me Out of Here!* In the end, he was unable to do the show, which was filmed in Costa Rica, because the government had revoked his passport. With the family in need of money, Patti took his place.

When Rod and I spoke, my potential liability rarely came up. Recognizing the enormity of what he was facing, I didn't want to burden him with my fears. I relied on my wife and my lawyer for support at this early stage.

On February 2, less than a week after he'd been impeached, Rod appeared on *Late Show With David Letterman*. I didn't watch. The next morning, my good friend from Nashville Paul Gaddis called to say he was surprised that Letterman had played one of the government's wiretapped recordings between Rod and me.

I was shocked. The snippet involved a conversation about Johnny Johnston, a racetrack owner whom Lon Monk had been wooing for a donation before the end of 2008. Less than a minute long, the Letterman recording offered no context. It had obviously been cherry-picked to put Rod on the spot.

I was also furious. No one had asked me if I wanted my words from a private conversation with my brother played for the entire nation, and more importantly, for the potential jury pool in Chicago. You might ask: if I was innocent, why worry? I worried because of the lack of context and, when I eventually watched Rod's appearance, his flip response to the recording.

Here is the pertinent part of the transcript from the show on which Rod also discussed his hair and glibly told Letterman, "Well, I figured I had to get impeached and thrown out of office to get the chance to get invited by you."

> Dave: Yeah, you set it up—this is you and your brother talking about Johnny Johnston, right? [*audience laughs, applauds*]
> Rod: I don't know. I don't know, I haven't heard it.
> Dave: Let's take a listen here. [*conversation is played and chyrons appear on screen*]
>
> [START OF RECORDING]
> Rob: Uh, I talked to Lon, and uh, he says Johnny Johnston's good for it.
> Rod: OK.
> Rob: He's gonna give you . . . ya know, he didn't get it. But he said, ya know, I'm good for it. I gotta just decide what, what uh, accounts to get it out of. And Lon's gonna talk to you about some sensitivities legislatively tonight when he sees you. With regard to timing of all of this.
> Rod: Right—before the end of the year, though, right?

Rob: Oh, yeah. Yeah, yeah.
[END OF RECORDING]

Dave: All right, so what have we got? What are we talking about there?

Rod: Well, I mean, you know, again, that speaks for itself—there's not a single criminal act in that conversation. I was afraid you were going to have some of those other tapes where I sounded like Christian Bale. . . . [*audience laughs*] And had I known somebody was listening I would not have said some of those words, but these were private conversations with top staff.

Dave: But what is it—is money going to change hands?

Rod: Oh no, campaign contributions, commitment to raise money.

Dave: In return for some favorable treatment for the track owners?

Rod: No, absolutely not.

(http://featuresblogs.chicagotribune.com/entertainment_tv/2009/02/blagojevich-letterman-governor.html)

Maybe I was overreacting, but as far as I was concerned, this was just another indication that I had a problem with Rod as a potential codefendant. I immediately called him. When I got him on the phone, he cheerfully asked if I'd seen him on *Letterman*. I curtly told him, no, but that I had just gotten off the phone with a friend who told me the wiretapped conversation had been played.

After Rod laughed this off as a mere nuisance, I responded angrily. "What the fuck are you doing on these shows? You put me in jeopardy by doing them when they play conversations that make us look stupid."

His lame response: "I didn't know he was going to play it."

"That is the reason why you don't do them!" I yelled. He just didn't get it. Nor was he willing to understand my point of view. I was troubled by our inability to talk logically about the potential risks of his being so public.

FROM THE DAY ROD had been arrested in December to the day the indictments were announced on April 2, the media speculated about who else the government would charge. Would it be Senate Candidate 5 (whom everyone knew was Jesse Jackson Jr.)? Fundraiser A? Patti?

Indicting the spouse or a relative of the principal target is a not an uncommon practice. Why? One word: leverage. The government reasons that a husband whose wife might be or is indicted will be more amenable to pleading guilty to some or all of the charges. What man wants to see his wife go to prison? Who will take care of the children? And so the threat of a spouse's indictment lingers like a dark cloud over the head of the target.

Such a strategy has a downside. If the government leans too hard on, say, a wife, it can look like mean-spirited overkill and thus alienate potential jurors and the court of public opinion. As indictment day approached, the prevailing thinking in some circles was that the DOJ would be hesitant to indict Patti, a mother of two school-age children. This left me more vulnerable as the family member to be charged and used as leverage to put pressure on Rod to work out a deal with the DOJ.

Why would the DOJ want such a deal? If a defendant pleads guilty, the government is vindicated. It also avoids a potentially lengthy, costly trial. Who knows? A jury might even find a defendant not guilty or, at least, may be hung—unable to reach a verdict. In Rod's case, the government knew it had a defendant who, despite the barrage of criticism from the press and fellow politicians, was still popular with many citizens in Illinois. And it would be these men and women who would be the jurors.

As I was to learn in time, the government's modus operandi is to take the path of least resistance to a conviction, no matter who they destroy in the process. Although I had been involved with Rod for only four months, I was vulnerable because I was his brother and because the FBI had amassed hundreds of hours of my conversations on tape. The prosecution could then be selective in choosing the intercepts they believed demonstrated a criminal intent, take them out of context, and make a case against me. At the same time, they could exclude all the calls that clearly showed I had done nothing wrong.

I've been told on good authority that Patti was fortunate I was a family target whom it was convenient to charge, or she may have been implicated in spite of the DOJ's reluctance to charge spouses who are parents of young children. I'll never know what the real reasons were or what the DOJ's strategy considerations were in ultimately making the decision to charge me. But what I believe is that the DOJ was more interested in getting the win than it was in getting at the truth. That can be devastating for the codefendant who becomes collateral damage. And it's sad, too, for those who believe in a fair system of justice.

All my life I was one of those people. I mistakenly believed the federal government was an impartial, truth-seeking arbiter. This naïvely held belief led me to think I wouldn't be indicted because I knew that the government knew, or should have learned from its investigation, that I had done nothing illegal.

My positive thoughts turned negative on April 1. My business associate Kevin Stinson rushed up my Nashville driveway in a panic and told me that all my business records had been subpoenaed by the FBI/IRS. This was no April Fools' Day prank. I realized then that I was going to be charged.

I immediately called Mike to tell him that Kevin had been served. He instructed me to tell Kevin, as he did me, not to turn over the documents. If necessary, Kevin should contact him for legal advice.

Julie was still home, getting ready to leave for work at Vanderbilt. She was as shaken as I was. I asked her not to go in to work because I didn't want to be alone. Our lives were about to go in an entirely different direction.

The next day, Thursday, April 2, Mike called me with a heads-up that the government was going to release the indictments later that afternoon. "Prepare yourself," he said.

How do you prepare yourself to be indicted? Was there something more proactive I should be doing to be ready? Should I pray for the best or meditate to clear my mind of negativity and let the universe handle it?

I'd already been following the plan that Alex and I had drafted back in December. But I guess I'd fallen short on one count. I could not contain my anger. If I had any chance of surviving the challenges ahead, I would have to figure out how best to channel my outrage into positive energy.

As soon as I got off the phone with Mike, I called Eric to tell him what was happening and to see if we could spend the next couple of days at his house. Aware from past experience that the media would show up at our doorstep, I wanted to avoid the cameras and reporters if we could. After Eric said, "Of course," Julie and I wasted no time. We closed all the blinds, packed a couple of overnight bags and got into our car.

We were barely down the street when we spotted a Fox News vehicle turn toward our house. Our neighbors later told us that Fox and another news affiliate camped out in front of our house for quite a while until they somehow realized we weren't there.

Late that afternoon, Mike called to inform me I had been indicted on two counts of wire fraud for conspiring with Rod to deny the citizens of Illinois their right to Rod's "honest services." Of the indictment's nineteen counts, these were the ones that applied to me:

Count Three

On or about November 1, 2008, at Chicago, in the Northern District of Illinois, Eastern Division, and elsewhere, ROD BLAGOJEVICH and ROBERT BLAGOJEVICH, defendants herein, for the purpose of executing the above-described scheme, did knowingly cause to be transmitted by means of wire and radio communication in interstate commerce signals and sounds, namely a phone call between ROD BLAGOJEVICH in Chicago, Illinois, and ROBERT BLAGOJEVICH in Nashville, Tennessee, in which ROBERT BLAGOJEVICH gave ROD BLAGOJEVICH an update on the solicitation of campaign contributions from Construction Executive and Racetrack Executive, and they discussed potential contributions from Senate Candidate C and Senate Candidate A.

Count Twelve

On or about December 4, 2008, at Chicago, in the Northern District of Illinois, Eastern Division, and elsewhere, ROD BLAGOJEVICH and ROBERT BLAGOJEVICH, defendants herein, for the purpose of executing the above-described scheme, did knowingly cause to be transmitted by means of wire and radio communication in interstate commerce signals and sounds, namely a phone call between ROD BLAGOJEVICH and Deputy Governor A in Chicago, Illinois, and Advisor A in Washington, D.C., in which ROD BLAGOJEVICH said that if he gave the Senate seat to Senate Candidate 5, there would be "tangible political support . . . specific amounts and everything . . . some of it up front."

It turned out that Deputy Governor A was Bob Greenlee, Advisor A was Fred Yang, and Senate Candidate 5 was Congressman Jesse Jackson Jr.

My first question for Mike was, "What did I do wrong?" I didn't understand how I'd broken the law.

Mike said he needed more time to study the indictment to better understand the government's theory behind its case. For the time being, he tried to explain as best he could. I was being charged for violating a federal statute that includes the following language: "For the purposes of this chapter, the term scheme or artifice to defraud includes a scheme or artifice to deprive another of the intangible right of honest services."

Honest services?

The *Chicago Tribune* explained: "Honest services fraud criminalizes schemes that deprive the public or the government of the right to have public officials perform their duties honestly." The statute had been used in recent years against former Enron CEO Jeffrey Skilling and former Alabama Governor Don Siegelman, as well as the infamous lobbyist Jack Abramoff (*Chicago Tribune*, December 8, 2009).

As former *Boston Globe* reporter Gary S. Chafetz wrote in the *Huffington Post*: "For years, federal prosecutors have aggressively exploited the honest-services fraud statute, charging public officials and private citizens with denying their 'honest services' to taxpayers, stockholders, or business clients. In an overwhelming majority of the cases, these white-collar defendants have been pressured into pleading guilty in order to receive a much-reduced sentence in a minimum-security prison camp."

Writing in *Forbes*, former federal prosecutor James D. Zirin noted that the "criminal statute . . . has become the darling of the prosecutor's nursery." He then offered a history and analysis:

> Honest services fraud evolved from a 1941 Supreme Court decision in which a public official received bribes in exchange for favorable action on a city contract. The court reasoned that, even though the city saved money on the deal, the element of bribery made the conduct "a scheme to defraud the public." Normally, in fraud, there is a certain symmetry. The fraudster gains something of value at the expense of the victim. Under the honest services doctrine, there need not have been that symmetry. Thereafter, courts did not limit the doctrine to fraud by public officials. It was applied to private individuals participating in public decisions and even private employees playing no role in public decisions. In short, the statute applied to any notional breach of fiduciary duty—whatever its boundary or legal source.
>
> In 1987 the court dealt a death knell to the denial of services fraud doctrine, limited the mail and wire fraud statutes to protection of tangible property rights, and challenged Congress to fix the problem if it wished to do so. The result was §1346, enacted the next year, which spelled out that a scheme or artifice to defraud "includes a scheme or artifice to deprive another of the intangible right of honest services." The prosecutors were off and running, dreaming up creative ways to apply the new statute. A criminal statute must clearly define the conduct it proscribes. An unconstitutionally vague statute, the cases say, fails "to provide a person of ordinary intelligence fair notice of what is prohibited, or [as being] so standardless that [they] authorize or encourage seriously

discriminatory enforcement." For example, a statute making it criminal to embezzle funds from a bank would be constitutional since everyone knows what it means. On the other hand, a statute making it a crime to do "something wrong" would be unconstitutionally vague. . . .

Honest services fraud is a titanically vague concept. On its face, it might apply to an employee who called in sick and then went to the ballgame—or even to a judge who used his office to get a first-rate corner table in a restaurant for himself and his significant other. (http://www.webcitation.org/6WjY2Ms13)

Confused? I was. And so were the nation's courts. As I'll explain later, eventually the US Supreme Court's interpretation of the statute would force the government to reindict me on other charges.

The first of many interactions I was to have with my now-codefendant brother occurred roughly fifteen minutes later when Rod called me from Florida, where he and his family were spending spring break. As he spoke, I could hear my nieces in the background laughing and carrying on like normal.

Rod was unemotional and seemed to be resigned to his situation. He acknowledged that he expected this to happen to him. Then, laughing, he said that I was the most honest guy he knew, and he couldn't believe they also indicted me. After all, he had been mired in Illinois politics and hounded by the feds while I had lived a quiet life five hundred miles away. I had worked for him all of four months when this came down on me.

His laugh and what seemed to be a dismissive attitude of my situation had me on edge. I got angrier when he said that I would be fine, that the feds weren't after me, but after him. I thought to myself: he might think that my circumstance is inconsequential compared to his, but I'm facing two felony charges. It sure feels like they are after me, too.

While he was laughing I snapped back angrily and told him I didn't think it was funny. He immediately retreated and said he wasn't laughing at me, just that he couldn't believe what had happened. I told him I didn't care how he tried to justify laughing, this was serious and I didn't think it was funny. This interaction, much like the unresolved one that occurred on December 6 after the Indian fundraiser, was indicative of a pattern of behavior between the two of us that was to severely strain our relationship. Unfortunately, we would have many more testy interactions with each other as we moved closer to trial.

The announcement of the indictment was big news all over the country. There was no escaping the fact that from now on, my quiet life in Nashville was going to be very different. Everybody in my circle now knew I was facing criminal prosecution with my more famous brother in Chicago. The local newspaper picked up the story and published an article about my alleged crimes. There was no hiding it. All I could do was to continue to believe in myself and deal with the visibility, ridicule, and speculation about my innocence until judgment day came sometime in the distant future.

In the meantime, I was determined to stay the course by following the plan Alex and I had drafted in December and to maintain a structured and disciplined lifestyle. By doing so I believed I could stay focused on the tasks that would lead to my vindication. I tried to keep it simple. I would control what I could, influence what I could, and try not to worry about the rest.

CHAPTER EIGHT

La-la Land

"Y ou'll have to call your pretrial case officer," Mike told me after the indictment was presented. The case officer, headquartered at the Dirksen Federal Building in Chicago, takes a defendant through pretrial processing. Phase One, before the arraignment on April 14, was a phone interview. Mike explained that I would be asked to provide financial data and information about my business interests. He compared this to seeing a loan officer—except in this instance the numbers would be crunched to determine my bond. The information I provided would be shared only with the judge presiding over our case, Mike added.

That assigned judge was James Zagel, a sixty-eight-year-old Harvard Law School graduate who had previously been a prosecutor and director of the Illinois State Police. During his more than twenty years on the bench, Zagel had presided over more than a few high-profile cases. Just prior to our indictment, the Family Secrets trial had been held in his courtroom. Here, members of the Chicago mob had been convicted of multiple murders. Another interesting factoid: in 2002 the judge had published a legal thriller, *Money to Burn*, about a federal judge involved in a plot to rob the Federal Reserve. (I'll have more to say about Judge Zagel later.)

My case manager was very professional. I sensed that he understood the gravity of what I was facing. Indeed, although I considered him a member of "the enemy," he seemed empathetic. He told me I would talk to him again the day of the arraignment when we would conclude the processing.

On the day before I was to leave Nashville for the arraignment, my brother-in-law and sister-in-law, Eric and Nanci, invited me to go to a tennis match at Vanderbilt University. My nephew Davis, an excellent high school tennis player at the time, joined us. Vanderbilt is a short ride from our home, and I figured watching a collegiate tennis match with my family on a beautiful spring afternoon would get my mind off the arraignment. Not so. I couldn't help thinking about the many times I'd watched my son play baseball in high school and college, a time in our lives when we were happy and danger-free. As I sat there lost in those sweet memories, my flashbacks were abruptly interrupted by the applause of the parents cheering on their kids playing tennis. As I snapped out of my daydream, I felt jealousy for the first time. Those tennis parents were experiencing happiness, while my reality was headed in a very different direction.

Earlier in the week, Eric had offered to fly up to Chicago with me. I'd already decided I didn't want Julie to accompany me because she had to work and I didn't want to expose her to whatever unknowns were awaiting me at the courthouse. She was under enough stress living with the fear of what might happen to me. The time would come soon enough for her to face the courthouse mob. Still, I didn't want to be alone. I immediately said yes to Eric's generous offer.

On April 13 Eric and I boarded the first flight on Southwest Airlines to a chilly and rainy Chicago. We took a cab through the gloom—literal and figurative—to Mike's law office in Palos Heights, a suburb southwest of the city. Cloaked in gray, the neighborhoods we drove through were tired and in need of repair. So was I.

Mike was at his office alone to greet us. This was only the second time we'd been face to face. I hadn't seen him since our meeting at the restaurant where he'd won me over despite the scrambled egg hanging from his lower lip.

Eric and I both had experience working with the biggest and best regional corporate law firms in Nashville. We were accustomed to meeting at law offices that were well staffed and richly appointed in high-rent space. Spacious, wood-paneled conference rooms with generous offerings of food and drinks were standard at these firms. The offices of Michael Ettinger and Associates couldn't have been more different. Mike had told me he abandoned downtown office space years ago because he preferred the lower overhead costs that came with an office in the south suburbs. Mission accomplished.

Mike's conference room was a disheveled mess "decorated" with stacks of legal papers everywhere—on the table, under the table, in all the corners.

His personal office was no better. We went there to look for jury instructions . . . to no avail.

Before I'd left Nashville, he had told me that his trial strategy was always the same: he began at the end of the process with the jury instructions he believed applied to the case. He then built his defense framework from that, working backward to his opening statement, which would emphasize the flaws in the government's case and outline our arguments as to why I was innocent. I didn't know if this was a typical way to put on a defense, but it sounded good to me.

Mike couldn't find the misplaced instructions, so he reprinted them. I made eye contact with Eric. We were thinking the same thing: who is this guy? Columbo again came to mind.

Mike was profiled by the *Chicago Lawyer* in a feature headlined, "Small firm lawyers sometimes handle big-time cases." Here's what reporter Amanda Robert had to say:

> Mike Ettinger worked in the Cook County state's attorney's office for a few years before he found his own niche in handling federal criminal cases in the suburbs.
>
> After Cook County State's Attorney Edward Hanrahan lost his race in 1972, Ettinger and several attorneys from the office opened their own firm downtown.
>
> Since Ettinger worked in the 5th Municipal District, he received cases from the area's lawyers, he said.
>
> He opened a satellite office in Oak Lawn and started practicing in federal court in 1974. He handled federal cases in Illinois, but also worked on federal cases in nine other states.
>
> "I represented some people charged with drug dealing, and they'd tell their friends about me, and they'd start hiring me," Ettinger said. "I started representing some Colombian groups who would get arrested around the country, mainly in Florida. We ended up buying a little townhouse in North Miami, because we got so much business in Fort Lauderdale and Miami."
>
> Ettinger decided to stay in the southwest suburbs when his firm split up in the 1980s. By that time, most of the municipal districts opened suburban courts and sent them their own felony calls, he said.
>
> He now practices with Mark Besbekos and Cheryl Schroeder, two former assistant state's attorneys who also worked in the suburbs. The trio handles 30 to 40 complex federal and state criminal and civil cases.
>
> Ettinger said working in a small firm at this point in his career gives him more freedom to tailor his practice.

"In the first 10 to 15 years, I'd be handling three or four cases a day," he said. "As you advance in age and in experience, you get the larger cases, and you can't run around like you did before. You either don't take the smaller cases or hire attorneys in your firm so they can do them." (*Chicago Lawyer*, Nov. 2011, http://www.webcitation.org/6WSkmKuVL)

As Mike shuffled about, we helped ourselves at the self-serve coffee stand he had set up in his break room. He also told us to take whatever snack food he had stored above the sink. Snack food was the last thing I wanted that morning. I declined, as did Eric. Again we exchanged glances. I hadn't known what to expect at Mike's office, but the disarray and lack of organization were disconcerting. We were off to a rough start.

Once we settled into his conference room with a fresh copy of the jury instructions, Mike began to outline his defense strategy. As the morning progressed, I was introduced for the first time to Cheryl Schroeder, who would be an integral part of my team. As "second chair," she would be Mike's alter ego, prepared to step in when necessary. She would have specific responsibilities and had to know the case inside and out.

Cheryl, who had been practicing for over fifteen years and had worked in the Cook County state's attorney's office, was much like Mike in her passion and belief that the government had overreached by indicting me. In the days ahead, her steady manner and calm approach provided a nice complement to his unabashed confidence and bravado. I really liked her, and was pleased to learn that she had read the indictment and had independently reached the same conclusion as Mike: that I was innocent.

At this early stage in our relationship, I didn't have enough experience working with criminal lawyers to know whether they always told their clients they believed them innocent and if they really meant it. Mike and Cheryl each seemed sincere, however. So, too, did the third member of the trial team, Robyn Molaro, a twenty-nine-year-old former state's attorney.

As an executive, I had been responsible for bringing the best from our company experts to achieve our annual goals and objectives. Dependent on others, my responsibility was to keep us cohesively moving forward. This was how I approached my defense. I didn't know any other way to organize myself. What did I know about criminal law?

When I don't know or understand something, my practice typically is to ask a lot of questions. So that's what I did. I asked the same question several times and in different ways to help me understand what I'd been told. This is what I immediately began doing when I was identified as "Fundraiser A" in the criminal complaint.

I had to rely on Mike, Cheryl, and Robyn to provide the legal expertise and trust their advice. I had to listen and learn from them to become knowledgeable in the field of criminal law as it applied to me as a defendant.

When I thought we drifted off subject to small talk or courthouse gossip, or I just became frustrated with something and got off track, I tried to refocus us on what we were working on at the time. This approach seemed to be effective with my legal team as we methodically moved forward.

In the months to come, Cheryl and Robyn were both incredibly supportive and genuinely concerned about my personal and legal well-being. They provided a unique mix of compassion and a fierce determination in their efforts to defend me. Mike would affectionately refer to them as "the hens" during our many hours together. He had no sexist intent in calling them that; he regarded them as two of the toughest attorneys he'd ever worked with. They became my "guardian angels," always watching over me as we maneuvered together to square off with the government.

We spent most of our time that first day going through the indictment and discussing our strengths and vulnerabilities. We really wouldn't know what we were up against until the government gave us their discovery documents and wiretap recordings. Mike, as he would do at virtually all our meetings over the next eighteen months, took the lead. He set the agenda of the issues he wanted reviewed, and we would have a thorough and rigorous discussion.

Mike's ego never got in the way of putting together our defense strategy. If Cheryl, Robyn, other attorneys, or even Julie or I thought we had a better idea, he would listen and oftentimes recognize its merit. Mike stressed to us that he was a team player and all he wanted was to win; he didn't care who got the credit.

His pretrial methodology was to break down a case into its smaller components, then thoroughly discuss and hash out the problems with the evidence until he was satisfied he had a grasp of how it fit into his defense game plan. He had a photographic memory and was exceptional in piecing random facts into a coherent strategy. As I watched him work, I marveled at how, after thirty-five years, he still had the energy and intellect to practice law at the federal level. This is not to say we didn't have our moments . . . or our clashes. We didn't always agree on everything.

Eric and I spent the night before the arraignment in a hotel not far from Mike's office. I didn't sleep well. Many thoughts raced through my mind. I feared the unknown and I worried whether I would have the strength to withstand the coming events.

As we waited in the hotel lobby the next morning for Cheryl to pick us up for the ride to the federal building downtown, my attention was drawn to the television mounted over the bar. I saw a picture of my face and Rod's projected on the screen. The reporter detailed the charges against us and the time we would be arraigned later that morning. The report ended with a shot outside the courthouse showing the growing media gaggle gathering. To paraphrase Dorothy in *The Wizard of Oz*: We weren't in Nashville anymore. Whatever invisibility had remained after the arrest and the indictment was now gone. I felt like I was already on trial, with the public, as opposed to twelve jurors, judging me.

Cheryl, Eric, and I arrived downtown to meet Mike at an Intelligentsia coffee shop located near the federal building. Our seats provided us a safe vantage point to view the growing media activity outside. As we sat there visiting, I couldn't help picking up on the energy of the early morning bustle of people going about their normal routines. In contrast, here I was killing time until I was to go before a federal judge. I didn't dwell on wishing I were somewhere else, because it wouldn't help me any. I tried to focus on the task at hand. Most of those in the greater Chicago area would be seeing me for the first time as I walked to and through the federal building. I had to be mindful that potential jurors could be sizing me up.

Fifteen minutes before we were to leave for the arraignment, Shelly Sorosky, my brother's lawyer, came into the coffee shop and sat with us. He was a family friend of many years and I always liked him. It was comforting to see him, a familiar face, walk in and join us.

After we exchanged pleasantries, I asked Shelly how Rod was doing. He chuckled, shook his head, and said, "Your brother's in la-la land." He explained that he didn't believe Rod had a grasp of the gravity of his legal situation and was delusional. Hearing him say that made me sad and concerned for Rod. Now was the time to be grounded in reality. I hoped Shelly was exaggerating a bit. I would soon see for myself where Rod's head was when I got inside the courtroom and met up with him. Sadly, Shelly wasn't too far off the mark.

A few minutes before we were to leave for the courthouse, a young woman walked into the shop. Mike surprised me by calling her over to our table. "Rob, meet Natasha Korecki," he said. I knew the name. Korecki covered the courts for the *Chicago Sun-Times*, and I had read some of her reporting about my brother's arrest.

This was the first of what would be many interactions with the press as my legal odyssey progressed. Initially these encounters were a bit awkward; I didn't have a lot of experience dealing with reporters and wasn't sure how to act. There was no instructional manual for a defendant in a criminal case, especially one that involved allegedly selling a US Senate seat.

I was guarded with Korecki. Feeling more comfortable posing questions than answering them, I asked her why she had chosen journalism as a career and how she got a job with the *Sun-Times*. To keep her from questioning me, I even asked about her family and learned she was the mother of a toddler. We finally got to the point where I politely told her I was sorry, but I would be unable to comment about anything related to the indictment or my brother because this experience was all new to me and I was still uncertain about what to say publicly. She was gracious and seemed to understand my predicament. Mike intervened and said that the time would come when we would be in a better position to comment, but not now.

What I didn't know then was that Mike had told Korecki when we would be at the coffee shop and to come over before the arraignment to meet me if she wanted. This was the first phase of Mike's plan to introduce me to the media, and through them, the potential jury pool, on his terms. He knew this would be a high-visibility case and he had to plan to leverage the press to our advantage if it was at all possible.

As Korecki left the coffee shop, she wished me good luck, motioning to the throng of TV, radio, and print journalists we were about to confront. We gave her a good head start before we left so it wouldn't appear we were together. Eric chose to remain in the shop and wait for me there until I returned. Mike and Cheryl led the way out and I followed.

As we crossed the street, we could see that the press had recognized us. Reporters have a way of swarming when they have you in their sites, not unlike the way the paparazzi react to celebrities. The difference in this case was that I wasn't a celebrity and didn't view my indictment as anything to share or broadcast. I didn't want the attention or the distraction as I headed into the toughest challenge of my life. I had no choice but to walk through the media as they took their pictures and asked me questions that I didn't answer.

CHAPTER NINE

Reality Check

This is what it means to be a defendant in a criminal case, facing all the firepower the federal government can muster. Even if you know you are innocent, you will at least consider pleading guilty to lesser charges rather than hunkering down for a long, costly trial that might result in a conviction and prison sentence. Such was the case shortly after my arraignment, when Mike called to tell me he had just spoken on the phone with the government's lead prosecutor, Assistant US Attorney Reid Schar.

According to Mike, Schar had asked, "What does your guy want? We've got the governor, but your guy can win this." Mike said he'd told Schar that I wasn't going to plead to felonies, but that we would be open to discussion if the charges were reduced to misdemeanors.

Mike and I had not discussed any plea deals. We were prepared to forge ahead to trial. So when he spoke with Schar, I believe Mike was simply staking out a negotiating position, nothing more. Still, facing hundreds of thousands of dollars in legal fees, I was open to any cost-effective resolution . . . even if it might mean being charged with a misdemeanor. If the terms were acceptable, I would have given it serious consideration to avoid the uncertainty of a trial. The system is so convoluted and weighted in the government's favor that it forces you to make choices you would not make under normal circumstances.

Schar said he couldn't make such a deal. With thirty years' experience trying criminal cases in federal court, Mike knew that wasn't true. He told Schar, "You can do whatever you want to do. I'll talk to Rob."

My first reaction? Relief. It's about time, I thought. The feds have finally realized that they overreached by indicting me along with my brother. Better late than never that they want to make things right.

My second reaction? Anger. "Why did they indict me in the first place if they thought I could win?" I snapped to Mike. I told him to tell Schar to drop the charges and leave me alone.

And my third reaction? Confusion. It didn't make sense that the prosecution would tell my attorney that I could win and then ask what I wanted now. Not after they had put me in legal jeopardy, professed how strong their case was, and proclaimed that Lincoln would roll over in his grave if he knew about this heinous criminal enterprise in which I had allegedly been involved.

Mike told me to forget about the charges being dropped. That wasn't going to happen at this stage. Then he explained that Schar had proposed a "global solution" that Rod and I should talk over as brothers.

"Global solution? What does that mean?" I asked. Mike explained that the government wanted me to talk to Rod about pleading guilty on some or all of his charges. If he did plead, the prosecutors might in exchange consider reducing or dropping my charges.

I was never going to ask Rod to plead guilty to save me from prosecution. If he had wanted to do that, he would have initiated it. He did not. Earlier, he had told me that he couldn't look his daughters in the eye if he pled guilty to something he believed he didn't do. I think this was his way of telling me that he wouldn't plead guilty to spare me from prosecution. That was his choice to make, and I accepted it. I never told Rod about the government's proposal of a "global solution." I did tell Mike to reject the overture.

While the prosecution's attempt to use me to get my codefendant brother to plead had failed, I've learned since that this is a common tactic employed to get leverage against the prime target. Threatening, pressuring, coercing, or actually indicting a family member is a standard practice in our justice system. Loved ones are used as bargaining chips. Three examples will illustrate the point: by chance, Bernie Madoff, of Wall Street Ponzi scheme infamy, was arrested on December 11, 2008, three days after Rod. It soon became known that federal prosecutors were investigating whether his wife and sons had also committed crimes. Although his brother was eventually indicted and convicted, his wife and sons were not. Did Madoff end up pleading guilty to eleven felonies to spare them? Even if he did, the ignominy and threat of indictment was so great that one son, Mark, committed suicide. More recently, it was suggested that former US Congressman Jesse Jackson Jr., who figures so prominently in this story, cut a deal with the feds and pled guilty to wire and mail fraud with the hope that leniency would be shown toward his wife Sandi, who was also facing jail time if convicted of tax evasion.

The third example involves two brothers, Michael and Lowell Milken. They worked together in the High Yield Convertible Bond Department of Drexel Burnham Lambert in the late 1980s. After a lengthy investigation of Michael, the innovative genius who pioneered the development of high yield corporate bonds, better known as "junk bonds," the brothers were indicted on numerous charges involving racketeering and securities fraud. Including Lowell in the indictment was viewed by legal observers as a means to put pressure on Michael to cut a deal to get the charges against his brother dropped. Not wanting his brother to be unjustly prosecuted, Michael agreed to plead guilty, and the charges against Lowell were dropped.

Unlike Madoff, Jackson, or Michael Milken, Rod showed no signs of caving in. As long as the government thought I could be useful in their prosecution of the governor, they would hold me hostage.

In the pretrial phase of a civil or criminal proceeding, the opposing parties are required to share certain information with each other. This, I learned, is called "discovery." The prosecution has no obligation to organize this information so that it can be readily understood or so that key pieces of evidence can be readily found. This, I learned, is called a "discovery dump."

Two weeks after our arraignment we received the first of two such dumps. (The second occurred a year later, shortly before trial.) Discovery dump number one featured twenty discs with more than four hundred hours of wiretapped and bugged conversations. Although the prosecution had the resources to transcribe and catalog these tapes and had no doubt done so in preparing its case, it chose not to share any transcripts with us. My legal team and I would have to start from scratch, listening to and then transcribing hundreds of conversations to determine what applied to my defense. Such an effort required reliable technology, a capable transcriber, the organizational skill to put everything into a format for the legal team to use and reference, and lots of my money.

Imagine the potential cost of hiring a secretary to transcribe four hundred hours of tapes. Imagine the hourly fee of attorneys listening to those tapes and/or reading the transcripts. Imagine my dwindling bank account, despite the fact that my wife Julie heroically assumed the burden of doing a portion of the transcription to save us money. Advantage: prosecution.

During this discovery period, we were also given a copy of the judge's wiretap authorization, which, to our amazement, gave the government the go-ahead to eavesdrop on all of Rod's and my telephone conversations. The broad authorization outlined the government's probable cause argument in support of wiretaps. That argument was based on information from Rod's friend and colleague John Wyma, whom we learned had been the government's mole, relating hours of conversations with the governor and me.

Why would such a friend turn informant? When Wyma's name surfaced in connection with the indictments, the press reported that he was a target of a federal investigation looking into his lobbying efforts on behalf of a health care company client. The feds were apparently investigating him for alleged bribes to get the company a favorable action through an Illinois health care facilities board.

The press further reported that he had been interviewed by the FBI about this and was threatened with prosecution if he didn't cooperate in their investigation of Rod. When he was ultimately confronted with possible charges stemming from illegalities in his lobbying business, he apparently capitulated to save himself from prosecution. As a result, he received full immunity and became the government's key witness against his friend the governor and anyone else in the governor's sphere, including me. I do not mean to appear bitter, but I often wonder how Wyma lives with himself these days, knowing how he hurt and betrayed people who trusted him and counted him as a friend.

As soon as we got the discs, and with Mike's guidance, Julie, my brother-in-law Eric, and I tried to figure out how best to organize the data into searchable spreadsheets. Eric had a full-time job, but worked overtime with us to help out. We not only had to listen to the conversation on the intercept, but also had to transcribe it as accurately as possible. These spreadsheets would be an easy reference guide to direct us and the legal team to specific times and days as we prepared for trial.

We organized the conversations into five categories: personal (we limited this category to conversations between Julie and me or my son Alex and me. This totaled 284 intercepts); fundraising (anytime I had a conversation with someone who was referenced in the indictment related to fundraising or that we thought would be helpful to me); business (discussions

I had with my business associates. Every Friday I had regularly scheduled conference calls with my staff that the government eavesdropped
on with, in my opinion, no justification); Rod (all my conversations with
Rod); person (anyone who was material in my case). Filtered out were
hundreds of personal calls I had with friends and relatives. Some of them
never knew they had been captured on FBI intercepts.

Imagine having to listen to scores of hours of personal and professional conversations that you had every reason to believe were private.
No doubt—as in my case—you'd smile at some exchanges and cringe
at others. You'd hear yourself being tender and profane, cautious and
off-the-cuff. You'd be proud of some portions, embarrassed by some
portions. Now imagine allowing strangers (your legal team) and family
members to listen to those same conversations . . . without the advantage that you have of context. Finally, imagine how you'd feel if your
brother cavalierly allowed David Letterman and others to play portions
to a national television audience.

Mike had decided that Julie could help transcribe a designated portion
of taped conversations at our home in Nashville while he hired a couple
of attorneys in Chicago to work on another. At this point, we didn't know
how discerning the government had been. Who all was on the other end
of the wiretapped conversations with my brother and me? All we knew
as it related to me was that my cell phone, the conference room where I
worked at Friends of Blagojevich, and Rod's office at FOB had all been
tapped or bugged.

Shortly after Julie began transcribing, I heard her loudly cry out. I rushed
over to find her sobbing after she had heard, for the first time, her voice and
mine on an FBI intercept. Few things can make you feel more violated than
knowing that strange people, working for your government, are listening
to conversations between you and your spouse. Nothing prepared us for
the anger, fear, and disappointment we felt when we learned what the FBI
had done to us. This was just the beginning of many indignities we would
endure together as we listened to each other talk about all kinds of things a
husband and wife talk about after thirty-one years of marriage. It took Julie
a couple of weeks of listening and transcribing before she was hardened
enough not to cry. She is a perfect example of the many people who became
collateral damage because of Wyma's betrayal.

After learning I had been wiretapped, I tried to recall the many conversations I had had during the time the FBI was eavesdropping. I

knew I had done nothing wrong while I fundraised at FOB, but that gave me no comfort. It was the "stupid talk" that worried me, conversations in which I might have said something flippantly or off-color that could be taken out of context by the government and used against me. With each conversation I listened to, I felt as though I were walking down a dark street at night, coming to an unlit corner, not knowing what I'd find when I turned. I couldn't remember everything I'd said in those conversations, and it was excruciatingly stressful to listen to every one of them, fearing that I may have said something dumb in an unguarded moment.

As we prepared to go to trial, I naïvely thought that we would have the opportunity to play any of the intercept calls favorable to me that would reveal the truth of how I conducted myself with donors. It only seemed fair that we should be able to submit conversations that would balance the government's overwhelming advantage to selectively pick what they could play to a jury. To my shock and outrage I learned we had to get the judge to approve what we could play. True, the prosecution had to do the same; however, it seemed Judge Zagel never said "no" to them. This, along with learning how easy it was for the government to get a wiretap application approved by a judge, was the beginning of my education in how stacked the deck is in favor of the government when they prosecute defendants in federal court.

The FBI has guidelines that stipulate how the agents doing the eavesdropping are to conduct themselves while they are listening. The guidelines specifically instruct that listening to or recording any conversation not related to the investigation should be minimized. Once it is clear the conversation isn't relevant or the voice recognized by the agent is not part of the investigation, surveillance should be terminated. Screening these calls for relevance is designed to protect the civil liberties of the targeted subjects, who we all know are presumed innocent until proven guilty beyond a reasonable doubt.

Sadly, we found hundreds of calls that we believed failed to meet the standards of the FBI procedures manual for wiretaps. These intercepts violated not only my family's right to privacy as American citizens, but also the right to privacy of many of my friends and business associates. One example: the FBI recorded a conversation I was having with my son who, unfortunately, happened to be urinating in the toilet while he was on the phone talking to me. You could very clearly hear what he was doing. There was no mistaking the sound. If the agent listening had any doubt, it would have been eliminated by the flushing of the toilet. We were not talking about anything related to the investigation. Nothing sinister was discussed in our non-conspiratorial, father-son conversation that could have justified the continued eavesdropping, but somehow the agent listening failed to understand that. (I share this embarrassing example to illustrate how slipshod and indifferent the government can be about protecting the civil liberties of the people they are investigating.)

I would argue that in many similar ways the government violated our fundamental right to privacy. Another was a twenty-two-minute conversation Julie had with Patti on the evening of November 21, 2008, discussing the menu for Thanksgiving. There was little we left out as the FBI overheard we were going to order mashed potatoes, collard greens, and yams from MacArthur's Restaurant, a family favorite place, to serve with our turkey. They also heard Julie telling Patti in the same conversation about a recent double bunionectomy Julie had had earlier in the year and how it had affected her jogging. In this same conversation, the FBI also managed to hear about Alex's love life and his girlfriend, Jessica. The sum total of this lengthy, non–Senate seat, non-shakedown, non-extortion conversation was a massive intrusion into the private lives of two women talking innocuously about life's challenges.

We filed a motion to suppress all of our personal calls. Unfortunately, the judge denied the motion, stating that the calls would not be played unless they were relevant to the case. They never were relevant to the case and were not played in court, thankfully, but they are allowed to exist somewhere in government archives.

I only wish that the judge had held the FBI accountable for violating their own rules. To my knowledge, no agent or supervisor was ever reprimanded for breaking agency policy. Had I the money and the energy at the time to pursue a strategy to reclaim our right to privacy, I would have done so, perhaps through a lawsuit claiming my constitutional or civil rights had been abridged. But I could only fight so many battles and had to move on to prepare my defense against the two charges that could potentially put me in prison.

Many weeks of hard work were required to listen to all the FBI-intercepted conversations that came with the discovery discs from the government. We thought we would never finish. Julie tirelessly transcribed nearly every day when she came home from work. We worked every weekend, only taking breaks for food and exercise. I can still remember hearing the awful high-pitched, shrieking sound of the wiretap recording cycling on each time we played a conversation. I hated it so much that Julie began wearing headphones as she listened and transcribed. Whenever I would start to feel overwhelmed and stressed, all I had to do to get back on track was watch my wife determinedly plow though those wiretaps. She was my rock.

As we had expected, of all the hundreds of taped conversations we heard, I would have to be prepared to explain only a handful when I was cross-examined at trial. (Unlike most defendants I would not be invoking the Fifth Amendment. I looked forward to taking the stand and proving my innocence.) My lawyers and I believed that when the recordings were put into proper context, the jury would see there was none of the requisite criminal intent in any of my conduct.

Only one conversation was somewhat troublesome. We knew from the complaint and the indictment that the prosecutors would attempt to argue that a particular phone call was evidence that I was conspiring with Rod to sell Barack Obama's vacant Senate seat to Jesse Jackson Jr. in exchange for sizable campaign contributions from him and his supporters in Chicago's Indian community. As I have previously described, two of those supporters, Rajindar Bedi and Raghu Nayak, had raised the subject with me, and I had told them in no uncertain terms that this was not the way my brother or I operated. If Obama did win the presidential election and his Senate seat did open up, Rod would follow a process to pick a successor, I continually explained. That process would not be influenced by campaign contributions.

The intercepted call in question occurred on December 4, 2008, at 2:43 p.m. while I was having coffee with Julie in a noisy Starbucks near our condo at Lincoln and Wilson Avenues on the city's north side. I had attended a fundraiser earlier in the day with Rod and slipped out afterward to be with Julie for a bit. Rod's able assistant, Mary Stewart, reached me on my cell phone and asked me to contact my brother, who wanted to talk with me.

The following is the transcript of that conversation played to the jury during the trial:

Rod: Where are you?
Robert: Well actually, I picked Julie up, we just had a coffee here. I've been trying you for twenty minutes.

Rod: So here, listen this . . .

Robert: Yeah.

Rod: This whole Jesse Jr. thing, you, you, gotta understand something, I, I'm fucking elevating him now. Because that whole Washington establishment's freakin out.

Robert: Yeah.

Rod: Okay?

Robert: Yeah.

Rod: And you, you know, my play here is to ah, hey, I'm not completely ruling him out, okay? I objectively need to look at the politics of that. But my play here to ah, make him look like, if this Lisa Madigan thing doesn't, if they can't put it together, then I'm going to him.

Robert: Yeah, I like that.

Rod: Okay. And I'm so fucking repugnant to them then fine, take Jesse Jr. Fuck you.

Robert: Right.

Rod: And they're already freaking out, and a Rasmussen poll came out today. He gets 36 percent of the Democrats, Tammy Duckworth 28 or 29 percent, Lisa Madigan 17, Emil Jones, 2. Lisa Madigan no support, zero support among African Americans.

Robert: Mm-hmm.

Rod: . . . in that field.

Robert: Mm-hmm.

Rod: With him. Okay? So why the fuck should I send fucking Lisa Madigan who gets zero support among African Americans, piss of my base.

Robert: Right.

Rod: Okay. And I don't get anything, fuck you, Harry Reid.

Robert: Right.

Rod: You know, here's fucking Jesse. The people want him. And so you know what? You're not giving me shit, so there. And I can cut a better political deal with the Jacksons and, most of it you probably can't believe, but some of it can be tangible up front.

Robert: Yeah.

Rod: And if nothing else, I've done something for the black community.

Robert: Yeah.

Rod: And we're fuckin gonna say Obama wants him.

Robert: I like it. Look. You're a clear thinker. I think you understand the landscape, obviously, very well. Sounds like a very interesting play.

Rod: I'm meeting with him Monday.

Robert: Yeah, nice.

Rod: We've invited him to our, he's coming to my poverty conference on Tuesday.

Robert: Nice.

Rod: It's a big public event.

Robert: Nice.

Rod: I'm trying to get a story written in the *Sun-Times* about how
close we are.

Robert: Yeah, nice, nice. Now are you, you're not gonna jack him
up and you know, create expectations in him and then fuck him
in the end?

Rod: Yeah, but oh I'm not gonna rule that out.

Robert: Yeah.

Rod: Oh look, if he doesn't get picked, he's pissed, no matter what
the fucking reasons are. Okay?

Robert: Yeah, um okay. But I mean he can't hurt you in any way
can he?

Rod: He can hurt me in the same way, if I pick somebody other
than, look, he can hurt me, equally the same if it's any white
person.

Robert: Yeah.

Rod: Um, if it's a black person, he can't hurt me quite as much but
he'll, you know, really be fucking vindictive and pissed off.

Robert: Yeah, well, ah, my thinking here is really just, the next two
years for you. Does it get further complicated or not. I mean you
gotta get that totally . . .

Rod: Oh yeah, yeah, yeah, I know that.

Robert: You know.

Rod: Yeah.

Robert: So good, I, I, hey, I'll stand by and listen to the news. Should
be fun.

Rod: Let's see how it plays out. I mean you know, let him, let's see if
we can get that, him looking more and more like he could be the

one. And maybe they'll say, okay, fine, we'll take him. Maybe it's not that bad from their point of view.

Robert: Yeah.

Rod: But you know my indication it is. And they sure would rather have her and they feel like he could lose the general, you know.

Robert: Yeah. Well I think if you do appoint him and I don't know who the money centers are in the black community, but you gotta get me focused on them or somebody focused on them.

Rod: What, here's, here's what you've got to do. You gotta talk to Raghu [Nayak]. You gotta call him and say hey, look. You know, Jesse Jr. you know, I think Rod's meeting with him at some point. Very much a realistic, and you should just let him know, you know, the Durbins and the other behind the scenes, they don't want him. They're afraid.

Robert: Yeah.

Rod: You know, and so he's getting a lot of pressure from the Obama Administration, you know, you can just tell him . . . don't quote me.

Robert: Yeah.

Rod: . . . but this is what is happening. Okay.

Robert: I'll do that, I'll do that.

Rod: Right, and ah . . .

Robert: Okay.

Rod: And the other point, you know, all these promises of help. That's all well and good but he's had an experience with Jesse and Jesse promised to endorse him for governor and lied to him. Okay?

Robert: Mm-hmm.

Rod: So, you know, we, if, if in fact there's, this is, you know, this is possible, then some of the stuff's gotta start happening now.

Robert: Yep.

Rod: Right now.

Robert: Very good.

Rod: And we gotta see it.

Robert: Okay.

Rod: You understand? Now you gotta be careful how you express that. And assume everybody is listening, the whole world's listening.

Robert: Right.

Rod: You hear me?

Robert: Right, right, right.

Rod: But if there's tangible political support like you've said, start showing us now.

Robert: Yeah, okay.

Rod: Okay?

Robert: Very good.

Rod: Ah . . .

Robert: I'll make that call, I'll make that call this afternoon.

Rod: I would do it in person. I would not do it on the phone.

Robert: Ah, okay, very good.

Rod: Have a cup of coffee with him like tomorrow or something.

Robert: Yeah, okay. I'll do that.

Rod: And I would, you know, put an urgency to it, listen, you follow?

Robert: Yeah. Ah, yes, I can do that. That's good.

Rod: Okay and then we'll talk some more about how, how to do it.

Robert: Yeah, ah, I'll get him lined up for tomorrow assuming he's in town.

Rod: Alright, okay. Bye.

(FBI Telephone Monitoring, Date: 12/04/2008, Time: 2:43 pm, Activity: Rod Blagojevich home line incoming call, Session: 1357, SPEAKERS: ROB BLAGOJEVICH: Rob Blagojevich, BLAGOJEV-ICH: Rod Blagojevich)

During this three-minute, forty-second call with Rod, I said "yeah," "a huh," "mm-hmm," "right," or "okay" thirty-two times. We had been to-gether only an hour or so earlier. I was anxious to get him off the phone because he had ignored the fact I was having coffee with Julie and he had continued the conversation as if she weren't there. If one had listened to all the other fifteen hundred conversations the FBI eavesdropped on and heard, as the government had, one would know I was not intending to commit a crime. At the conclusion of the conversation, I wasn't sure what Rod wanted me to tell Nayak, but I agreed to set up a meeting and did so shortly after this conversation. This call was interpreted by the government as a felonious furtherance of a criminal act—a scheme to deny honest ser-vices to the citizens of Illinois.

Prior to hearing the surveillance tape and all throughout trial prepara-tion, I struggled to remember the specifics of this particular conversa-tion with Rod. No matter what I did to jog my memory—repeatedly listening to the call, going back to the Starbucks several times and sitting there, researching our credit card bill for the purchase we made at the time—I still couldn't fully recall all the particulars. I can only conclude that this call was so incidental to everything I was doing at FOB that it didn't stick with me.

Typically, when Rod wanted to talk with me, his conversation seemed to be triggered by something that happened just prior to his call. It was not part of a coherent strategy or follow-up. It was an impulse. After four months of working with him, I became frustrated by his pattern and reacted with a kind of impatient tolerance. I cringed when I knew Rod wanted to talk with me because I knew the conversation wasn't likely to be productive or helpful to me as a fundraiser. This was the case during that fateful call on December 4. As we later said during the trial, Rod and I had not talked about Nayak or Jackson for more than a month when he called me out of the blue at the Starbucks.

When I reviewed the complaint for the first time on the morning of Rod's arrest five days later, I read the government's reference to this conversation and to the call I had made to Nayak. At the time, I was so worked up that I couldn't remember if I initiated the call to Nayak or whether he had called me. I frantically reviewed the call history on my phone to refresh my memory only to find that, in fact, I did call him as the complaint alleged. As I sat there after looking at my call history, I felt a sense of resignation and realized that forces more powerful than I were aligning to misconstrue my actions and use them against me.

The transcript reveals that Rod said that I should "be careful how I expressed that and assume everybody's listening, the whole world's listening" and that "we'll talk some more about how, how to do it" before I had a conversation with Nayak. The key point from this statement, I believe, is that it was unresolved, not clear to me, as to what Rod really wanted me to tell Nayak. I never had a chance to hear him explain what he meant.

When I came on board in August 2008 to help Rod fundraise, I told him I would only talk straight with donors. I would not play anyone for a campaign contribution. He understood that. As a result, I wasn't sure what he wanted me to discuss with Nayak. I still don't believe my brother ever wanted me to accept the bribe that had been suggested to me by Bedi and Nayak on behalf of Congressman Jackson.

In preparation for trial, I listened to all the conversations Rod had earlier that day with some of his staff. They discussed the possibility of appointing Jackson and the political implications for Rod in Illinois if he did. I was not aware of any of those discussions at the time. Consequently, I didn't have the full context of where Rod was coming from when he called me in the coffee shop.

Rod may have wanted me to play Nayak, but then again, I couldn't be certain of that—even after listening to our conversation many times. All I can conclude in retrospect, having never discussed it with Rod since, is that he might have had some delusional strategy to play the leadership in Washington, believing that if he showed signs he was elevating Jackson, they would help him politically in Illinois in order to avoid a Jackson appointment. Rod believed the Washington establishment didn't think Jackson could win in the general election, and he might have thought he had some leverage with them to get their help in Illinois.

The day after that Starbucks phone call, I canceled the meeting with Nayak. An article published in the *Chicago Tribune* that morning alleged that John Wyma had worn a wire for the government in the campaign fundraising meetings he had attended at FOB. Needless to say, this revelation gave us great concern because we didn't know what was going on with Wyma and the feds. (Wyma later denied that he wore a wire and said he had verbally related conversations to the prosecutors.)

Wyma! This news forced us to step back and evaluate what was happening before I went forward with fundraising. Rod conferenced me in to a conversation he was having with his chief legal counsel, Bill Quinlan, to discuss how to proceed. In addition, Rod wanted me to help him recall what we may have said in front of Wyma during our meetings that could have been misunderstood. I couldn't remember anything we'd said that could be harmful, even if misunderstood. Quinlan didn't overreact to the Wyma news and calmly told us he was going to make some calls to see what else he could learn about Wyma talking to the feds.

After Quinlan dropped off the call, I reminded Rod about the meeting I had scheduled with Nayak and asked him what he wanted me to do in light of the article. After first telling me he didn't think I should have the meeting, he said he needed a little time, but was sure it would be "no." I had already decided that I didn't want to meet with Nayak. After all, I was going to see him at that previously scheduled Indian community fundraiser the following day. I didn't know what Rod wanted me to talk about with Nayak, and the only thing I would have spoken with him about was my hope for a good turnout for the event.

One thing I knew from working with Rod: there was always less drama and less possibility of argument between the two of us if he came up with the idea to do something rather than if I did. When he said he thought it would probably be a "no" on having the meeting, I instantly told him I took it as a definite no, and I would cancel. I also tried to reinforce his decision by telling him there was no way around it, given the new developments with Wyma. He agreed that I should cancel and tell Nayak I would see him the next evening at the Indian fundraiser. I would be rigorously cross examined at trial about this call.

During the four-month period that I worked with him, Rod had never intentionally put me in a compromising position, and I don't believe he was trying to do that in this conversation. If one listened to all the FBI taped intercepts of me, one would conclude that I conducted myself properly and never misled or played anyone for a contribution or for a fundraiser. The government, I believe, knew from listening to all my conversations and the many people they interviewed during their investigation that I was a forthright and honest guy. I think that taking into consideration the total body of information they had collected on me, the government should have followed their own Department of Justice's mission statement, "to ensure fair and impartial administration of justice for all Americans," and given me the benefit of the doubt and not indicted me. Instead I was corralled, to be used to leverage a "global solution."

When the FBI and DOJ are listening, if your guard is down, as it is in most casual conversations, you are in great danger that your words can be misconstrued and used against you. As the saying goes, "You can indict a ham sandwich." The powers that be can make a federal case out of anything they want. I was too good a target because I was Rod's brother.

Through all the many weeks of hard work and transcribing my conversations, Julie never complained about having to do it. She endured because she believed in me and knew it was necessary for my defense. Her work was meticulous and helped accelerate the formulation of our defense strategy. When we finished listening to the last conversation on my cell phone on June 29, some six weeks after we began the process, we high-fived and hugged in brief celebration. There was some stupid talk on the tapes, and there was the coffee shop phone call that would have to be explained. But there was no "smoking gun" conversation we had to fear.

Even though we still had a long way to go, we couldn't help feeling a strong sense of accomplishment and hope. A major step in getting prepared for trial—listening to the tapes of my cell phone—was completed. Although the legal team and I had listened to the recordings of all of the other relevant conversations relating to me, the task of getting those fully transcribed would still take several more months.

The world had already heard a snippet of one conversation thanks to Rod's February appearance with David Letterman. In May, a few weeks after arraignment, a second FBI-recorded conversation went public, and then viral. This was an intercept of a seven-minute November 13, 2008, phone call between me and Roland Burris.

Rod's appointment of Burris to fill Obama's vacant Senate seat had created a stir . . . and spurred investigations by the Senate Ethics Committee in Washington and the Sangamon County state's attorney in Springfield, Illinois, the state's capital. The investigation centered on whether Burris had perjured himself when testifying under oath on January 8 to the Illinois House impeachment panel.

As the *Huffington Post* reported: "Burris has come under fire for changing his story about the circumstances surrounding his appointment. He initially said he hadn't contacted a key Blagojevich adviser about the seat but later released an affidavit saying he had spoken to several advisers, including the governor's brother."

The lead prosecutor, Reid Schar, asked Mike if we had any objection to the release of the tape. When Burris had initially testified to the Illinois House, I had told Mike that, contrary to the new senator's recollection, he and I had spoken three times in November and all the conversations had been appropriate. There were no quid pro quos—just the opposite. Neither Mike nor I had any objection to its release. Indeed, I was excited that the public would have a chance to hear it because it clearly showed how I behaved as a fundraiser in a delicate conversation. Even the government had chosen not to cite this conversation in the charges related to me.

When the Senate committee released the tape on May 26, the media feeding frenzy began. The recording was played by the major network and cable news affiliates, as well as the Chicago stations. Major print media around the country—the *New York Times, Washington Post, Los Angeles Times,* and *USA Today,* among others—also covered the story. All I cared about was how the Chicago media would respond and thus impact potential jurors.

My optimism that the media would note the conversation reflected well on me was misplaced. Here's what the *New York Times* said:

In the call, [Burris] seemed almost in a crass negotiation with Mr. Blagojevich's brother—also his chief fund-raiser—over how he could help the governor win the appointment and not run into trouble over negative connotations that he might be trying to buy an appointment by fund-raising for him.

"If I do that, I guarantee you that that will get out, and people said, 'Oh, Burris is doing a fund-raiser,' and, and then Rod and I both going to catch hell," Mr. Burris said in a phone call shortly after the presidential election that opened the Senate seat held by Mr. Obama. By the end of the call, Mr. Burris had promised to send a personal check within a month.

"God knows, No. 1, I want to help Rod," he was recorded as saying. "No. 2, I also want to, you know, hope I get a consideration to get that appointment."

At another point, Mr. Burris reminded the governor's brother, "Tell Rod to keep me in mind for that seat, would you?" (*New York Times*, May 27, 2009, http://www.webcitation.org/6WSl4ajmT)

And here's a portion of the *Chicago Tribune*'s article:

The transcript provides a behind-the-scenes portrayal of the give-and-take world of Illinois politics. During the conversation, a restless Burris makes a hard pitch for the greatest job of his political career while Robert Blagojevich politely pushes back to try to get fundraising cash from a longtime supporter. In the end, little is agreed upon. (*Chicago Tribune*, May 27, 2009, http://www.webcitation.org/6WSlJSuAT)

I still see nothing wrong with this conversation. The media found ways to make it sound like Burris had perjured himself and that he was trying to get something from me in exchange for the Senate seat. None of these observers commented on how properly I had dealt with Burris, telling him, "Roland, I can't help you with your dilemma."

As it turned out, I failed to grasp the extent of the lynch mob mentality in the Chicago and national press against Burris. I even had a Fox News crew from Chicago knocking on my door at my home in Nashville for an interview. I politely declined to comment, but still was featured on a national broadcast standing in front of my home. I was shaken by all of this. Were my view and the view of the press really so divergent? If so, my confidence that the tapes were exculpatory rather than damning might be off base. More important than the media: how would the jury interpret my conversations?

Later I would take heart that Sangamon County state's attorney, John Schmidt, cleared Burris of perjury and concluded that my conversation with him was just a routine call. In his June 19 letter to Illinois House Speaker Michael Madigan, Schmidt wrote: "It is clear from the conversation that Robert Blagojevich's call was to raise money for Governor Blagojevich and not to discuss the vacant Senate seat."

Unfortunately, as far as I was concerned the damage was done. Although none of my conversations with Burris were charged in the indictment against me or Rod, the perception was out there that I had been a party to something that sounded corrupt, whether anything had happened or not.

AS A DEFENDANT FOR the first time and never having been to law school, I had no idea how one got ready for trial. I figured that, like most things, there was a standard format or template that all lawyers followed. It seemed to me there would be a clear organizational methodology that focused on each critical task, completed in its proper sequence, which would organize the evidence into a cohesive work product, ready for trial.

This wasn't what I experienced during our trial prep. It seemed more art than science with no standard textbook way that I could detect. Although Mike was a student of the law and understood the "science of the legal process," he was more the artist than the scientist in how he organized us for trial. For example, as noted, he began every defense by working on the instructions that would be given to the jury months or even years later. This, he said, helped him frame the issues for himself.

If I were to explain my experience with Mike during our preparation for trial, I would describe the process as fluid. As facts and information would reveal themselves, and in no particular order, we would discuss them as thoroughly as possible and attempt to put them into context and prioritize them for importance. We oftentimes went back to information we reviewed only to come to a different interpretation of the material.

Mike would call me at least twice a day every day during our eighteen-month ordeal. I'd hear from him at seven in the morning and five in the evening. He would call me from his car on his way to work and at the end of the day going home. Because he was so reliable, if he was a little late, I would begin to worry that something may have happened to him.

Our conversations weren't always about the case. I believe Mike often called just to help me cope with the stress of my legal predicament. Our topics covered the gamut—exercise, family, work, and, of all things, psychology. The science of psychology has always been important to Mike. He advises college kids who want to become lawyers to major in psychology, rather than the more common political science or English. He believes that no other college major can have more practical application to a future lawyer. One example: jury selection.

Mike practiced what he preached by the way he managed me as a man who faced an uncertain future and the possibility of prison. In countless conversations, my anger, outrage, and frustration about my situation would boil over. And on countless occasions, Mike would take a deep breath, calm me down, and help give me perspective. He listened and then shared his wisdom and experience.

"Rob, life is a series of body blows," was one of his mantras. "Life's not fair, and the body blows don't stop coming." I already understood the spirit of his message, but to hear it at the right time, said the way he said it, helped.

Another Mike-ism that has stuck with me is: "You've got to take things one day at a time." Stressing that I should enjoy the good things in my life each day, he would constantly remind me there was nothing more important than my health and a wife and son who loved me. For sure he was right, but I had to be reminded of the obvious to know how special my life really was in spite of all the crap related to the case. He really was a good counselor, both legally and psychologically.

I believe all criminal defendants deal with the same emotions, insecurities, and doubts that I dealt with. Loss of reputation, cost of defense, fear of the unknown, and the potential loss of freedom weigh heavily on a defendant. Worrying is normal when you're indicted and going to trial. How could it not be? Mike understood this very well from his many years of defending clients and knew how to add value beyond his legal expertise. What I didn't realize until nine months into our working relationship was that Mike lived with an insecurity and fear no one could help him with. I learned this in an unexpected way after my first interview with the press. By this time we had covered a lot of ground and pretty much sized each other up, building a bond of trust and friendship. We pulled no punches with each other. He knew I expected him to shoot straight with me, leading with the bad news first. He expected nothing less in return. There was much at stake.

We were under immense pressure, sifting through mounds of information, absorbing everything that might matter. Of course, we had our disagreements. Sometimes we each pressed too hard to make a point on an issue, even raising our voices, only to back off moments later. We methodically made our way through discovery, gaming all kinds of scenarios we might face during trial.

I even began pushing Mike to cross-examine me because I wanted to know what it was like. His only answer was a curt, "You're not ready yet." I couldn't understand why he wouldn't accommodate me and figured he just didn't feel like it when I asked. After one of his numerous "you're not ready yet" responses, he surprised me with something else. He had somehow decided that I was ready to give my first interview to the media.

CHAPTER TEN

Two Different Profiles

A longtime military man and successful businessman, Rob Blagojevich—the brother of our controversial ex-governor—lived in relative obscurity. But just four months after reluctantly agreeing to act as the fund-raising chair to the former governor, Rob Blagojevich was an unnamed co-schemer in a federal complaint. By the next spring, he was indicted. For the first time, Rob and his wife, Julie have agreed to break that silence in a wide-ranging interview with the *Chicago Sun-Times*. (*Chicago Sun-Times*, September 4, 2009)

Memo to potential criminal defendants in high-profile cases: dealing with, if not controlling, the media is essential in the months before trial. Bad press can poison the jury pool, eventually resulting in a loss of freedom.

Among the many professional attributes Mike brought to his client, one in particular surprised me when I learned he had developed a wide network of very good contacts with the major local newspapers and TV news stations. These contacts were based on a mutual respect . . . and mutual self-interest. Lawyers and reporters used each other to share inside information off the record.

Here was one more quid pro quo to add to the mix. The press was anxious to get the inside story surrounding whatever high-profile defendant Mike might be representing. In turn, Mike was anxious to learn about any rumors that might be circulating around the courthouse or the US attorney's office. Was an indictment of so-and-so imminent? Was so-and-so thinking of a plea bargain? Reporters wouldn't breach any confidentiality promised to a source—be it Mike or a prosecutor—but there were still ways of legitimately passing along "the word on the street" in return for a nugget about Mike's strategy or access to a client like me.

Mike had another reason for playing the this-for-that game: to introduce a defendant to the pool of potential jurors in a controlled situation. By the summer of 2009, much had been written about Rod's inner circle of friends and operatives, including the two indicted fundraisers Tony Rezko and Chris Kelly. I was still relatively unknown—by design. Mike wanted Chicagoland to "meet" me on our terms. Now he believed I was ready. My mind and body were back to normal and I had spent enough time with him since the indictment in April that I could talk intelligently about the case without sticking my foot in my mouth. The interview could serve as a dry run of sorts for the trial, giving me practice telling my story to a stranger. I would be doing exactly that on the witness stand.

As Julie and I were coming in from Nashville over the Labor Day weekend to see Alex, Mike set up an interview in his office with the *Sun-Times*'s Natasha Korecki, whom I had met briefly many months before at the coffee shop the day of my arraignment. She had expressed to Mike that her editors had proposed doing two front-page exclusives over Labor Day weekend: one that focused on me and the other on Julie.

Although Mike thought I was ready, Julie and I both had misgivings about doing the interview primarily because we were not public people and were not accustomed to being interviewed by major news organizations. On the other hand, we knew we really had no choice but to do it because it was a good opportunity to get some of our story out. In the end, we believed the potential reward outweighed the risk.

There was a safety net, too. Mike said that if I got uncomfortable with the questions or Korecki's tone I could refuse to answer or just walk away. He said that he would be there, and if any questions were beyond the scope of what he wanted, he would intervene. Interestingly, as after the arraignment, he didn't instruct me on what to say or how to say it for the interview.

Korecki interviewed Julie and me for almost three hours. She was thorough and detailed in her questioning, spending almost as much time on our personal background as she did on the subject of the indictment. I believe we were able to convey in a forthright way our frustration with how the indictment had affected us and how it consumed our lives. Julie talked about how our "quiet, private lives" had been upended and described the horrifying, sick feeling she had knowing the FBI had violated our privacy. "I am frustrated with the government because I believe he is being held hostage by them. I believe that they indicted Rob to get his brother to plead."

Julie did a wonderful job by accurately portraying who we were and maintaining her steadfast belief in my innocence. As Korecki reported: "Julie Blagojevich said she has listened to all of the tapes and can't understand why her husband was charged. 'My husband is an innocent man, wrongly accused,' she said. 'He's done nothing wrong. He's been portrayed to be the bagman for his brother. . . . He is so not that person. He's the most honorable, forthright, direct . . . moral person you will ever, ever meet.'" Any objective reader would see that I was a lucky guy who had a loving and loyal wife standing by him during his darkest time.

Much of what I talked about centered on my background, growing up with Rod and my desire to help out my brother when he said he had no one else he could trust to fundraise for him. Korecki, who gave us every opportunity to say what we wanted, wrote:

> Rob Blagojevich, who spent 21 years in the Army, said he has always lived by the rules and takes it as a personal affront that the country he has served has, in his view, turned on him.
>
> "We're not perfect people, but I'm not a criminal," he said. "This is just not fair. It's absolutely not fair."
>
> And though his brother has frustrated him at times, Rob won't turn on him.
>
> "I do not plan to plead guilty. I plan to go to trial. We're codefendants, and we are not guilty on those charges," said Rob Blagojevich, "I would not testify against my brother."

What I didn't know at the time of this interview was a conversation I would have with a stranger many months later during the trial. He was a young African American man who shared an elevator ride with me down the lobby during a break. It was just the two of us, no one else was there. He broke the awkward silence by telling me that he admired me for how I was conducting myself during the trial. I was somewhat surprised and asked him why he would say that to me. To my astonishment he told me he had been through a similar situation involving his brother, but in his case his brother had flipped and testified against him. He said Rod was lucky I didn't turn on him. I told him I was sorry for what happened to him but that I had nothing bad to say against my brother. Nonetheless, I told him I was grateful for his kind words of support and wished him well as we exited the elevator. This stranger would never know how meaningful his words were to me on the elevator ride we shared that day.

I ALSO ADDRESSED WITH Ms. Korecki the conversation I'd had with Roland Burris on November 13—the one that had been released when Burris was being investigated by the US Senate. The following excerpts are taken from Korecki's article:

> Rob Blagojevich declined to discuss the specifics of the criminal case. But he pointed to an exchange last November between himself and Roland Burris, who eventually got the Senate appointment. The secretly recorded conversation was made public as part of a US Senate ethics inquiry. Burris can be heard telling Rob Blagojevich that he's feeling conflicted, that he wants to give to Rod Blagojevich's campaign fund but worries how it would look as he sought the Senate seat appointment.
>
> • • •
>
> On tape, Rob Blagojevich presses Burris to donate to his brother. But, regarding the Senate seat, he's heard essentially telling Burris: Get in line, that others also were seeking the appointment.
>
> "How I conducted myself with Burris is how I conducted myself with everyone when no one was looking," Rob Blagojevich told the *Sun-Times*.

As we concluded the interview and were getting ready to leave, Korecki asked me if I thought Congressman Jesse Jackson Jr. had gotten a pass. Her question seemed to come out of nowhere and surprised me. Although I believed that Jackson had empowered Bedi and Nayak to approach me on his behalf with the bribes they offered, I had not spent any time thinking about it. I told her I really had no way of knowing and felt that I needed to concentrate on my own predicament before I started to think about anyone else. She accepted my answer and we finished for the day. Almost two years later, when I was ready, she would give me a second opportunity to talk about Jackson.

Mike called me later in the day to tell me he thought the interview went well. He was particularly impressed by the way Julie handled herself and thought she came across as a class act. He took a deep breath, and then told me something I didn't expect. He said he watched and listened carefully to all the questions Korecki had asked and the way I answered them. He then told me that from his experience defending people, 95 percent of them were guilty of something when they were charged. He explained his job in those circumstances was to use the law to the best of his ability to mitigate the punishment for those clients. He had my attention. Was a shoe going to drop?

Mike went on to tell me that what kept him up at night were the other 5 percent whom he knew were totally innocent, like me. "Rob," he emphatically stated, "you're innocent! Do you realize how much more pressure that puts on me?"

Knowing a client is innocent put even more pressure on him to win because he knew that if he didn't, an honest man would be wrongly punished, he explained. Listening to him talk this way comforted me. It was nice to hear that my attorney truly believed in my innocence and felt the same stress I felt, albeit in a different way. Fortunately, I had chosen a man to defend me who recognized the enormity of his responsibility and the consequences if he failed. We shared the same fear and insecurity, but from very different perspectives.

Although I would go to prison and Mike would return to his home and practice if I lost, I felt bad for him. There was no way I could help him cope as he helped me. However, I knew that if I did my part, whatever he required of me as a defendant, I would be helping him do his job for me. By remaining united in our objective, each of us doing his part, attorney and client, maybe we could beat Goliath, the United States of America.

THE TRIAL WAS SCHEDULED to start on June 4, 2010. Mike, Cheryl, Robyn, and I spent the rest of 2009 getting ready for my day in court. They'd all had an opportunity to review the discovery evidence— the tape-recorded conversations and statements of witnesses the government expected to call. The good news was that each of my three lawyers concluded I had no criminal intent and was innocent. Their collective belief in my innocence was the cornerstone to the exceptional working relationship we developed. Our team dynamic matured over the months as we diligently worked with a unified and coordinated purpose of beating the government. Any time one of us found something in the evidence that needed to be flushed out, we would immediately call and not let time pass without talking about it. We were all determined to leave no stone unturned and to be optimally prepared when we went to trial.

The bad news was that this was not true of my codefendant brother. I didn't get the same constructive vibe from him that I had expected. From the time we were kids, Rod and I had very different approaches to managing life's challenges and solving problems. When a conflict with a neighborhood kid popped up, Rod's tendency was to verbally inflame the problem and, thus, unnecessarily escalate the situation. My approach was to be less combative, trying to avoid a fight to figure out how to move on before fisticuffs broke out. Often I would have to step in and save Rod from himself, protecting him from the bigger kid he angered. These differences once again began to express themselves at a most dangerous time in our lives in ways that caused me great concern.

When we were kids, Rod's behavior had put me in harm's way a few times. But that harm might have been a black eye or fat lip at the hands of a neighborhood kid. Now, as an adult, I found myself in harm's way thanks to my little brother. But this time what was at stake was five to seven years behind bars.

Because Rod was responsible for putting me in this predicament, I had an expectation that he would try to be helpful in any way he could to ease the impact on me. Much to my disappointment, he failed to be there when I needed him. Having been arrested, impeached, unemployed, and trying to figure everything out for himself, Rod had a lot to deal with. However, I thought he never understood or took responsibility for the position I was in because of him. Several times he dismissively told me not to worry. The government was after him and not me, he insisted. My name, however, was still on that indictment along with his. Rod and I spoke with most frequency the months right after the indictment. We were both still stunned by what had happened to us. I, more than Rod, needed time to assess what the implications of being criminally charged actually meant. He seemed to take this next phase of his life in stride, trying to figure out how to make a living and defend himself at the same time.

As noted, with the help of his publicist, he had already secured a book deal in which he was able to earn some money, tell his side of the story, and occupy his time during the day. Although he couldn't leave the country to appear on *I'm a Celebrity…Get Me Out of Here!*, he was able to accept a spot on Donald Trump's *Celebrity Apprentice*, which was filmed in New York. This ensured additional income and a national following for the former Illinois governor who was under indictment. It also guaranteed additional ridicule.

I felt sad that Rod had been reduced to doing reality shows to make a living, but I understood. To be supportive, I told him he needed to do whatever he believed was in his family's best interest. Had I not been indicted and facing financial ruin having to defend myself, I would have been able to help him some.

The strain on our relationship escalated when Rod went on a national media tour proclaiming his innocence. Months before the trial he appeared for a second time on Letterman. He also did *The Daily Show with Jon Stewart*, the *Today* show with Meredith Vieira, *Fox News Sunday* with Chris Wallace, *Larry King Live* on CNN, *The View*, an ABC *World News* interview with Brian Ross, and all the local Chicago news outlets. He even did a stint as host on WLS 890, a local Chicago radio station.

During this time, I questioned him about why he was being so public. I feared I would in some way be collateral damage from negative public opinion that might result from his excessive media exposure. I told him a national media strategy didn't help him with a Chicago jury. Naturally, he disagreed with me, rationalizing that if it helped him, as he believed it did, it would be good for me as his codefendant. As politely as possible, I told him he was way off base to think it was helpful and stressed that he was putting me in greater jeopardy. This subject led to a heated argument leaving me very disappointed in him once again. He didn't care what I thought, nor would he objectively consider my opinion. Sadly, I could only conclude he didn't care as much about me as I once thought he did.

It's hard for me to pass judgment on the wisdom of Rod's media blitz. There was a sense of desperation I believed drove him to action. Sitting at home worrying about being prosecuted wasn't going to cut it for him when he could be out in the public making his case, much like what he'd done in all the campaigns he'd won in the past. That's what he knew; that's what sustained him when nothing else could. What made me worry was his detachment from the reality of the danger he was in. It was too painful for me to watch him on any of those shows—I didn't have the stomach for it. But I honestly believe he thought the media exposure was helping him make the case for his innocence. My friends who saw Rod interviewed thought he did a good job. Perhaps they were telling me this to be supportive, but I was happy to hear it anyway. Maybe he knew what he was doing after all, but I still didn't get it and still worried.

While Rod was busy working on his public image, I was getting the impression he was too detached from the real problem and not focused on going to trial. As my concerns grew, I asked him a couple of times if he'd listened to any of the FBI intercepts. It was obvious from his lame explanations that he had not. He would blow me off and try to change the subject.

I knew how tedious and time-consuming it was to learn what was on the tapes. By that time I had listened to the majority of those that involved me—and mine were a fraction of what Rod had to process and know. I thought he should have had his nose to the grindstone, doing the hard work and spending less time on the media circuit.

At a certain point when the subject of preparation came up I'd hold back my opinion to avoid an argument. In Rod's mind, doing all the interviews was getting ready for trial. His approach couldn't have been more different from mine. All the time he was doing his media tour, my energies were focused on plowing through the discovery. There was no higher priority for either of us, but Rod didn't seem to see it that way. I knew and understood he was in a tough spot and had to make a living. However, it became apparent to me that while working on all these side projects Rod was getting caught up in his own celebrity and not focusing on what really mattered: getting ready for trial. His head wasn't in the game and there was nothing I could do about it. As his codefendant. I was really bothered by this.

In August of 2009 Rod and I had a conversation that significantly worsened an already strained relationship. For the first ten minutes we had a nice conversation talking about family and how each of us was coping. I told him about some of the tapes I'd listened to earlier in the week—tapes that I thought were very helpful to him. They clearly demonstrated to me his intention to do the right thing and I wanted him to know that.

His response surprised me. He instructed me in a condescending tone that I was too caught up in the minutiae and needed to see the big picture of what the possibilities were after this was behind us. I couldn't believe what he was telling me. Somehow he was able to diminish the importance of knowing the evidence and could convince himself that everything would be fine, as if preparation was a secondary detail to be magically overcome without the hard work. My response was right to the point, that there wouldn't be a chance to live the big picture, whatever that was, if he didn't get acquitted!

Rod then took the conversation in a different direction, telling me I was too negative and needed to be more optimistic. I'd heard that from him before and in no uncertain terms had told him he couldn't be more wrong about me. I emphasized to him that I was a realist who dealt with facts. With eyes wide open, I was one who wanted to confront the problem in order to fix it, not run from it. We went back and forth on what the words negative, optimist, and realist meant with neither one of us giving ground.

Finally I'd had it with him. Raising my voice, I told him that of all the people who should know me, he didn't. I told him how disappointed I was in him as a brother and believed I could no longer count on him in the most dire time of our lives. I even reversed the circumstances, telling him if I had been the reason he got into legal trouble, I would feel a great sense of responsibility to him to do all I could to be helpful and supportive. I wouldn't do anything to put him in further jeopardy and would be there for him as a reliable ally in the fight we both faced.

This was a devastating conversation, but it needed to happen for Rod to know where I stood as his brother. We were having a major failure to communicate and a clash of styles that I could no longer afford to ignore. I felt I had no choice but to set a course that would distance me from him.

CHAPTER ELEVEN

"Is That All There Is?"

"Would you rather be indicted or have your arm cut off?" Julie asked me. The question came out of nowhere, as we drove to watch our nephew Davis play in a tennis tournament.

"What?" I said. I noticed Julie was smiling.

"Just answer the question," she said. "Would you rather be indicted or have your arm cut off?"

This, I believe, is a good example of what they call "gallows humor." Here we were, the rug suddenly pulled out from under our comfortable life, with prison and financial ruin passengers in the car—and she was asking me to make a choice between two surreal options. Well, actually only one of the options was surreal. Being indicted would have seemed surreal six months earlier—but not now.

I thought for a moment, then said: "I'd rather have my arm cut off." I meant it. All I wanted was to have the pressure I was under go away. I just wanted to get on with my life. Here's my arm, take it. Move on.

With the gallows now open for business, the humor continued. We got really silly with this game, sacrificing any body part imaginable, except one. We were even reduced to figuratively throwing acid into each other's faces only to draw the line at that one and be resigned to an indictment instead. Nonetheless, it helped break the tension and got us laughing for a few mindless moments.

My Julie! She had, at least for the moment, defused the time bomb. Later, we told her family about the game. They found it strange at first, but when they saw we were okay with it, they started their own version. The game—Would You Rather Be Indicted Or—became such a stress relief for us, that even to this day we use it to put bad things into perspective. Of course I didn't have the option of giving the government a few pounds of flesh in return for dropping the charges, but if I had, who knows what they could have gotten from me in return.

AS I'VE PREVIOUSLY EXPLAINED, I had been charged with violating the honest services law, a twenty-eight-word clause in a federal statute that most scholars found confusing and many found unconstitutional. I, therefore, took heart in December 2009 when the US Supreme Court agreed to hear three cases (Weyhrauch, Skilling, and Black) challenging the validity of the honest services law. It would be argued that the law was unconstitutional because it denied the right to due process, which requires that criminal laws offer an understandable explanation of the conduct that is prohibited. That made sense. If a layperson can't understand what conduct is forbidden, how can you know when you've crossed the line?

In my case the government alleged I had conspired with Rod to deny the people of Illinois "their intangible right to his honest services." From the day I was indicted, I repeatedly asked Mike, "What did I do to break the law?" I read the statute, but it seemed so vague.

I wasn't alone. Supreme Court Justice Antonin Scalia was an outspoken critic of the law, noting its vagueness and the expanding use of the law by "headline-grabbing prosecutors." Scalia opined that the average citizen could break this law without realizing that what he or she was doing was wrong. Taken to its logical conclusion, the justice said, the law may apply to a government worker who called in sick and then went out to the ballpark, or even a mayor who used his position to get a table in a restaurant without a reservation.

Mike, an avid Supreme Court watcher, said it was unusual that the justices had agreed to hear three different cases challenging the honest services law. He explained that the court typically didn't hear multiple cases unless they had significant concerns about the constitutionality of a law. He thought it was an indication the justices were going either to trim the law substantially or deem it unconstitutional. He said it was possible that if the court did void the law, the charges against me might be dropped. During our trial preparation, he sometimes said, "If you're still in this, Rob." Knowing Mike, he would never have said that to me unless he really believed it and thought it was reasonably possible.

Mike wasn't the only one speculating on the outcome of the Supreme Court's review of the honest services law. Three months after the court announced it was going to hear the appeals, Fitzgerald hedged his bets by charging me with three more felony counts. He now charged me with bribery, conspiracy to bribe, and extortion. As a result of his maneuver the burden of defending myself at trial (and of conviction) increased exponentially. I now faced a total of five felonies. Even if the honest services law were ruled unconstitutional, I would still be in legal jeopardy with these additional charges.

By this point it had become clear to me that as long as Fitzgerald thought I could be useful to him to convict my brother, he would remain determined to keep me in no matter what. This maneuver only hardened my cynicism about the criminal justice system and the lopsided advantage federal prosecutors have to play with peoples' lives. What I will never understand is why I wasn't charged with the three additional felonies at the time I was first indicted. If I was so guilty, why didn't the government throw the book at me in April 2009 instead of waiting until February 2010? Nothing had changed. The evidence was the same!

Unfortunately for me, Fitzgerald's agenda had not changed. Unless you have lived it, you have no idea how difficult and frustrating it is to withstand the machinations of a government that does whatever it chooses, even to an innocent person, in order to win. My expectations for a good outcome from the Supreme Court were low in spite of Mike's optimistic opinion. I couldn't take the emotional risk to count on a favorable ruling only to be disappointed if it didn't happen. I wouldn't learn the outcome of the court's ruling until we were in the thick of the trial in June.

Trying to take the new indictment in stride and not let the process get me down, I once again flew to Chicago to be arraigned a second time. This time I did it differently. I had been in the legal meat grinder long enough to get a feel for the system. When Mike told me the date of the arraignment, I asked him if Rod and I were scheduled to go before the judge together. The feds had also re-indicted Rod.

When Mike said he believed that we were to be arraigned together, I told him I did not want to be arraigned with Rod again. "Please get me another date," I said. I had many reasons for the request. Over the last ten months, Rod had been painfully visible to the public with his national media tour and other events that he believed helped him for trial. I did not. It was also becoming evident to me that Rod and his lawyers believed I was tied to his legal coattails. They believed that if Rod did well at trial so would I. This meant I should just accept the wisdom of their strategy and buy into his public antics even if I thought it was harmful to him and me. Thankfully, I had my own legal team to defend me properly; the risk was too great to look to Rod and his lawyers for any help.

Sadly, I had no choice but to deliberately separate myself from Rod. The realization that I could no longer count on him or his lawyers to consider my interests factored critically into my changing view on how I should proceed as his codefendant. As a result, my defense strategy began to take on a distinct shape. Mike and I agreed to a strategy of separation from Rod that we believed would be beneficial to my defense.

Separating myself from Rod did not mean I would do anything to intentionally hurt him to advance my defense. On the contrary, I knew I could be helpful to us both at trial by taking the risk to testify and tell the truth about what really happened. Standing alone at my second arraignment was the first step in advancing this new strategy. This was a calculated move to separate me from Rod and demonstrate to the public I was my own man. I'll never know if this ever resonated with anyone in Chicago, but I liked it. My attorneys were continuing to proactively manage my public image in spite of the distractions of an unreliable codefendant and a US attorney who would stop at nothing to win. During a time when I felt almost helpless to influence things around me, something as small as this gave me a psychological lift that I could.

Initially, Mike and I disagreed on how far to go with the separation strategy. He did agree that we would only use my proper name Robert in public, not Rob, so that I would not be confused with Rod. After my second arraignment I instructed Mike to file a severance motion, but he resisted. Translation: I wanted to be tried separately from my brother. I didn't think I could get a fair trial if we were tried together. The jury, I thought, would reason that if one Blagojevich was guilty, the other was guilty, too.

The practice of assigning cases to judges in federal court is accomplished through a random draw. Our indictment had been superseded onto the indictment of Chris Kelly and William Cellini, a power broker in Springfield of whom I'd never heard, whose case was before Judge Zagel. (Note: A superseding indictment is filed subsequent to an original indictment.) Although our charges had nothing to do with Cellini or Chris Kelly who had two other indictments pending, we were automatically assigned to Judge Zagel.

We most likely would have been assigned a different judge had the court followed the customary practice. However, in what I consider another underhanded maneuver, US Attorney Fitzgerald was somehow allowed to add us to the Cellini indictment because he knew Zagel was a pro-government judge. By superseding our indictment onto Cellini's to get Zagel, Fitzgerald knew his prosecutors would have an easier time at trial. Subsequently Cellini asked for a severance from us and got it. As a layman who knew nothing about the federal court system, I'm appalled at how rigged the system appears to be in favor of prosecutors' ability to unfairly manipulate a case.

Mike didn't think a severance was a good idea. He believed I was better off being tried with my brother and not separately. However, he did as I'd asked and filed for severance. The logic of the motion was sound—at least to me. We argued that the vast majority of the charges were against Rod; that I'd worked for Rod only four months, only 5 percent of the eighty-four months of the alleged conspiracy; and that the publicity surrounding Rod would hurt me if we were tried together. I also believed that Fitzgerald's inflammatory press conference the day of Rod's arrest polluted the jury pool with a bias against Rod and adversely affected me as well. In the interest of fairness I thought a severance was justified.

There were other considerations, although we didn't have grounds to argue them in our motion. The prosecutors estimated the trial would take up to six months. The case against me was thin. I had two wire fraud charges, of five total, for out-of-state phone calls, one of which I wasn't even on and had no knowledge of. (This call would eventually be dropped by the prosecution the day before the case went to the jury. We never understood why I was charged with it but nonetheless still had to deal with it at trial.) The preponderance of the evidence was against Rod. Mike believed if I were tried alone, it would take only two weeks. The cost of my defense would have been substantially less in a trial estimated to take one-twelfth as long. The additional financial hardship of a six-month trial in Chicago when I lived in Nashville seemed unfair as well.

The prosecutors objected to our request for severance, and Judge Zagel agreed with them. Denied! The government succeeded in keeping me in the case to continue to attempt to leverage me against my brother.

AFTER THE SECOND ARRAIGNMENT, Mike, Cheryl, and I had stopped at the Marquette Inn on Adams near the federal building to have a bite to eat. It would become our favorite place for lunch during the trial. We went there so often that the owner, Tom, reserved a spot for us in the back of the restaurant, away from the public. While we were eating, Mike reviewed where he thought we were in trial prep and what still remained to be done. He had an idea he wanted to run by me that he thought might help us prepare our case.

Mike explained that Cheryl had a good friend, Cindy Rafter, who had years earlier been on a federal jury. She was willing to help us in any way needed. Given her experience, Mike thought she could be useful as a jury of one in a mock trial. We'd present our case to her and see what she thought. Mike and Cheryl would represent the defense, while Robyn played prosecutor. The mock trial would give us a great opportunity to test-drive our defense theory with someone who had been a juror. The process would reveal our weaknesses, which, we hoped, would give us insight into how to fine-tune our strategy.

I loved the idea and told Mike to do it when he thought the time was right. As I continued to struggle with my personal frustrations about loss of control, this idea inspired me to believe I was getting some of it back. Thanks to a legal team that was passionate about winning and willing to do anything that would help us, my spirits were rising.

Later that month, Cindy came to Mike's office for a mock trial that lasted a few hours. According to Mike, she was attentive as "US Attorney" Robyn tried to make the government's case against me. Robyn pulled no punches and did her best to flush out any weakness in our defense so Cindy would get the worst of it for her verdict. Mike and Cheryl presented the defense case armed with the substance of our many hard months of preparation.

As I waited for Mike's postmortem, I felt the same kind of anxiety I felt before I took a big test in school—hope, confidence, and the fear that I might not pass. Every possible scenario ran through my head. Cindy could come to the conclusion I was guilty or come in undecided, not sure about my innocence. I tried hard not to worry too much, assuring myself that whatever the outcome, we would have her valuable input to help us improve.

"How'd it go?" I asked when Mike called late in the afternoon.

"It went fine," he said.

One year after my first indictment, I'd learn where we stood with at least one qualified and objective person. I was so anxious to learn Cindy's

verdict that I didn't pay close attention to Mike's explanation of how specific arguments went over. As Mike briefed me on the presentation, I
expected an up or down, guilty or not guilty verdict.

What I got was far better than a not guilty. Mike said that when they
finished putting on the case, Cindy didn't render a verdict. She just asked,
"Is that all there is?" Those were the five best words I'd heard in my life. I
couldn't believe she got it! I was elated that she was left wanting to hear
more evidence. But there was no more, what she had heard was all there
was. Cindy confirmed for us the government had a weak to nonexistent
case against me. We believed the only chance they had for a conviction was
to discredit me. We also knew they would try their hardest to do just that.

From the time of my brother's arrest, through our indictments I never
felt at peace with my situation. How can you when you're facing years
in prison? But after hearing those liberating five words, I moved a little
closer to feeling better about what lay ahead. This was the mental lift I
needed before going to trial.

With the mock trial results still fresh, Mike pressed on. He suggested I
travel to Chicago one last time before the trial to review our case together
with Cheryl and Robyn. Despite my reluctance to be back in Chicago
I thought it was a good idea, so in the middle of May I went. The only
thing that helped ease some of the pain of all the recent bad Chicago
memories was being able to hang out with Alex for a few days.

Hoping to optimize my time with him, I was able to persuade Alex to
go with me to Mike's that weekend so he could see firsthand what I was
going through. Over the past many months, we had talked a lot about the
case, but he had never been exposed to the evidence nor met my lawyers. I
thought it would be good to prepare him for what was coming at trial and
to get his thoughts on what he learned from observing Mike and the team.

From Alex's condo on the north side, we drove south on Lake Shore
Drive, by some of the most beautiful city views in the world: the Gold
Coast, the inspiring architectural variety of downtown, the green space
of Grant Park, Buckingham Fountain (a place my dad would take us to
play), past McCormick Place to a much less aesthetic I-55 west to the
South Harlem exit that eventually led us to Mike's office. The drive was
long, but the time went fast because I always had fun with Alex. Despite
the circumstances, just being with him made me feel better.

I gave Alex a quick overview of what we were trying to accomplish over
the weekend and encouraged him to ask questions and be as involved as

he wanted. I did not tell him that I was going to once again ask—more likely insist—that Mike cross-examine me this time. With all the preparation, and studying the evidence and the positive feedback from the mock trial, it was the only element missing for me to be ready for trial. I needed to know what it was like to be crossed. I knew I was ready.

ALL THE TEAM WAS assembled when we arrived at 9:30. Mike lived in Northbrook, a nice suburb way north of the city, and it took him about an hour to get there. He had no sympathy for me when I repeatedly complained to him about having to come so far to meet at his office. I once asked him why he lived so far from work. He told me that over the years his legal practice seemed to flourish in the southwest suburbs so he moved his office from downtown to where the business was concentrated. Aside from the fact he liked the long drive, his main reason for living so far was he didn't want to be recognized by his clients on his days off and be bothered.

After I introduced Alex and we exchanged pleasantries, we moved into the conference room and got to work. To my surprise I noticed Mike had managed to mount a television on the conference room wall and connect it to a laptop that had all the wiretapped transcripts on it. We were all able to simultaneously read whatever conversation Mike chose to review and discuss it right off the screen. Robyn was our designated techie, and she did a great job finding everything we needed, including the FBI 302 witness statements we'd recently received from the prosecutors. Also notable, the conference room looked organized and lacked the clutter I witnessed back when I visited Mike's office the day of my first arraignment.

Federal discovery guidelines require the government to turn over to the defense all the FBI 302s no later than thirty days before trial. That's when we got them—exactly thirty days before trial. I still don't understand why they're allowed to withhold these very important documents from the defense for so long. It's just another example of the unfair advantage the prosecution has in federal court. When the 302s had arrived, Mike and I had spoken by phone about how we should digest the additional discovery dump. I immediately went to work with Julie organizing and systematically reading everything that might pertain to me. We were scrambling, trying to quickly prioritize the relevant pages from the scores of interviews and thousands of pages.

At Mike's, we dissected a number of the 302s, focusing on Raghu Nayak, Rajindar Bedi, Congressman Jesse Jackson Jr., Babu Patel, Lon Monk, John Wyma, and a few others that we thought were relevant. Both days of the weekend were jam-packed with work. We started at 9:30 a.m. and stopped around 4:00 p.m., only taking breaks for restroom runs and a dine-in lunch. Mike was able to keep the mood light, and we managed to laugh when least expected. I always felt energized when I was with the team. We had a chemistry that kept me strong and gave me confidence. Now it was on to cross-ex.

Early in life I discovered I learned best by doing and not by watching or being lectured at in class about how to do something. That's not to say I wasn't a committed student; I studied hard when I had to, but unless I had some hands-on experience along the way, it didn't stick for long. I don't think that's unique to me, but I knew myself well enough to know that if I was going to testify, especially be cross-examined by a well-prepared prosecutor, I had to have the learning experience that came with having been through it.

After more than a year of studying all there was to know about the case, hearing the tapes, and talking with my lawyers nearly everyday, I thought I was as ready as I could be to stand up to the tough questions that would come at trial. In addition, I believed that my experience as an army officer and corporate executive gave me a good practical foundation to draw from in my preparation to testify.

As a young lieutenant serving in Germany, I had constantly been tested. I once had to brief sixteen NATO generals on the tactical deployment of the three Pershing nuclear missiles that I was assigned to lead. Also, I was aide-de-camp to a brigadier general whom I had to brief regularly, oftentimes extemporaneously while under a lot of pressure. My corporate career exposed me to examinations by the Securities Exchange Commission (SEC), National Association of Securities Dealers (NASD), and the Federal Reserve. As I held positions of responsibility, I was accountable if there was a violation of a regulatory nature.

Fortunately I was always well prepared for these career tests and succeeded in meeting the required standard each time. All these challenging career experiences gave me the self-confidence that I could handle anything that came my way from the government, especially when I knew I had done nothing wrong. Being cross-examined by a skilled prosecutor couldn't be that hard.

Wrong! Although Mike didn't think I was ready to sit in the witness chair, he bowed to my wishes and cross-examined me in his office. The grilling took only ten minutes. And it was a grilling.

Mike took control of the cross immediately. His deliberate use of rhythm and pace lulled me into a false sense of confidence. Then suddenly he'd ask rapid-fire questions that would catch me off guard. He was way ahead of me, leading me into logical dead ends, because he knew where his questions would lead me and I didn't. I felt like I was a step or two behind him, running to catch up to provide an answer while trying to figure out where he was coming from. He was relentless in pushing me to answer when I hadn't had time to think. In short, he chewed me up and spit me out.

After we finished, I sensed I hadn't done well. Alex seconded that emotion. He leaned over to me in frustration and told me to "listen to the question and tighten up, Dad!" These were the same words I used with him while he was growing up and I thought he needed to focus on something.

To hear my son tell me I screwed up was bad enough. Then Mike rubbed it in. "I told you so. You weren't ready yet." I realized that my confidence had been misplaced and that I still had a long way to go—and a short window of time—to be ready for the government's assault. Cheryl tried to console me by saying I'd do fine when the time came. I sure hoped so.

While the cross-ex was ugly, I soon realized this had been the most valuable ten minutes of my trial preparation to date. It was exactly what I needed: to feel the emotion and learn what it was like to be in the hot seat. Next time I would have to be much more aware and try not to surrender control of my testimony to the pace of the prosecutor's interaction with me, as I had done with Mike. I needed to listen much more carefully to the entire question before I jumped in to answer.

I'd have to try to slow it all down so I'd have time to think about what I had been asked. That may be simple enough for most people, but for me it was more challenging because my natural impulse is to answer quickly. I had no choice but to learn to control it, so that later I wouldn't regret it. Equally important, I had to try to prevent the prosecutor from leading me though rapid-fire questioning like I had just experienced with Mike and not let him lead me down logic paths that could trap me. It was a good thing I learned these lessons the hard way before it was too late.

On the long drive back to Alex's place, we had plenty of time to talk about what had been accomplished that day. Alex offered some constructive criticism he thought I should heed the next time I testified. Again he told me I needed to tighten up and listen more closely to the question. He feared I might do the same thing at trial and told me it wouldn't be good for me if I did. He was right and I knew it.

I'd already concluded that in spite of how bad it may have looked, I had made real progress. I told Alex not to worry about me, I was fine and that this was the best thing that could have happened to me in my preparation for trial. Further, I explained to him that the best way for me to learn was from the mistakes I'd made that day. "I'll be more aware not to repeat them when it really matters," I said. When it really mattered was rapidly approaching.

CHAPTER TWELVE

Stay Focused

There is no way to explain the empty feeling of leaving your home and your life behind to spend many uncertain months in a city where federal prosecutors are waiting to ruin you. On Memorial Day weekend 2010, Julie and I packed up our car and, with our dog Shelby, a bichon/ poodle mix, in tow, drove the five hundred miles from Nashville to Chicago to settle in for the fight of our lives. The prosecutors had said it would take them about six months to put on their case. This meant we would likely be away into November, so before we left we shipped several boxes of our winter clothes to Alex's condo, where we'd be staying.

As apprehensive as I was about facing a determined US attorney's office, I was glad we were finally going to trial. Waiting really wore me down. I don't think I could have survived very long without the plan that Alex and I had drafted almost eighteen months earlier. Structuring my days with a regime to strengthen me mentally and physically had allowed me to focus on my defense.

As I've mentioned, I was more worried about the toll this ordeal would have on my family than on myself. Julie and Alex had each had their moments, but, thank goodness, they had each held up pretty well since the day Rod was arrested. And then . . .

A few days after we settled in, three days before the trial was to start, Alex started to have some discomfort in his chest. I didn't think much of it. Julie did. She was sitting with him in his bedroom when she frantically called to me to take him to the hospital. "I think it's his heart," she said. How could that be? He was twenty-six years old, healthy, athletic and in better shape than most people his age. I told Julie that it was probably just indigestion.

She would have none of it and shamed me into taking Alex to the Weiss Memorial Hospital emergency room around 11:30 that night.

By the time we got to the hospital, he was feeling fine, with no pain. I knew it was nothing. It was late, I wanted to go to bed, I was going on trial in a few days, and I needed to focus. But the nurse on duty insisted on doing some tests and drew blood. She and the doctor determined there was an elevated protein enzyme count that was symptomatic of a heart problem. A few hours later they admitted Alex for observation.

I waited until Alex was settled into his room to confer with the doctor. He assured me Alex was not having a heart attack. Diagnosis #1? An infection of the lining of his heart. Thankfully, with treatment this cleared up after a couple days in the hospital. Diagnosis #2? Mothers know best.

One morning when Julie and I were visiting Alex in the hospital, I found a Chicago newspaper prominently reporting that our trial would be starting in two days. It gave the readers a quick reference guide to all the players going on trial, including me.

After I read it, I stuck the paper under my chair and had another of those clarifying moments I seemed to be having lately. This time it was real simple—the realization that the health of my son and loved ones was more important than any of the worries I had going to trial—even prison.

Speaking of family! This last bit of perspective couldn't have come at a better time for me because the drama between my brother and me was wearing thin. While I was still at the hospital, my cell phone rang. It was Rod. We hadn't spoken to each other for more than a month because of a conversation we had had over family. Part of it involved his father-in-law, Dick Mell, the man whom I believed initially endangered Rod and his family by publicly speculating that Chris Kelly was offering state contracts in exchange for contributions to FOB. I could never understand why a sophisticated man like Mell would put his daughter and her children in harm's way with reckless allegations to the press about her husband.

During that conversation, I also reminded Rod that I hadn't flipped on him to cut a deal, like his close friends Wyma and Monk had done. I went on to tell him how hard it was for me to comprehend why he failed to recognize the personal sacrifice I was having to make during a family crisis he brought on. As a brother this was my biggest disappointment with him. If just once, he had acknowledged what I was going through instead of telling me the government didn't want me. It was clear to me from reviewing the tapes during discovery that Rod, while serving as governor, was still concerned about the possibility of being indicted. So I'll never understand why at that July 4 meeting, he and Patti had not been forthcoming when they told me the feds' investigation was behind them, that they had a clean slate. Julie even recalled for me later, that during that same conversation, when she inquired about the corruption allegations and problems swirling around them, they looked at each other and laughed at any possibility of an indictment.

Rod didn't know Alex was in the hospital so I knew he wasn't calling about him. We were miles apart on many big issues, and I no longer had the emotional energy to deal with him. I didn't answer the phone.

Within one minute of Rod's call to me, Julie got a call on her phone from Patti. She hadn't talked to Julie for nearly a year and a half. Julie asked me if she should answer. "No," I said, explaining that Patti would leave a message if she really needed something. As it turned out she left a message telling Julie that she was calling to "coordinate court." We didn't even know what that meant.

Sadly, neither Rod nor Patti called Julie to check in on her at all during this time. I remember having a conversation many months earlier with Patti when I suggested she give Julie a call. Patti disappointed me when she said she didn't believe it would be welcome. To me it sounded like an excuse not to take responsibility to reach out to someone you'd known for well over twenty years to express your sorrow for what you brought on her. I told her I had no idea what she was talking about and asked her to explain. She couldn't and merely repeated her belief that her call would not be welcomed by Julie.

I tried to assure Patti that Julie would love to hear from her. They both had husbands facing prison time and could at a minimum comfort each other. Months went by and she never called. I can only conclude she didn't care.

At this late date, Julie was hesitant to call Patti back. We were not going to pretend everything was all right between us just as we were about to be in the public eye. Regrettably, as a family we had a lot of unresolved issues that could have been properly addressed much earlier. Unfortunately we were to carry this emotional family baggage with us to court.

Julie and I had agreed before we left Nashville that she would not go to court with me every day. I wanted some normalcy when I got home from a long day at trial and didn't want us to have to scramble every night to prepare dinner and get ready for the next day. We decided it would be best for us as a family that she come only on the days that mattered to my defense.

All through our marriage Julie and I have been a team. But I have to admit she is a much better teammate than I am. I know this may sound a little selfish, but it really did help me get through the long court days knowing when I came home that Julie was there making the evenings as comfortable and relaxing as she could. In doing so, she made my life in the legal trenches a little easier to manage. I don't know what I would have done without her.

On the evening before the trial was to start, Julie, Alex, and I talked about how we should act in public given that this trial had local and national media interest. We had never had to think about that until then, and I figured it would be a good idea for us to anticipate and plan accordingly.

Our approach was simple. I wanted for anyone watching our behavior to be taken by our ability to conduct ourselves with dignity, strength, and courage. It didn't matter what these strangers thought of us personally. All I wanted was for us to control our own behavior and show the public nothing but strength and determination in the face of adversity. We all agreed and did our best to live up to it.

Months earlier, management consultant/sounding board Dan Haile had suggested I keep a journal. I did every day of the trial—which, thankfully, turned out to last for three, not six months. I wrote in my journal during trial testimony as well as away from the trial. I filled two white legal pads with my observations.

The journal was my safe place to record my observations, emotions, and frustrations during the most challenging days of my life. In telling the story of the trial here, I have relied on those entries to refresh my memory. The quoted portions that follow are taken verbatim from my journal writings.

Day One: Thursday, June 3, 2010

As I would for every day of the trial, I got up at 5:30 a.m. I either went for a run or to the gym to work out. In any way I could I tried to get a mental edge over the prosecutors. I convinced myself they didn't have the same discipline to get up early and exercise, which I believed gave me the advantage over them. Plus it just made me feel better, sitting in a court-room all day, knowing at least I was productively getting some exercise.

The morning routine also included eating a breakfast of scrambled eggs, crisp turkey bacon, and grits, which Alex prepared every day before he drove me downtown to the federal building. His office wasn't far from where he dropped me off so it gave us quality time together in the car to talk about the day ahead.

After he dropped me off that first day, I met up with Mike and the team in the cafeteria of the federal building, as I would for the entire trial. Then we went together to the courtroom. When I walked in I was once again struck by how big the place was—just as it had seemed over a year earlier when I was first arraigned. I was already seated at my desig-nated defense table when Rod came in and sat down beside me to chat. He asked me how I felt, I reciprocated, and after that we had little to talk about. Patti came over and we hugged. We perfunctorily exchanged pleasantries, talking about what my nieces were up to, and we moved on.

Noted in my journal this day:

- ◆ "Feel strong, confident, and undaunted!"
- ◆ "I stare at the prosecutors and have to contain my outrage with them. They know I did nothing wrong."
- ◆ "Judge Zagel late 45 minutes."

We were all gathered, defendants' lawyers, media, and others for an 11:00 a.m. start, except for Judge Zagel. He showed up forty-five minutes late with no explanation. This happened throughout the trial. I kept track in my journal each time he was late because it bugged me. On average he was forty minutes late every day. This included any time we had to be ready to either start for the day in the morning or return from lunch or breaks.

My legal team and I were always there on time, ready to go. I did the math and calculated the total number of minutes he was late, times the hourly rate I was paying my lawyers. Judge Zagel cost me roughly $15,000 in additional legal fees due to his tardiness while the meter was still run-ning as my lawyers sat by idly. This may sound petty, but I came from a mil-itary and corporate background where I was always on time for meetings.

When the judge came in that first morning, he immediately commenced with *voir dire*, the legal term used to describe jury selection. It comes from the French meaning "to speak or seek that which is true." The objective is to question prospective jurors about their backgrounds and biases for fairness and impartiality. The process Judge Zagel followed to seat the jury allowed the defense ten peremptory challenges and the prosecution six. Unless both sides agreed on a juror, this meant either side could boot a prospective juror for any reason whatsoever without explanation up to their number of challenges. Whoever was left became a juror.

Mike had a very well-thought-out approach to jury selection. In general he tried to avoid pro-government types such as former police officers, military veterans, city, state, and federal workers. Asians were also not an optimal choice because he believed they had a pro-government bias. He preferred women over men. Women had more compassion, he explained, and would be more likely to give a defendant the benefit of the doubt. A person whose family member had a brush with the law might be inclined to be more sympathetic than not for a defendant and got a green light from Mike.

Much more nuance went into his formula for a good jury, but I couldn't grasp it. As my attorney, he not only had to consider Rod's lawyer's preferences, but also those of the prosecutors, who likely followed a strategy far different from ours, trying to neutralize our choices. I had no clue if we got a good or bad jury; I had no way of knowing. With no background in the law, I was astonished to see firsthand how tenuous it was to get the right people to sit in judgment.

As I watched the selection process, I worried about the corrupting influence of Fitzgerald's egregious exaggeration of criminal activity at the press conference the day of Rod's arrest. I strongly believed the jury pool was tainted because of it and the chance of getting a fair trial was lost then. My fears were justified after reading all the answers on the questionnaires the prospective jurors were instructed to fill out before voir dire. Questions included: What's your occupation? Have you formed an opinion on this case? Have you heard about the defendants? It was obvious from reading them that most of the prospective jurors had already made up their minds about Rod, and I believed, by default, me. There was a bleed-over from Rod to me, with many of the respondents confusing our names and mistakenly ascribing facts and attributes to me that did not apply.

The potential jurors seemed to be familiar with the sensational headlines surrounding the case. Many admitted they had already concluded that Rod had sold the Senate seat and was corrupt. As I read the questionnaires, I was concerned and wondered how a defense attorney could ever really filter out the jurors committed to convict. At the same time, I crossed my fingers that Mike, with all his experience, could find at least one juror willing to say "not guilty" and stand by his or her decision in the face of pressure from the other eleven.

After three long days, six men, six women, and five alternates were selected. The jury included an Asian American man who ended up as foreman, a retired naval officer, a young woman whose parents were in law enforcement, a retired postal worker, a twenty-something young man, and a mix of others who would ultimately sit in judgment and decide if I went to prison or went home. They were supposed to be a jury of my peers.

On top of having to worry what the jury might think or how the prosecution would attempt to discredit me, I also had the burden of dealing with my virtually estranged brother. Managing my emotions while on trial with him was difficult. Issues unresolved since the arrest—heck, issues unresolved for years before the arrest—followed me into the courtroom every day.

I eventually had to recognize that—as with most everything else in life—Rod and I had different approaches to the situation at hand. I had to let go and detach my feelings for him as my brother. This was serious stuff and I wasn't going to risk my well-being for him this time. I would never do anything to intentionally hurt him, but I wasn't going to pretend everything was right between us.

I was polite and civil with both Rod and Patti, not much more. When court adjourned, I left through a side door and did not stick around to socialize with them or anyone else. How sad that it came down to this during a horrible family crisis. My lawyers would eventually catch up with me in the lobby. We would discuss the events of the day and anticipate the events of tomorrow.

Unfortunately my quick departure from the courtroom on the first day of the trial created some unwanted drama. Cheryl later told me that right after I left, Patti came up to her and Robyn in tears. She couldn't understand why I left without saying good-bye and why I was treating her and Rod that way.

All three of my lawyers knew the relationship was strained and understood the challenges I had with Rod. Numerous times I asked, even pressed them to be honest with me: was I being a jerk and overreacting to things Rod said or did as we had prepared to go to trial? I didn't want them to side with me because I was their client. I genuinely wanted to know if I was the problem. They told me they thought Rod was self absorbed and only cared about himself. "You aren't the problem," they said. They told me not to worry about him, but to take care of myself. And so I did.

Day Four: Tuesday, June 8, 2010

Opening statements commenced with the prosecution leading off. The government was represented by three seasoned prosecutors: Reid Schar, Christopher Niewoehner, and Carrie Hamilton. They would rely on a deep bench of FBI and IRS agents, hundreds of hours of wiretaps, and an expert on jury instructions from Washington to systematically lay out their case against us. Hamilton was selected to give the prosecution's opening, which went on for nearly three hours.

Almost all of her presentation was directed at Rod. She spent less than five minutes describing the government's case against me. She accused me of shaking down numerous people. Whether it was clever or blatant, it didn't matter, she argued. Robert Blagojevich's message to the donor was clear: You aren't going to get what you want, unless you contribute to my brother. Once again I was struck with the vagueness of the accusations and a failure to attribute a specific action to my alleged crime.

Shortly after the lunch break, Rod's lawyer Sam Adam Jr. offered his opening statement. I thought his opening was long on passion and short on substance. But what did I know about giving opening statements in federal court?

Then it was Mike's turn. On a number of occasions before trial, I asked Mike what he would say in his opening. I wanted to review his outline and have a copy that I could follow as he spoke. Each time I asked him, he told me he had it all memorized, not to worry. I couldn't help worrying, I wanted it to be perfect and not leave anything to chance. I'd never been on trial before and just figured he would have a thoroughly prepared outline to guide him through this most crucial phase of the trial.

Mike told me he did best when he didn't have to refer to an outline or notes because he wanted to come across to the jury as authentic. His objective for an opening statement was to get the jury to like him and garner empathy for his client. He likened himself to Columbo, who came across as less than perfect but smart as a fox. Another note to potential criminal defendants: check your stylistic preferences in the courtroom closet. You are not going to change the way your lawyer goes about his business.

When Mike finished, I had no way of knowing whether he succeeded in connecting with the jury as he'd intended. I thought he fell short, and he seemed a little nervous and got some details wrong. Mike was the trial expert and I deferred to him. At this late stage I had no choice but to trust that he knew what he was doing even if I thought he should have done it differently. Later on during the trial, I asked him to prepare an outline that he and I could review before he gave his closing argument. I thought he would push back and ask me not to tell him how to do his job, but instead, he said he had no problem doing that. Watching Mike operate over the course of the trial, I gained a real appreciation that being a successful trial attorney was at times more art than science.

Day Six: Thursday, June 10, 2010

Noted in my journal this day:

♦ "Today is Friday! Oh not really, it's Thursday. Tomorrow no court cause it's Friday."

Judge Zagel held his trial court from Monday through Thursday each week. Ordinarily having a three-day weekend is not a bad deal. However, by the time a trial workweek ended, I was worn out and needed to regroup. We didn't do much other than exercise, get groceries, and relax. These long weekends gave me a temporary sense of security. I was safe from the government for at least a few days. Unfortunately, Mondays always came and with them the renewed threat of a guilty verdict.

In a criminal trial, the government presents its case first. The defense is under no obligation to present a case at all if it thinks the government has not proven its case beyond a reasonable doubt. When a particular side calls a witness whose testimony it thinks will supports its case, the Q and A is called direct examination. This is followed by cross-examination by the opposing side.

This day started with Lon Monk taking the stand as the first major witness for the government to testify against my brother. Monk had known Rod for more than twenty-five years. They had met as students at Pepperdine University Law School. During the last eight years of their friendship, he would head up Rod's campaign for governor, fundraise, and parlay his relationship into a lucrative lobbying business. Over those years he had spent more quality time with Rod than I had and likely knew him better.

It was hard to sit there and listen to Monk's damaging testimony against Rod. I couldn't understand why he wouldn't accept responsibility for his own criminal behavior and face the consequences instead of turning on his good friend. As Rod's chief of staff, he had compromised himself by taking $70,000 to $90,000 in bribes from Tony Rezko, justifying his acceptance of the money as gifts. In my eyes, Monk simply didn't have the strength to fight the temptation of easy money.

The government exploited this shortcoming, giving him little choice but to cut a deal to minimize his punishment and cooperate with them against Rod. The entire time he was up on the stand he frowned and looked very uncomfortable. In a strange way I felt sorry for him. It was painful to watch as he was revealed to the public as a man of weak character and no backbone. His testimony lasted well into the next trial day, when Mike would have a chance to cross-examine him.

During the lunch break I was standing in the lobby of the federal building with my two brothers-in-law, Tom and Eric Thrailkill, who had both flown in for the first couple of days of trial. As we killed a little time before we had to get back to court, I turned to look toward the street. There he was, coming in through the revolving door, an average-looking, balding, middle-aged man returning to work perhaps after having had a pleasant lunch. I stared at him like a laser beam as he walked toward me, my eyes locked with his. As he approached me, he nodded in acknowledgment and I just stared as he walked by us.

This was the first time I saw the man who was cynically playing with my life, Patrick Fitzgerald. Seeing him live and in person actually gave me a psychological lift. He really was just another guy, human and fallible, but with one exception: he had unchecked power to do whatever he liked. This made him very dangerous to me. Seeing him stoked my resolve not to be intimidated and to continue fighting. I would see him one last time the day the verdict was announced.

Seconds after he passed, Tom, a senior executive with the Boeing Corporation in Los Angeles, turned to tell me he heard Fitzgerald say, "Hi Rob." I thought I had heard Fitzgerald say something, but I couldn't be sure what.

A few more words about Patrick Fitzgerald—and they're not my own. In March 2007 *Chicago Tribune* reporters Rudolph Bush and Matt O'Connor profiled the man they called the "controversial top prosecutor." In their balanced story, the reporters cited colleagues and objective observers who had kind things to say about Fitzgerald in the wake of his successful prosecution of Scooter Libby, then–Vice President Dick Cheney's assistant for national security affairs, for perjury and obstruction of justice in the criminal investigation into the leaking of Valerie Plame's identity to the media.

But the reporters also wrote this:

> Mark Corallo was the top Justice Department spokesman when Fitzgerald was named special counsel. He recalls being taken aback by the decision to subpoena and then jail reporters until they revealed their sources.
>
> "There has always been a great respect for reporters privilege [in the Justice Department]," said Corallo, whose public relations firm now represents Libby.
>
> But Fitzgerald brushed aside long-standing guidelines for justice to get his man, Corallo said.
>
> Meanwhile, Fitzgerald failed to charge anyone with the original crime he was supposed to investigate: the leak of Plame's name.
>
> "This was not about the Bush administration," Corallo said. "This was about Patrick Fitzgerald. There were no checks on his authority. There was no one who could say no to him."

Bush and O'Connor further noted:

> Some critics, though, say Fitzgerald's judgment is skewed by his one-dimensional career as a prosecutor.
>
> Ronald Safer, a criminal-defense lawyer involved in a number of high-profile corruption cases in Chicago, gives Fitzgerald high grades for energy, independence, and fearlessness, but a D-minus "for empathy."
>
> "Until you have a client, until you hear firsthand the other side of the story, it's impossible to fully appreciate that perspective," said Safer, a former federal prosecutor.
>
> "I think it is very difficult to not see things in black and white if you haven't walked a mile in the other person's shoes." (http://www.webcitation.org/6WSlZSllj)

In my opinion, US Attorney Fitzgerald had no interest in walking even a few steps in my shoes.

Day Seven: Monday, June 14, 2010

I went into the second week of trial after having had a difficult week-end with Julie reviewing our worsened financial condition. We had already spent a considerable amount of money on legal fees, more than $650,000, and had to figure out how to continue to feed the beast. In addition to liquidating our IRAs and other cash investments, we were still confronted with some hard decisions. Even after taking out a second mortgage to pay the lawyers, it seemed we would have to sell our home.

I knew that I could have stopped the financial bleeding months ago if I had offered to testify against Rod or perhaps plead guilty to one count. But I wasn't going to turn on my brother and I wasn't guilty. What does it say about a justice system that maintains that if you want to stand your ground and prove your innocence, you must be prepared to spend all the money you've made over a lifetime, give up your retirement account and home, and spend weeks away from the business you built over the years? Yes, the court will provide an attorney if you are indigent. Many of these attorneys are competent advocates. But the record is replete with examples of court-appointed attorneys who have failed to adequately represent their clients.

Noted in my journal this day:

   ♦ "Judge Zagel, late again, 25 minutes."

While the direct examination of Monk continued that morning, I got a text from my CPA in Nashville, Jeff Bridges. He requested I call him as soon as possible. As if I didn't have enough to worry about, he told me he had just been subpoenaed by the government to turn over my income tax returns from 2002 to 2008. What? Why? I thanked him for the heads-up and went straight to Mike. I was furious. After all this time, even now while we were on trial, the government was still digging, doing all it could to try to find something to discredit me. As it turned out, they found nothing they could use against me in those returns. We learned later that the government called Vanderbilt, the YMCA, and Red Cross to verify our charitable contributions during those years.

While examining Monk, the prosecution played a number of wire-tapped conversations. These included routine conversations about fundraising that I had with Rod and Monk (one of which had been played on the Letterman show months earlier). They specifically focused on two donors: Jerry Krozel, a paving contractor, and Johnny Johnston, whose family owned racetracks in Illinois.

There were no wiretapped conversations of Krozel or Johnston talking with me. I never called or had any direct involvement with either of them; they were Monk's contacts. He had a long-standing relationship with both men and was the lead in cultivating them for contributions. The prosecution was trying to imply that I was involved in soliciting these donors, who would later testify they were being pressured to contribute. In truth, all I was doing was getting updates from Monk on his progress.

Mike's one-hour cross-examination of Monk was a masterful example of how an experienced trial attorney extracts information from a witness. During his questioning, Mike got Monk to concede it took him more than six months to learn the ins and outs of fundraising when he started working on Rod's first gubernatorial campaign in 2002. He also got Monk to agree that it was very likely I was still trying to learn how to fundraise after only four months at FOB. Establishing that I was not an experienced political fundraiser was important for the jury to know. When listening to the tapes one could observe that I was still tentative, not knowing all the donors, their circumstances, or their history of giving. All I was really doing in those conversations with Monk was getting updates on his fundraising activities. My objective with him was to know where he was in the process of securing contributions and to see if any follow-up was necessary, just as I did with all the other centers of influence who were helping to fundraise on Rod's behalf.

Mike also got Monk to acknowledge that I was always professional and never lied to him. A government witness was describing a defendant as honest and truthful. Weeks later in his closing argument, Mike would use Monk's words to my advantage against the prosecution.

Day Nine: Wednesday, June 16, 2010

Noted in my journal this day:

- ♦ "We had a couple of good days with Monk on the stand but I can't get too comfortable, despite the positive feedback we were already getting from the media attending. A very seasoned AP court reporter, Mike Robinson, told Mike that the consensus of the people in the courthouse watching the trial was that I'd been taken out."

While I don't know how the trial watchers were coming to that conclusion so early, it was nice to hear the gossip was trending my way. We still had a long way to go as Harris, Wyma, and Bedi all had yet to take the stand.

In the meantime, several more witnesses testified against Rod, supporting the government's charge that Rod had personally benefited through a consulting arrangement Patti had with Rezko. Rezko had agreed to pay Patti a generous monthly retainer in return for her real estate expertise. The prosecution's witnesses, including Monk, testified that contrary to what the contract required, Patti didn't earn the money she was paid.

Rod had told me years before that Patti was consulting for Rezko, and they had thoroughly reviewed the legality of the arrangement with their attorneys before executing the contract. I had asked him at the time how it would look to the public even if it was legal. He had dismissed me and said other politicians' wives had business arrangements like Patti's and that it was nothing to worry about. It was hard for me to listen to the testimony about Patti's contract because it was so damaging to Rod. I felt bad for him. At the same time I realized that if the government wanted to indict Patti—perhaps instead of me—it might have done so.

During the afternoon recess, Rod came over to my table to tell me he thought I was "coming off clean so far." As he said that, I thought, what does he mean "so far"?

"Of course I should come off clean. I am clean." I said sharply. "I never did anything wrong and this has nothing to do with me." I then told him he should have known better than to have asked me to join him. He said he wouldn't have asked me if he knew this would happen and added that I knew about the investigations that were going on that summer of 2008. I told him yes, I was aware, but reminded him that both he and Patti had reassured me that everything had calmed down and that the investigations were no longer an issue. Once again, we were at loggerheads. I wished I could have contained my anger, but he kept pushing the wrong buttons.

Listening to the prosecutor's case, I could only conclude that the government was still actively investigating him when he told me things had calmed down and asked me to help him. Rod had boldly miscalculated what was going on around him and was oblivious to the danger of bringing me into it all. Even in this very direct conversation, standing in the courtroom, he could not take responsibility for the jeopardy he put me in. All I wanted to hear and never did hear from Rod was a sincere recognition of the consequences of his actions.

The tone of the conversation escalated to the point that Patti came over to the table to tell us to lower our voices. This was not the place to talk, she reminded us. By then the courtroom was pretty much empty and no one was around to hear us. After she left, I went on to tell Rod how much it was costing me to pay for my lawyers and the personal financial sacrifice I was having to make because of him. His legal bills were paid out of the same FOB campaign fund for which I helped raise three quarters of a million dollars during the months I worked for him.

We'd made a motion requesting the campaign fund help pay some of my legal expense because I was employed by FOB. Once again, denied, even though it would have been fair and appropriate for me to get some help from the fund. This irony was not at all lost on me.

During this conversation, Rod also tried to counter the harmful testimony Monk and the others had given against him. He insisted that Patti had earned the money she was paid by Rezko. I told him I was concerned for him and hoped that Patti could refute the accusations of the witnesses by showing how she earned her substantial retainer. I was under the impression she was going to testify and would have to be prepared for such questions.

Rod caught me off guard when he responded that Patti had added more value working for Rezko than I had working for him at FOB. How low could he go? I was stunned, considering the fact that I wouldn't have been standing in that courtroom if it weren't for him. He didn't seem to realize that.

Staring daggers at him, I spit out: "Shame on you. Don't talk to me anymore. How could you say that?"

I swore at him several times and angrily told him how much he had disappointed me with what he'd said. Then I again told him we were done talking and motioned for him to leave. He wanted to talk more but I was livid and told him to get away from me. For the remainder of the day I sat in dazed disbelief until court adjourned. I no longer knew my brother.

Day Fourteen: Thursday, June 24, 2010

Every day you're on trial is important, but this day was special. While we were sitting in the cafeteria as we did every morning waiting for trial to start, we learned the Supreme Court had finally handed down a ruling on the honest services law. Mike and Rod's lawyers were huddled around a laptop frantically reviewing the decision before court was called to order to determine how it would affect us, as the original two counts against me before the re-indictment alleged violations of the honest services law. If the court had ruled the entire law unconstitutional those two counts would be dropped. But it appeared the justices had not gone that far. Our initial reading was that the law could now only be applied to kickbacks and bribery—charges conveniently added by the government at my second indictment.

Noted in my journal this day:

- "First blush it looks like it will not help me. The vagueness of the law and the process are killing me. As a citizen I can't believe this is still happening to me and no one in power cares—unchecked, unrestricted power. Zagel's preliminary reading to the court is that it will not be as helpful as you might think. This whole thing is spiritually demoralizing. It wears you down."

- "This honest services buildup, with all the leading pundits that said it would be overturned, is par for the course for me. Not one break has gone my way in this legal ordeal. Now I only have my lawyers and finally have to put faith in the jury. I am very concerned about the ultimate outcome and my future. This really sucks!"

I had quietly held out hope that something good might come from the Supreme Court. Their questions during the oral arguments led us to believe they might rule honest services unconstitutional. I had believed that justice might finally prevail at the highest levels so my case would be dismissed and I could get on with my life. Instead, I had to continue to focus on the things I could control and keep my mind right. Hard as it was, I managed to stay strong in the belief that everything would turn out fine for me despite all the disappointments and setbacks. One important advantage I had was my family and close friends, who loved and believed in me.

Aside from the Supreme Court's ruling, this proved to be a full and eventful day for other reasons. While I was in the cafeteria waiting to buy some coffee, I noticed a tall African American man in a light brown suit staring at me. He surprised me as he approached because he looked as though he knew me. As he reached to shake my hand and we made eye contact, he wished me luck. He said he was rooting for me. I thanked him and asked his name. Jonathan Jackson! He was the younger brother of Congressman Jesse Jackson Jr. Later, I couldn't help thinking of the potential trouble his brother faced because of his instigation of the bribe offer made to me by Bedi and Nayak on his behalf.

Later in the day, the prosecution played a wiretapped conversation Rod and I had on November 11, 2008. In it he posed a scenario in which he would appoint his deputy governor, Louanner Peters (Senate Candidate 4 in the criminal complaint), to the Senate seat and then replace her at some future point with himself in the unlikely event he got impeached by the state legislature. Rod believed he could trust her the most to work with him. Like many conversations I had with Rod, this was a great example of how he just threw harebrained ideas out there to be provocative and get a reaction. I didn't, and still don't, believe he would have tried this.

Here is an excerpt from the recording played in court:

> Rod: See, another factor is Louanner could conceivably, if it ever got hot on impeachment, which we think is an unlikelihood, but if it ever did, you know, she's the one I can most trust if we told her, 'you have to quit that, you have to resign the Senate seat and let me have a place to go parachute and avoid that.' You know what I'm sayin?
>
> Robert: Boy, that's, I mean how do you pull that off?
>
> Rod: What do you mean?
>
> Robert: You, you, you put her in the Senate seat and then, and then tell her to step aside and put you in there? I don't get it.
>
> Rod: Then I, then I appoint myself, yeah.
>
> Robert: Oh, you mean quietly tell her . . .
>
> Rod: Of course, quietly, yeah, yeah.
>
> Robert: So, what, come July they're impeaching you, you step down and . . .
>
> Rod: Correct.
>
> Robert: . . . oh, Jesus, that's ugly.
>
> Rod: Why is that ugly?
>
> Robert: Oh, it's self-evident. I don't have to explain it.

Rod: What are you, nuts? What's uglier? That or being impeached?
Okay? [*chuckles*]

Robert: Neither one. Neither one. I mean, it's so transparent. I mean
in the middle of July, she's already senator. She's been in sessions
and she steps aside so you can step in and replace her? What is
the public gonna think? It would be an outrage.

I didn't mind that my accusers offered this conversation into evidence.
My outrage at Rod's "plan" was apparent. One reporter in the courtroom
immediately texted Mike: "Awesome! Big Bro Smack Down of Little Bro."

Noted in my journal this day:

- "I have no idea how that came across. My heart is pounding. Shelly
  told Mike this tape could very well win the case for your client."

- "Rod throughout his life surrounded himself with weak personalities. Always had flawed people around him. As a kid and as an
  adult. He didn't have people around him with strong personalities."

- "While discussing strategy with the team outside the courthouse,
  I looked inside and saw JH (John Harris) walking with his lawyer
  and made eye contact. We acknowledged each other and he walked
  on. We'll see if that little gesture has any significance."

Day Fifteen: Monday, June 28, 2010

Noted in my journal this day:

- "Paid Mike another $50K this morning. Painful fact."

John Harris, Rod's former chief of staff, was the only other member of the
alleged conspiracy to be arrested. Months before I was indicted, Mike told
me that he was told by an attorney friend who was vacationing in Mexico
at the time that he had gotten numerous frantic calls from Harris's lawyer.
He claimed Harris's attorney didn't have a lot of experience dealing with
the feds and was panicked about how to manage the government's men-
acing threats to punish his client if he didn't cooperate. I don't know if it
was the attorney who represented Harris at trial or another lawyer. None-

theless, his lawyer was told that the government was threatening Harris with some very severe consequences if he didn't cooperate with them and testify against Rod. Evidently Harris had been questioned by the government for days and was resistant to becoming a prosecution witness. Mike's read of this anecdote was, "This is what happens to people who talk to the government and don't plead the fifth."

Also noted in my journal this day:

- "Mike spoke with Terry Ekl, JH lawyer to find out what JH was going to say about me. He told Mike to ask whatever we wanted about what JH thought of me. He supposedly feels bad for me and has a high regard. We'll see? Cheryl will cross him today."

- "Julie is here today to watch Harris's cross. She really looks good sitting in the first row. I'm very proud of her. Patti said good morning to Julie. Julie said, 'Hi Patti.'"

I liked Harris. He was a family man, hardworking and dependable. He told me when I started working for Rod that if I ever came across a donor who wanted something in return for a contribution to refer them to him and he would handle it. Harris understood the pitfalls of fundraising and wanted to keep me out of trouble. On several occasions I did call to get instruction on what to do when someone was pushing the envelope. He was always clear in telling me how to handle the situation and never let me down. I trusted him.

Harris testified as a prosecution witness for five days. His testimony was not helpful to Rod, but he didn't mention me. We found out what he thought of me in Cheryl's effective twenty-minute cross-examination.

Noted in my journal this day:

- "11:15–11:35 Cheryl's cross. She did a very good job. She got JH to agree I was honest & truthful and professional. Also established that I was not in various calls with him or others to discuss policy issues. Cheryl was very organized, soft-spoken, and knew where she was going in her cross. A very professional performance. Made me feel proud she was my lawyer."

- "Juror, black hair, Oak Park. No expression usually, smiled and acknowledged Cheryl when she sat down after she crossed JH. We believe this is a good development but not going to read too much into it."

- "Natasha Korecki (*Sun-Times* Blago Blog reporter) immediately had a blog hit stating that JH was the second major witness to say I was 'honest and truthful.' Mike texted her, while she sat in the courtroom, to be sure to get the 'honest and truthful' into the blog. AM (Andy Martin) sent me an email from Nashville with her blog entry not 10 min after Cheryl stopped."

- "I sit here with a heavy heart today feeling very sad for Rod. Days and more days of witnesses who have not and likely will not say good things about him. At times I think he grasps the gravity of what is happening and others I wonder. He works hard to keep a good face and seems to take it all in stride, mixing it up with people in the hallway and courtroom. It makes me sad to watch him."

- "At break we left the courtroom, JH made a point to make eye contact with me and nodded after having been crossed by Cheryl. Actually he almost stumbled into the holding room for witnesses as he made his gesture."

Day Seventeen: Wednesday, June 30, 2010

Noted in my journal this day:

- "Holly Garland, a WLS reporter, asked if I was keeping a journal. I told her yes, for therapy. She said I should consider writing a book. I told her I had no plans and asked, why would anyone care what I have to say? She very emphatically said there are a lot of people who want to hear what you have to say. I said I don't understand why. She said we all have siblings and want to hear how you've dealt with it and your brother's situation. You will have a lot to say that people will want to hear. She said my situation is biblical, the conflict of family loyalty and self-preservation. This whole experience must be taking an emotional, physical toll on you and you can write about it. Title idea she suggested was 'Brother's Keeper.'"

- "Another interaction with Rod. He said, 'You should be feeling pretty good right now. You're better off tried with me and not alone. You can just sit back.' I said no, I would rather have a short two-to-three-week trial and get it over, this is killing me financially. I looked him in the eye and said in light of all the people testifying against you who you trusted, I'm the only one standing. He said I would do the same for you. I said we'll never know. He said you never know. I said I know so. I would never put him in a situation like this in the first place. He said let's not argue, we're getting along, and he walked away."

- "Prior to lunch the judge called the lawyers regarding two motions pending. My request for legal fee reimbursement from FOB was one. He denied it because I had yet to prove my indigence. Once again no breaks, not a single procedural item has gone my way. Nothing has changed for me. I sit here and bleed financially with three great lawyers who babysit me everyday. Actually about the only thing that makes this nightmare bearable when I come to court everyday is that I genuinely like my lawyers. They believe in my innocence and steadfastly support me every day."

Day Eighteen: Thursday, July 1, 2010
Noted in my journal this day:

- "We've been at this a month now, time really has gone fast."

- "Mike was told by the government that they had about three weeks left to complete their case. This information put him into a mental storm, trying to figure out how to get ready for my direct and redirect in three weeks. (Note: Redirect allows the side who conducted the direct examination to ask more questions of the witness—but only to qualify or clarify testimony brought out during the opposing side's cross-examination.) He told me we'd probably have to work on Saturday and very possibly on Sunday. I told him that would be fine and that I would do whatever was required of me to get ready. For me this is very good news if it pans out. Seems unlikely to me that they'll be done by the last week of July."

- "People who watch a trial probably and rightfully think the lawyers are exclusively and seriously focused on the trial they are a part of.

That is not exactly the case, at least not with my legal team. The vast majority of the testimony has nothing to do with me so we all get a little bored. My guys, actually gals, Cheryl and Robyn, somehow started matching Rod's team of lawyers and staff with the seven dwarfs from Snow White. They listed out all the dwarfs' names and lined them up on a blue sticky note matching them with Rod's legal team. When they showed me their line-up, I asked if I could name Dopey."

- ◆ Snow White—Lauren Kaesberg
  Grumpy—Sam Sr.
  Sneezy—Jason
  Bashful—Elliot
  Happy—Sam Jr.
  Doc—Mike
  Dopey—I'll keep this one to myself
  Sleepy—Sheldon

- ◆ "There you have an example of the creativity going on behind the scenes of the Blago brothers' trial that no one sees. Actually they did a pretty good job with the names of the lawyers and staff matching them with the nature and character of the dwarfs."

- ◆ "Huddled as we often do outside the courthouse on the corner of Jackson and Dearborn in a private spot in the shade. Mike said the reporters asked him about next week and observed to him that I was the only one to tell Rod no of all the tapes and witnesses that were entered into evidence. I clinched my fist in victory and said, 'I'm so happy, they got it.'"

- ◆ "Mike also said he spoke with AUSA Reid Schar after court, who asked if I was going to testify. Mike told him, yes. Schar was surprised and said we haven't touched him, 'why would you put him on?' According to Mike, Schar didn't expect me to take the risk, alluding that they had a weak case against me. I immediately, for the thousandth time asked, 'Why the hell did they indict me?' His response, "Robert, we are way past that. We'll deal with it after." I backed off and we got back to the subject. I asked whether Schar showed his hand, having a weak case against me. No was his answer, 'they don't know how to cross and believe you'll be a good witness for your brother.' I don't buy any of this, it means nothing. We are going to get ready, hopefully for anything. Time will tell who was better prepared, me or them. I have seen nothing from them to show they are not thorough, well prepared, and organized."

♦ "After today's developments, I can for the first time see the finish line."

We were given four days off from court to celebrate the Fourth of July. Cheryl had invited all the team and our families to her lovely home in Lemont, a suburb southwest of Chicago, to decompress for an afternoon on the Fourth. This gathering was the only time we had any social life for the entire trial.

Day Nineteen: Wednesday, July 7, 2010

Noted in my journal this day:

♦ "Mike spoke with Schar again this morning, Schar wanting to know if I was going to testify. Mike told him I was. Schar's response was that he had other tapes that haven't been played that he could play if he needed. Mike told him to bring it on. I told Mike I won't testify if they drop the charges against me. That was a nonstarter for Mike, he just looked at me. This means they are threatening to use more tapes to get me not to testify."

♦ "Another sidebar with the lawyers. (Note: A sidebar is when the prosecution and defense lawyers approach the judge's bench and confer out of earshot of the jury.) I sit here wondering what it will be like to get up and get my testimony out. How will it come across and what will people think of what I say, most importantly the jury. As we close in on the time I'm to testify, I'm beginning to feel some anxiety. The unknown is the toughest part of this whole affair. I face it everyday. Unusually I eagerly face it because before all this I understood the rules. Now I don't and it causes me to worry."

♦ "Can't believe that I'm sitting here even after over a month of trial. This seems so unreal to me. I'm a half-glass-full person and that's how I have to continue to be. Can't forget that Cindy, our juror of one, concluded after our mock trial, 'Is that all there is?' My favorite five words ever spoken on my behalf. In most cases it could be a diminishing statement, especially if you are discussing physical features or anything of substance. More is usually better. Not for me! I just have to hope the jury concludes the same. I feel tired today, low energy. I worked out and I'm still dragging ass."

Day Twenty: Thursday, July 8, 2010

Mike cross-examined Jerry Krozel, the road builder whom the government alleged I conspired with Rod to shake down for a contribution.

Noted in my journal this day:

- ◆ "Mike was exceptional in his cross! Established how fundraising works, that I never saw nor spoke to Krozel again after having briefly met him on (August 22). Especially did not ask him for money or a fundraiser. His cross was logical, focused, and led you to the right conclusions. The jury was listening and taking notes. I like Mike! He was outstanding!"

- ◆ "By myself again, sidebar. More people than usual in the courtroom today. I try not to stare at the jury but can't help it. I want them to like me. I suppose that's a self-serving desire but I can't help it. How pathetic am I?"

- ◆ "A reporter for WLS, channel 7, Paul Meincke, talked with Mike before lunch and inquired about a directed verdict from the judge on my behalf to release me for lack of evidence. (Note: A directed verdict is an order from the presiding judge to the jury to return a particular verdict. Typically this order comes from the judge after finding that no reasonable jury could reach a decision to the contrary.) Up to this point there has been little presented against me."

- ◆ "Over lunch we discussed Bedi. We are anxious because we believe big points can be made with him during cross. We'll know so much more after Bedi testifies and the December 4 call between Rod and me is played. Then we'll find out if the media changes regarding me."

Rajindar Bedi, the man who first approached me with the offer to fundraise for Rod in exchange for Congressman Jackson's appointment to the Senate seat, took the stand at 2:20. If it wasn't for Bedi, Raghu Nayak, and Jesse Jackson Jr., I would never have been indicted or a defendant in that courtroom. During Bedi's testimony, the government entered two wiretapped conversations into evidence: the December 4th call I had with Rod regarding Jackson while sitting in the Starbucks with Julie, and one of the few conversations I had with Rod about Jackson, which occurred on November 12, 2008.

In the November 12 conversation, Rod asked me if I had any thoughts about the Senate seat. I told him no, I had none, no insights to offer him. Eventually I did finally offer the name of Gerry Chico as someone Rod should appoint. I'd met him a couple of times and thought that with his legal, civic, and political background, Chico was uniquely qualified to serve. He had served as Mayor Richard J. Daley's chief of staff and had then gone on to head the Chicago Public School system and Chicago Park District.

Rod brought up a few names during the conversation that he said were in play as possible choices. Jackson's name came up and I gave Rod my opinion of him, not knowing it would be played in a federal courtroom with me as one of the defendants. "Jesse Jr. is not emotionally stable to do anything other than, hell, cry. I mean he shouldn't even be a Goddamn congressman. He's a fucking articulate incompetent."

I was all too accurate about the emotional instability. Later it would be revealed that Jackson allegedly suffered from bipolar disorder.

As the taped conversation further revealed, Rod and I went back and forth, with me calling Jesse Jr. an "articulate incompetent" two more times before we moved on to another subject. Rod had told me that during the Democratic National Convention in Denver earlier that summer, the Illinois delegation was gathered for a luncheon when Congressman Jackson took the podium and tried to make peace between Rod and Speaker Madigan. During his plea, according to Rod, Jackson started crying in front of everyone as he tried to bring the two to the podium to hug. That was why I said he was emotionally unstable and did nothing other than cry. I'd never met the congressman and had only observed him through the media and by hearing him speak. With no major policy achievements in his many years in Congress, I concluded he was in fact an "articulate incompetent."

Noted in my journal this day:

- "I'm embarrassed by all the fucks and swearing from this call. I'm hot and red-faced. I said fucking articulate incompetent. Very embarrassing."

Two weeks later when I testified, I would apologize to the court about my language.

- "Bedi was directed by AUSA Niewoehner. Two-thirds of the way through his testimony, as the government was about to attempt to enter hearsay about the October 28, 2008, 312 Restaurant meeting with

Bedi, Nayak, and Jackson Jr., Mike sprang from his seat like a panther to object. The judge sustained Mike's objection and asked the jury to leave the courtroom and take a break. The lawyers gathered in front of the judge. He asked the government where they were going with their questioning. They explained that it was the core of their case to show that Nayak and Jackson were the instigators of the conspiracy and it had to come out through Bedi. Mike explained it was blatant hearsay and why doesn't the government call Nayak? The judge sustained the objection and allowed the government to get from Bedi only that fundraising and the Senate seat were discussed."

This was a very important juncture in the trial because the government wanted to sneak in hearsay testimony that would have spared them the risk of calling Nayak to testify about his role in the pivotal breakfast meeting. The prosecutors did not want to expose him to cross-examination by the defense, which would likely open a can of worms regarding his relationship with Congressman Jackson. We knew from reading the 302s as did the prosecution that Nayak and Jackson had conversations about the Senate seat that the government would not want the jury to hear. They instead tried to slip in Nayak's participation at the breakfast through Bedi and limit the testimony to only what they wanted disclosed to the public. Mike wisely put an end to that with his objection.

We also knew that Jackson and Nayak had met earlier in Washington when Jackson persuaded Nayak to offer money and a pardon for Rod, in return for the appointment to the Senate seat. Jackson rationalized that if he was a senator, he would be close to the president and could be helpful getting a pardon if Rod needed one.

Mike and I believed the government was protecting Congressman Jackson by not directly calling Nayak to testify. We knew that Nayak got a call from Congressman Jackson to tell Nayak the government was investigating whether the Senate seat was for sale. We also knew that conversation occurred in early November when Congressman Jackson told Nayak not to talk to them, meaning the Blagojevich people, about money after he had already told Nayak to approach us. What is evident from this conversation is that Congressman Jackson had to have been tipped off about the investigation.

We also knew that Congressman Jackson had called Bedi later in the day on October 28, after the breakfast, to find out how his meeting with me had gone. We knew Bedi didn't answer when he saw Congressman

Jackson's number appear on his phone. In addition, we knew Bedi was reluctant to call Congressman Jackson back to tell him I killed the deal. So instead, when Bedi called Congressman Jackson back, he lied to the congressman and told him the meeting had been canceled.

Mike and I talked about what his strategy would be in his cross-examination of Bedi. He knew exactly what he needed to get from him to show that I was forthright and direct with Bedi when I rejected the Jackson proposal on October 28.

Noted in my journal this day:

◆ "I asked Mike before he crossed Bedi to get Bedi to testify at least three times that 'I killed the deal.' He did exactly what I asked not once but twice got Bedi to say I killed the deal. When Mike had completed his cross he came back to our table, as was his practice, to ask if he forgot anything. I told him he needed to ask Bedi one more time about me killing the deal. I wanted to make sure nobody missed it. Third time Mike asked, the government objected and Mike said to the judge, 'asked and answered, I agree.' The jury laughed and the judge smiled."

Day Twenty-one: Thursday, July 8, 2010

Noted in my journal this day:

◆ "Sitting for these many weeks, one of the random thoughts that floats in my mind is the concept of sitting in a defendants' chair being judged. I am smothered in a legal system with jury, codefendant, media, and observers all passing judgment on me for alleged crimes I know I didn't commit. Under normal circumstances you accept some people will like you and others not. So what, no big deal, that's life. But now I'm hypersensitive about what people think of me and I want them to like me. I can't believe what I've been reduced to."

◆ "Mike spoke with two reporters during the morning break. They both told him that we had a good day yesterday, referring to the Bedi testimony. I didn't get the details and particulars. I told Mike jokingly I thought they were just feeding the 'Ettinger Ego.' I hope they were sincere."

CHAPTER THIRTEEN

"Where Did That Come From?"

Day Twenty-two: Monday, July 12, 2010

Noted in my journal this day:

- ◆ "Very busy weekend, spent Friday, Saturday, and Sunday with the legal team. We spent three to four hours each day together. So far we've met almost every weekend except for one or two. Weekends bleed into the week, it all bleeds together, no breaks."

- ◆ "We made real progress this weekend primarily because we finally got to Mike's direct examination of me. I learned as we went, Mike asking the questions, me answering truthfully and together working to synthesize the message/truth down into crisp statements and concepts. I kept falling into the same trap of answering some of his questions without hearing them entirely. I did that weeks before when he shamed me in his cross at his office. As we went on, I believe I made the adjustments necessary and listened more carefully and waited for him to finish his question before I answered. I left our weekend sessions with reinforced confidence in my ability to articulate the truth."

Day Twenty-three: Tuesday, July 13, 2010

Noted in my journal this day:

- ◆ "I have concretely concluded that I am sitting at this table this morning because of Jesse Jackson Jr. He is the one who put into motion actions thru Bedi and Nayak that got me indicted. I have to ask the question: why weren't Jackson, Nayak, and Bedi indicted instead of me? They offered the bribe. I was the guy who said no. But it shows again, life is not fair and that the government selectively prosecutes to achieve political objectives. There is something wrong about all this. The system is broken."

♦ "In spite of the situation I'm in now, having dug a deep financial hole, I want to fight not just for my freedom but for justice and fairness after this trial ends if I'm able. Somebody needs to talk about the selective, unchecked power the US attorney has to do whatever he wants without consequence. I've never lived my life without taking personal responsibility for my actions. I expect the same from people in government. This is an unbelievable place I find myself when the DOJ empowers its prosecutors to pursue an agenda, no matter what the cost to innocent people, just to win. I don't know at this moment how to get this done or whether it will even be possible for me to warn people about government overreach."

♦ "Rod tells me his autograph is going for $100 on eBay. He thought that was strange because he could give it away as governor."

♦ "Everyday, several times a day Mike talks and socializes with the prosecutors. I don't know if I should worry or rejoice at his ability to genuinely connect with people. I think it's a unique skill that can only help me and of course all his clients."

John Wyma took the stand next. The last time I saw Wyma was back in October 2008 when we'd met at FOB for a fundraising meeting. Unknown to us at the time, he'd already been cooperating with the government. I remembered him looking stressed and even told Rod after that meeting that Wyma seemed different, just stared deadpan and didn't interact much during the meeting.

The Wyma I saw on the stand looked a lot different from the last time I saw him. He was tanned, his hair was dyed a shade of yellow, and he seemed composed and comfortable. The reason for his new calm must have had something to do with the deal he cut with the government. He had negotiated an immunity agreement for himself that protected him from future prosecution in exchange for his cooperation and testimony. In effect a legal quid pro quo—the same theory the government used in its indictment of me with charges of extortion and bribery. I will never understand why when a citizen allegedly does it, it's illegal and when the government does it, it's legal.

Like all the prosecution witnesses before him, Wyma offered testimony that was not helpful to Rod. He was another close confidante-turned-lobbyist who made millions off his friendship with Rod. He betrayed him to save himself. In October 2008 Wyma was named in a subpoena by investigators for records from Provena Health, a lobbying client of his. I don't know any of the details of Wyma's involvement. However, whatever he allegedly did, the government scared or threatened him enough to get him to cooperate in exchange for immunity from prosecution.

Chicago Tribune reporters Jeff Coen and Bob Secter wrote the following about what happened in court on Day Twenty-three:

> As Wyma described it, Blagojevich was pulling him into fundraising schemes in 2008 just as federal authorities were looking into Wyma's lobbying activities years earlier for a controversial hospital plan that had moved through a corrupt state regulatory panel stacked with members loyal to Blagojevich fundraiser Antoin "Tony" Rezko.
>
> Wyma said he already was set to meet with the FBI when he was unnerved by the talk at two fundraising meetings he attended in early October. Blagojevich was stoking up pressure to stockpile money because a new ethics law would soon rein in his ability to raise donations from companies doing business with the state—a fertile avenue for cash.
>
> At several points, Wyma said, Blagojevich appeared to link spending on certain state projects to campaign cash from donors likely to benefit from the state help. "If they don't perform, (expletive) 'em," Blagojevich allegedly told Wyma at one point.
>
> At a meeting Oct. 8, Wyma said Children's Memorial Hospital came up. The governor, Wyma said, mentioned how he had recently been called by former Cubs manager and ex-hospital board member Dusty Baker about raising Medicaid reimbursement rates to pediatric specialists at the hospital by at least $8 million. The hospital had been seeking the boost for years. Wyma said Blagojevich told him he was going to give the go-ahead—but with a caveat. The governor wanted Children's CEO Patrick Magoon to kick in a $50,000 donation to his campaign, Wyma said.
>
> It was left to Wyma to follow up with Magoon, but he said he didn't. "I was very uncomfortable with the notion that there's a pending state action and a fundraising request at the same time," Wyma said.

Instead, by Oct. 13 Wyma was telling federal authorities what was happening, delivering information that would break the case against Blagojevich. The meeting had previously been scheduled, not to talk about Children's but rather about questions investigators had about Wyma's involvement with the earlier hospital client—Provena Health—and the hospital board manipulated by Rezko. Wyma told investigators about the fundraising push and Blagojevich's efforts to extract donations.

With another fundraising meeting coming up Oct. 22, Wyma said he was asked to wear a wire for the FBI, but he declined. He did, however, agree to attend the meeting to keep the government's investigation moving forward. Armed with Wyma's details, prosecutors on Oct. 21 obtained court approval to record conversations in two rooms at the offices of the Friends of Blagojevich, records show. The recordings proved critical to the government's case against the governor.

Wyma said it was during that meeting at the campaign office that Blagojevich asked his brother to keep the pressure on Magoon to donate. As the meeting broke up, Wyma was confronted by two *Tribune* reporters waiting outside, and a story that ran in the paper the next day about the Provena subpoena began to cost Wyma lobbying clients, including Children's.

The final government witness was Magoon, who found himself in the middle of the alleged shakedown by Blagojevich. Magoon said that Medicaid reimbursement rates for specialists at Children's Hospital had for years been so low that the hospital was reimbursed for only 33 cents on the dollar. The hospital had long been unsuccessful in prying more money out of the state, said Magoon, prompting him in June 2008 to pen a handwritten plea to Blagojevich, who fancied himself a champion of expanded health care coverage for children.

The letter was ignored, but Magoon said the hospital then turned to Baker in a strategy to play on Blagojevich's fanatical devotion to the Cubs. Baker served on the Children's board when he was with the Chicago team.

That caught Blagojevich's attention, and by October the governor had reached out to Magoon and told him the rate increase would be on the way, the hospital CEO said. Magoon said Blagojevich asked one favor—keep word of the increase, worth $10 million, quiet until after New Year's.

Then six days later, Magoon said the governor's brother called and left a message saying he wanted to introduce himself. When the two connected, Magoon said Robert Blagojevich asked whether he would be willing to raise $25,000 in donations for the governor before New Year's.

Magoon said the one-two punch of securing a promise for the rate increase and then being quickly asked for fundraising help was unnerving, especially since the governor had sought to keep things quiet until after the fundraising

deadline set by his brother. He feared the rate hike could be in jeopardy. "I felt
threatened, I felt at risk and I felt a little annoyed," Magoon testified. (*Chicago
Tribune*, July 13, 2010, http://www.webcitation.org/6WSlhxrkd)

Although I wasn't charged with anything related to Children's Memorial Hospital and had not known about Rod's call to Magoon, listening
to Magoon's testimony made me sick. For a sophisticated hospital chief
executive with the governor's personal friend as his lobbyist, I found it
very hard to believe he felt threatened by my request for a modest fundraiser. (I asked him to raise whatever he felt possible, suggesting a range
from $10,000 to $15,000 or whatever he was comfortable with, but that
we shot for $25,000. I never told him to raise $25,000.) His testimony was
not at all credible to me given how I behaved toward him on my calls.
Listening to him, you would have thought he was an unsophisticated
neophyte. I wondered if he was hiding something and was eager to cooperate with the government as their witness.

Noted in my journal this day:

- "My heart doesn't pound as fast as it did earlier on in the trial. I guess
  I've been at this too long. Now with Wyma on the stand and Mike
  crossing, I feel a sense of calm and confidence at the moment. Mike
  made all the points: I was not in the meeting regarding the pediat-
  ric rate increase for Children's, Wyma was the key point of contact
  with CMH. Also on the October 9th voice mail, I was looking to
  Wyma about the next steps for his client. The key point was he got
  Wyma to agree he was the lead contact for Children's till he was
  fired in mid-November."

- "The reporter for the *Sun-Times* commented in her blog that Mike
  got Wyma to say he was not sure I was present when the rate increase was discussed or that CMH was getting state money."

The only time I could have been in a meeting when rate increases were
discussed would have been one of the fundraising meetings I ran. If the
subject came up then, I had no recollection. I tuned out so much of what
Rod, Wyma, and Monk talked about in those meetings because usually it
had nothing to do with me or fundraising.

◆ "Carrie Hamilton redirected Wyma. She did well questioning points that Mike made in his cross. Mike recrossed and got Wyma to again agree that I was not in the October 8th meeting when rate increase was discussed, and the message I left on the 9th was open to interpretation. I have no idea if we got it back or not?"

◆ "I ran into Elizabeth Brackett from WTTW, *Chicago Tonight* in the hallway during break. She seemed to be genuine when she asked me if I was ready to get up there and 'blast them.' I said I didn't know if I would call it blast them but that I did look forward to telling the truth. I told her if that's a blast, so be it. She seemed very warm and sincere. You never know with a reporter. While we spoke I made eye contact with an FBI agent who happened to be standing beside us. Wouldn't be surprised if he was trying to listen in."

To our surprise, after six weeks of presenting its case highlighted by dozens of recordings and nearly thirty witnesses, the government suddenly rested. We were a little caught off guard. We thought based on what we were told by AUSA Schar that we still had another week to go. This was a good thing as far as I was concerned. It meant the trial would be considerably shorter than the six months we were first led to believe it would last.

I told the team when the trial first started that I would pay them a "winner's bonus" if we got a good result by Labor Day. That meant that I could go home free to resume my life. They just laughed at me and didn't take it seriously. What they didn't realize was that I had every intention of paying them if we met the target. At the time I challenged them it seemed like a long shot but now with the government resting, we had a chance to hit it.

After court adjourned, Mike laid out his plan for the next few days. Rod's legal team decided to let us put our defense on first, so we had to be ready to go on Monday. We all reconvened at Mike's office a couple of days later to start working on my testimony. Julie was going to be the first defense witness to testify and also had to be prepared.

The three days we spent preparing to testify were some of the most intense and important hours of my life. It was far worse than cramming for finals in college. Mike drilled me on the substance of the wiretaps and the context of my words, and tried to trap me when he could. He tested my memory on dates, times, people, and places on which he thought the prosecution would focus. As I took the pretend stand in his office, he practiced taking me through my direct examination a number of times to make sure we were in sync. Cheryl, Robyn, and Julie all watched as Mike questioned me. They were constructive and supportive in their criticism and made me better.

On Sunday, the final day of preparation, Mike invited several people not familiar with the details of the case to listen to my testimony and critique my performance. We started at 9:00 a.m. and finished around 4:30 p.m.—nearly eight hours of concentrated focus. Mike knew exactly what he was doing every step of the way, optimizing our time and challenging our observers to be objective about me and think like jurors. This was the culmination of a year-and-a-half process that armed me with the confidence that only the truth and preparation can provide. When we finished that day I believed I was ready. Mike did, too.

Day Twenty-four: Monday, July 19, 2010

Noted in my journal this day:

- ◆ "I'm sitting in the cafeteria writing before we start court. Today I testify. This is the day I finally get to tell my story. Can't help remembering back when I was first arraigned sitting here visualizing this very day. Got up at 5:30, ran, cooled down, showered, shaved—same routine as everyday up here. Alex made me a great breakfast of scrambled eggs, bacon, and grits. I woke up with a sense of calm confidence. I believe I'm ready to face these people who stole my life. I want it back and hope today will help move me closer to that."

- ◆ "As I told Julie this morning and last night, these people, the government, know what they have done to us, and the outrage we feel being falsely accused should fuel our resolution to beat them and show people what they really are."

- ◆ "Julie is a little hesitant because she has no idea how she might be crossed. I told her I had complete confidence in her to get through this. She is a very special person, and until all this happened I never fully appreciated her."

- ◆ "Alex is here. I'm watching him talk with his Uncle Eric smiling and carrying on. I love that boy more than anything. I'm a lucky dad.

Tom, Eric, and Andy all made a special trip to be here with us. I'll
never forget them for their support."

Before court started, the prosecution told Mike that they would probably
not cross Julie. An unexpected, nice gesture. Knowing she would only be
questioned by friendly lawyers gave Julie some relief. As she prepared to
take the stand, I glanced over at her to see how she was doing and saw
Alex sitting next to her with a comforting arm around her.

Moments later Julie looked confident and spoke clearly as Cheryl took
her through direct examination. She testified that we were not close
to Rod and Patti and typically saw each other only once a year. When
Cheryl asked her about my relationship with Rod, she said she felt Rod
didn't know me and hoped that working with him would perhaps give
us a chance to get closer. Julie also said that when she met with them to
discuss the job at FOB her impression was that, to the best of Rod and
Patti's knowledge, the federal investigation was behind them.

As she made her way back to take her seat next to Alex, she looked at
me and smiled. I would be next to testify, ready as I could be to finally tell
my story and defend my name.

Seated on the witness stand looking out at all the people in the courtroom staring at you is surreal. I knew this diverse collection of spectators
was anxious to hear what I had to say. They would benignly sit in judgment, watching to determine if I was credible, while I sat there with the
weight of the world on me, my future hanging in the balance. I didn't realize it until I got up there that I had to adapt quickly to a lot of distractions.

Most surprising was the level of activity and noise that you would expect from any large group of people assembled in one place, but not in a
courtroom. I can't blame this on Judge Zagel. He maintained an orderly
court. It's just the nature of the beast that people will cough, quietly chat
with each other, and come and go in and out of the courtroom without
permission. When the stakes are high and everything is on the line with
a prosecutor gunning for you, sitting there by yourself, everything seems
to be magnified. Not only are you trying to look calm and collected, act-
ing like you have command of the moment, but you are also attempting
to process the vastness of the space in front of you to get as comfortable
as possible.

I never got comfortable. It was impossible under the circumstances.
Seated directly in front of me was the prosecutor's table and right behind
that were two rows filled with federal reinforcements. They were typically

IRS, FBI, and other government staff seated in force to make the defendants feel dramatically outnumbered.

There was even a day when the lead prosecutor brought his family in to watch the trial. It reminded me of parents going to their child's sporting event to cheer them on. In this case, however, the loser could go to prison instead of out for hamburgers after the game. Just behind the government staff were rows filled with local and national media looking for something worth reporting before deadline. The rest of the rows were filled by average citizens who got to the court early enough to get a ticket to sit inside. An overflow courtroom handled the unlucky ones who couldn't get in.

To the left and parallel with the prosecutors was a defendant's table where Rod and all his team of lawyers sat. Looming to my right was the jury box, to my left elevated on a higher platform was the judge, and what seemed out of reach, beyond my field of vision on the distant left, was my defense team. I couldn't really see them from my chair. It probably wouldn't have done me any good if I could. You can't help feeing alone sitting there by yourself.

In the other half of the courtroom in the row next to the government were family and friends of the defendants. The only familiar faces I saw when I looked out were the faces of Julie, Alex, my brothers-in-law, and Andy, the people who really mattered to me. Everyone else was a blur.

With no previous experience or frame of reference for modeling my behavior, I did what came naturally: I tried to be myself. When you're being judged by a packed courtroom, you hope that both the truth and the way in which you handle yourself will carry the day.

You would expect that in federal court the playing field would be level for both teams. I learned the hard way that wasn't true. The home team gets the advantage. As far as I was concerned, any idea of the presumption of innocence I should have had was long lost before the trial began—starting with Fitzgerald's comment that Lincoln would be rolling over in his grave if he knew what Rod had done. With major hurdles to overcome, I sat there ready to go, prepared to forthrightly answer all the questions I was asked and hope the jury would be able to conclude I was telling the truth.

After I took the oath, Mike began his direct examination. We believed the jury needed to get to know me and we wanted to distance me from the Illinois political scene. Mike took me through a complete review of my background. His strategy was to present a character sketch of me to the jury, starting from the time Rod and I were kids, through high school, college, my military years, and my business and charitable experiences, to the day Rod asked me to help him fundraise.

Mike then went into detailed questioning of my activities as a fundraiser at FOB. I testified that I never conditioned a campaign contribution in exchange for a government action, even when the temptation was proposed by donors. To corroborate this, we played an FBI wiretapped conversation I had with the Indian donor, Babu Patel, on November 11 in the campaign office. He wanted to warn me about the reckless overtures made by Congressman Jackson's emissaries, Bedi and Nayak, in the effort to get him appointed to the Senate seat. On that tape you could hear me telling him Rod would do what was best for the people of Illinois in filling the vacancy. Trying to stress the point in that conversation, I told Patel twice that money was not going to be a factor in Rod's decision.

From the trial transcript:

> RB: No. Let me tell you. I've been approached. [re: Bedi and Nayak]
> Patel: Yeah.
> RB: And I told them, I just want you to know, Rod has made no decision.
> Patel: Yeah.
> RB: He will go through a very thorough process.
> Patel: Right.
> RB: And he is going to make a pick that he thinks that's best for the State of Illinois.
> Patel: Right.
> RB: And nothing else matters.
> Patel: Yes.
> RB: Yes, let me just assure you money is not going to be a factor here.
> Patel: INAUDIBLE.
> RB: Money is not going to be a factor.
> Patel: Absolutely. I know.
> RB: Let me make that clear.
> (Trial Transcript: pp. 38–45, July 19, 2010)

Playing this tape to the jury was important. In another unguarded moment I had rebuffed Bedi and Nayak when they tried to bribe me with the promise to raise money for Rod in exchange for the appointment of

Congressman Jackson to the Senate. After nearly five hours of questioning, Mike felt we had accomplished all our objectives. He finished and let
the prosecution take its turn.

At 4:15, AUSA Christopher Niewoehner, a Harvard Law School–educated
prosecutor, began his hostile cross-examination and wasted no time trying
to trip me up. One newspaper reporter commented that from the start, the
prosecutor had me off balance with a hypothetical about me quashing a
military investigation in exchange for a job. Playing a wiretapped conversation between me and Rod, Niewoehner alleged that I was trying to get Rod
to quash the federal investigation into his past fundraising in exchange for
the appointment of Valerie Jarrett, Obama's choice to replace him. Had the
entire tape been played—and it wasn't—Rod would have been heard telling
me that wasn't going to happen. On that same tape, I'm heard telling him
that it was a bad idea anyway. This was one of many isolated conversations
Niewoehner cherry-picked to try to make me out like a criminal.

Niewoehner pressed me, saying I wanted the federal investigation of
Rod stopped by urging my brother to "horse trade" with Obama to stop
the investigation in exchange for the Jarrett appointment. I told him as a
brother I wanted to see the investigations stopped, but emphasized that
it wouldn't be proper if it was in exchange for the Senate seat.

The prosecutor repeatedly tried to trip me up with a number of hypothetical situations designed to corner me into admitting I had done or
would do something wrong. One such exchange involved Rod taking
cash for his family in exchange for a political action. Niewoehner asked
me if that would be improper. I emphatically answered yes, it would be
wrong to take governmental action in exchange for a contribution.

Then he asked whether it would be wrong if Rod took governmental
action in exchange for someone else taking millions of dollars and putting it into some organization my brother controlled. I again responded,
yes, that it would be improper if he directly agreed to that. The prosecutor reiterated by asking me if it was proper whether it was cash or a
campaign contribution. I again agreed with him and said no, it was not
proper, it didn't matter, not in my mind.

At this point in his questioning I had no clue what he was getting at. I
could tell by his demeanor he was anxious to get to the big question he
thought would catch me in an inconsistency that would discredit me. He
then proposed another hypothetical, asking me if I thought it was wrong
if someone walked into a room with Rod, dropped a bag of $100,000 on

the table, and asked to be named senator. The answer was obvious to me; without emotion I looked straight at the prosecutor and said that Rod would tell him to pick up the money and get out.

Immediately after I answered, I could hear people in the courtroom laughing at my response. I didn't think it was funny and maintained my focus on Niewoehner after I answered, expecting a quick follow-up from him, but it never came. I could see from his expression that he was now off balance, looking down at his notes and the other prosecutors for help. Surprised by my response, he had nothing else to ask me. This exchange ended my first day on the stand. The judge adjourned court, with cross-examination to be resumed the next morning.

When I made my way back to our table, my lawyers immediately huddled around me with words of encouragement and support. They thought my first day of testimony had gone well. So did my family. It was way too early to celebrate, but we all felt good about where we were in the process. I left the courtroom that day satisfied I had done my best and knowing I had at least one more challenging day on cross before I could let up.

Julie, Alex, and I spent a quiet evening together hidden away in Alex's condo. We continued our media blackout by not watching the local news or reading any reports about my day on the stand. My practice had been to keep out negative or distracting influences, and I wasn't going to change in midstream to find out what people thought about my testimony. We knew I was taking a risk to testify, so we remained committed not to let our guard down, trying to keep our emotions in check.

Day Twenty-five: Tuesday, July 20, 2010

Noted in my journal this day:

- "Slept well last night. Woke up energized and ready to get back on the stand. Ran to the lake this morning. Felt good."

- "I have to continue to keep my anger in check for what the government has done to my life and focus it into something constructive while I testify today. Can't let it get away from me."

Keeping my anger in check was a real challenge for me even on the stand. I had to constantly remind myself not to show it. My buddy Andy thought I had more work to do to improve on that score as he watched me testify those two days. He took me aside in the hallway during one of the breaks to advise me not to be too testy or combative answering Niewoehner's questions, lest I alienate the jury.

Andy cared enough about how I was testifying to approach one of Mike's good friends, retired Illinois Appellate Court Justice David Sterba, who had come to watch the proceedings. He was sitting with his daughter Lisa, a law student at the time. The judge presided over twenty-four other judges and oversaw the court operations of thirty-five municipalities in Illinois. Obviously, his opinion would be valued. Fortunately Judge Sterba told Andy I was doing just fine and should continue on as I was. Looking as serious as I've ever seen him, Andy had rushed back to me before I returned to the stand to tell me to forget about everything he said to me about how I was testifying and continue on and not change anything.

AUSA Niewoehner picked up right where he had left off the day before. He continued to try to trip me up with a repetitive, rhythmic, dogged reframing of the same question. His style of questioning was much like Mike's during our practice cross-examination, which I had failed miserably months before in his office. This time I was ready and didn't let it happen again.

The prosecutor's methodology was to ask a question, listen to my answer, then ask the question again another way, either putting words in my mouth or suggesting a criminal intent, when it didn't exist. Niewoehner did all he could to keep me off balance with leading questions, which forced me to counterpunch to challenge his premise. I couldn't afford to let him get away with it and would interrupt him, to clarify what I actually meant before it was misunderstood by the jury.

It was a tedious and difficult process not to fall into his traps. Throughout the day I reminded myself to stay focused and listen to the question. It took everything I had not to drift off or be distracted by the side noise in the courtroom. He never stopped trying to find an inconsistency in my testimony so he could discredit me.

One example: During my time at FOB, I had several phone conversations with Tony Freveletti, an attorney from Springfield. His firm had fundraised for Rod in the past but was not getting legal business in return as it had hoped. Freveletti's name was on the initial donor call list I worked from at FOB, and I had talked with him about hosting a fundraiser for Rod. For nearly thirty minutes, Niewoehner dissected my conversations with Freveletti, intimating by his questions that I was going to intercede on his behalf with Rod to help his firm get state business in exchange for a contribution. He asked me multiple times, each time a different way, leading questions designed to trap me into admitting that I was shaking the lawyer down.

Niewoehner kept citing my statement that I was sorry that Freveletti's donors had spent their time and treasure to help Rod and didn't get any work in exchange. I kept trying to clarify, explaining that the firm evidently wasn't qualified for the work and that I was sympathetic about Freveletti's firm's failure to get state business.

The following is taken from the trial transcript:

> AUSA Niewoehner: You said that you're sympathetic you're not qualified for the work even though you spent all the time and treasure, is that what you're saying?
>
> RB: That's kind of what I'm thinking without saying it. Why would I be rude to someone who might hold a fundraiser for us?
>
> AUSA: Right. Somebody who might still hold a fundraiser for you.
>
> RB: Yes, no question, I was a fundraiser.
>
> AUSA: Particularly if his firm is able to get some work?
>
> RB: No, no, that's a leap that I will, in no way, step into, no.
>
> AUSA: But you didn't understand Freveletti saying because the firm is not getting work, they're not going to contribute?
>
> RB: Listen, he's nibbling around trying to get a state contract for a contribution, that's how I was reading this.
>
> AUSA: Which is wrong?
>
> RB: Yes.
>
> AUSA: Absolutely wrong?
>
> RB: Yes.

After several more questions in this vein, Niewoehner pressed me.

> AUSA: You wouldn't think that one thing for the other? [clarification: campaign contribution in exchange for state business]
>
> RB: It's definitely not one for the other, no!
>
> AUSA: Well you understood that is what Freveletti wanted, though, yes?
>
> RB: Yes, and so do you!
>
> AUSA: Sir, I'd just like you to answer—

RB: Fair enough. I apologize. That was out of line. I shouldn't have said that.

A reporter wrote that Niewoehner appeared paralyzed for a few seconds, just staring back at me before I apologized. He finally looked down at his notes, trying to regain his composure. I felt for him. He was caught short in front of everyone. Still, I reminded myself this guy was doing all he could to get a conviction and put me in prison. I was pumped—there was no way I was going to roll over and be polite.

This line of questioning eventually ended minutes later. In response to a question, I said to Niewoehner, that with all due respect my conversation with Freveletti was an isolated one and that I had no intention to help him get a state contract for a campaign contribution.

I believe Niewoehner selected this conversation only to discredit me because there was no evidence on the tapes or from witnesses to show I was trying to exchange state business for a contribution. Niewoehner's style of questioning was frustrating and, I believe, structured to wear me down into making mistakes.

The prosecution contended that Rod and I had schemed to get him something of personal value in exchange for the Senate seat. The distinction between political horse trading and an illegal political deal is what the following exchange highlights.

AUSA: In fact, in terms of the Senate seat appointment, your brother told you that he wanted to get a job with Health and Human Services in exchange for appointing Valerie Jarrett to the Senate seat, didn't he?

RB: No.

AUSA: Well, in fact, he did so on November 3rd, didn't he?

RB: That's not how I understood it.

AUSA: Well, would it be helpful for you to look at the transcript of your conversation?

RB: Certainly.

AUSA: This is November 3rd, 2008, isn't it?

RB: Yes.

AUSA: That is actually the date before President Obama won the election?

RB: Yes.

AUSA: And your brother says: "Unless you can really negotiate this and get Health and Human Services or something." And you understood at that point your brother is talking about the possibility that he might be appointed to become the head of Health and Human Services?

RB: It appears that way, yes.

AUSA: And he uses the word "negotiate this," doesn't he?

RB: Yes.

AUSA: He is talking about negotiating with Barack Obama at this point, isn't he? That's what you understood?

RB: It could very well mean that because someone from Barack Obama's administration had approached him about a particular person they wanted in that seat. So I guess this would be Rod's response to their overture.

AUSA: Right. It would be a negotiation between your brother and Barack Obama or his people?

RB: Yes, between two politicians.

AUSA: And so after he brings up Health and Human Services, your response is: "I think that would be, that would be f'ing awesome."

RB: Yes, I did.

AUSA: And you continue: "That would be awesome 'cause that's a whole different world of possibilities for you."

RB: Yes.

AUSA: So you actually were interested in the idea that your brother would become head of Health and Human Services?

RB: Yes, I would have been very proud if he were appointed to that secretary position. He had a strong background and achievement in healthcare, All Kids, and it seemed like a very good fit. If he said he wanted to be Secretary of Defense, I'd laugh at him.

(Trial Transcript: pp. 15–35, July 20, 2010, vol. 27)

The *Chicago Sun-Times*'s "Blago Blog" was chronicling my testimony and on July 20 wrote: "While the witness isn't laughing, the courtroom gallery did. His former governor brother smiles big, moving forward in his chair."

The questioning continued:

> AUSA: So your brother continues on at line twenty-two he says: "No, but these are big asks." And you understood when he said "big asks," that it would be a big ask to be asked to be made head of Health and Human Services?
>
> RB: Evidently.
>
> AUSA: But then he continues: "But I mean, so is the US Senate seat a big ask." And you understood at that point he was referring to the request of Barack Obama to give Valerie Jarrett to make her senator, you understood that's the big ask he was referring to there?
>
> RB: It appears that way, yes.
>
> AUSA: So in the same sentence when he is talking about his ask for Health and Human Services, he's also comparing it to Barack Obama's ask for Valerie Jarrett, isn't that right?
>
> RB: Yes.
>
> AUSA: Because you understood that he was interested in trading Valerie Jarrett's appointment for Health and Human Services?
>
> RB: I wouldn't—I would say negotiate and discuss with another politician another political position. And it seemed very logical to me because of his background in healthcare and Barack Obama was taking a number of people with him to Washington and I figured, why not Rod?
>
> AUSA: Sure. He can make that big ask, right?
>
> RB: Well, Obama was making the big ask and Rod was responding to Obama's ask.
>
> AUSA: So you understood your brother was negotiating to trade Health and Human Services for appointment of Valerie Jarrett?
>
> RB: Call it what you like. It's two politicians or potentially their representatives trying to work a political deal.
>
> AUSA: Well, isn't it your brother who used the word "negotiate" in the conversation?
>
> RB: Yes, and that's what I believe politicians do.
>
> (Trial Transcript: pp. 15–35, July 20, 2010, vol. 27)

Until I took the stand, I didn't understand the enormous amount of energy it takes to testify—so many things are occurring at the same time that require intense concentration. You have to listen intently to the question, understand what the prosecutor is really asking, formulate a concise answer that does not trap you into the corner he is trying to get you into . . . and not get distracted by anything going on in the courtroom. While you're managing all this, you still have to try to display an outer confidence and command. Much like in the old deodorant commercial, you can't let them see you sweat.

This takes a lot of effort, grinds you down over time, and can be a defendant's toughest challenge. The prosecutor knows this and uses it to his advantage by intentionally asking the same question various ways to confuse, misdirect, and catch a defendant off guard. As the hours pass, the movement and noise in the courtroom becomes amplified, making it even harder for a defendant to focus.

Just before the lunch break AUSA Niewoehner questioned me about another call I had with Rod—when we had discussed Rajindar Bedi's $1.5 million approach on October 28th. This is the call I believe inalterably changed the course of my life. It shows how a prepared defendant with right on his or her side can score points while on the witness stand.

> AUSA: Now, at this point in time, October 28th, you did not think your brother was going to appoint Congressman Jackson to the Senate seat correct?
>
> RB: Correct.
>
> AUSA: You knew your brother, in fact, had a negative history with Congressman Jackson?
>
> RB: Which was precisely what I told Rajindar Bedi in the meeting on the 28th.
>
> AUSA: You told him you didn't even know who the president was yet?
>
> RB: Among other things, yes.
>
> AUSA: Now, when you're talking to your brother, this is an important conversation with Bedi, isn't it?
>
> RB: How do you mean that?
>
> AUSA: Well, he just said an outrageous thing, is that right?
>
> RB: Yes.
>
> AUSA: He made an outrageous wrong proposal to you about trading the Senate seat for campaign contributions?
>
> RB: Yes he did.
>
> AUSA: It was outrageous enough that you felt compelled to tell your brother about it?

RB: Yes, because we were going into a steering committee meeting a couple of days later and I didn't want him stepping into land mines. I wanted him to be aware of what was in the community, the Indian community.

AUSA: So it was important to tell your brother about Bedi's proposal so he wouldn't make a mistake three days later in front of the entire community?

RB: I don't know what you mean by "mistake." I wanted him to be aware that there were people who had these objectives and just have it in the back of his mind.

AUSA: And it would be important for your brother to understand the details of what's happening, correct?

RB: He needed to know that there was a danger there, that's basically what I was communicating.

AUSA: But you didn't actually report to your brother all the things you claimed you said to Rajindar Bedi in response to that, did you?

RB: Right, I didn't need to. Because what you didn't hear in the rest of the call, which was not surveilled, is that he dismissed it and I dismissed it, and we moved on, because it was so outrageous.

AUSA: But you didn't actually tell your brother in this conversation what you testified you said to Bedi, did you?

RB: No.

AUSA: You did not tell your brother, "Oh, I told Bedi it's going to have to be in the best interest of Illinois." You didn't say that to your brother?

RB: No.

AUSA: You didn't tell your brother, "Oh, money, I told Bedi money will not have nothing to do with it," did you?

RB: No, but I did tell that to Bedi, I told that to Nayak, and as you heard yesterday, I told that to Babu Patel.

AUSA: You just didn't tell your brother?

RB: Not in that conversation, no. But that's a given, I mean, I didn't need to tell him that.

AUSA: Because so many people had come to you in the past with outrageous suggestions, that you knew what your brother's response was going to be?

RB: Yes.

AUSA: How many people have come to you in the past and offered to raise campaign contributions in exchange for some kind of state action?

I then went on to testify about the out-of-the-blue call I had gotten from Barry Aycock on November 12th. As I have noted in chapter 7, Aycock offered a substantial contribution to FOB in exchange for my help in getting his PhD processed through Southern Illinois University. As soon as I finished explaining that outrageous attempt to Niewoehner, I asked if he wanted to hear another one. To my surprise he said yes.

AUSA: Okay, when was that?
RB: I was organizing a fundraiser in the Greek community in Long Grove to meet with some restaurateurs who claimed that they were going to raise $25,000 at a fundraiser for Rod. And so when I went there to sit down with them, they pulled out these architectural drawings of a desired road that they wanted to have changed, a state road change to give access to their restaurant. I mean, it was egregious. It was a plat about this big (indicating) and they pulled them out and they showed me where they wanted the road to go, the access road off a state highway into their restaurant because it was hurting their business. I told them: "I don't do that, I can't do that, you need to go through IDOT." And as a result they cancelled—eventually cancelled a fundraiser. They did not hold a fundraiser. So there's another example of how people were picking at me as a fundraiser to get something in exchange for campaign funds which I resisted. (Trial Transcript: pp. 79–84, July 20, 2010, vol. 27)

I believed these two examples of outrageous donor asks made it very clear to anyone listening that I was a responsible fundraiser determined not to break the law when it would have been very easy to do so.

Noted in my journal this day:

 ◆ "This is a written reminder to listen to the question before answering and to stay focused."

During the afternoon break I felt a little tired from the rigor of the day's cross examination. Knowing I couldn't afford to let down when I went back on the stand, I wolfed down a protein bar for energy. I also wrote myself a note on a bright blue sticky. "STAY FOCUSED!" it read in all capital letters.

When I sat down again in the witness box, I placed the note on the lectern directly in front of me. If I lost my concentration, I could glance at it. Harmless, you would think?

Unknown to me initially, one of the FBI agents, Special Agent Daniel W. Cain, was surveilling me, even in the courtroom. From the stand, I noticed him looking at me and then watched him get up from his seat and approach the prosecutor's table. He showed them a sticky note and demonstrated to them what I had just done with mine.

Niewoehner then got up and walked over to our defense table to talk with Mike. I was shocked when Mike came to the stand and asked me what I had taken up with me. I showed him my sticky note. He snatched it from me and brusquely told me I couldn't take anything to the witness stand. I was surprised to hear that. No one had told me that defendants were prohibited from having anything with them during testimony unless permission was granted by the judge.

Mike walked over to the prosecutor's table and stuck the note on his forehead to show them the "dangerous" material I had taken up to the lectern. I was outraged that the government, my government, could be so petty as to take away my innocent little note. It was childish. We were in a federal courtroom, not on the school yard playground. After that episode I didn't need anything to energize me for the rest of the afternoon.

The bulk of my remaining, adrenaline-fueled testimony centered on the Senate seat. Niewoehner played the phone conversation I had with Rod on December 4th in the Lincoln Square Starbucks and grilled me about the approach by Congressman Jackson's two emissaries Bedi and Nayak.

The prosecutor asked questions about something I had said during my direct examination by Mike—my comparison of Nayak's Indian origins to the Serbian community I grew up in. I explained that I observed the same clumsy awkwardness in Nayak that I saw growing up in the Serbian community. Like the immigrants I'd known in my youth, Indian Americans seemed naïve about our political system, and I told Niewoehner I put Nayak right at the top of the chart. Niewoehner played off my comments and asked if it was naïve of Nayak to offer $6 million to sway the governor for the Senate seat. I curtly answered that it was naïve of Nayak to think he could approach a guy like me and get it done. After that response, he quickly moved on with a new line of questioning.

The following are selected excerpts of a ten-minute exchange during cross. They further illustrate how the prosecutor tried to trip me up with repetitive variations of the same question to get me to concede that I had mixed government action with fundraising. The conversation in question was between Rod and me on December 6th, the day of the Indian fundraiser. I was following up with Rod to make sure he understood how I planned to talk to Nayak if he should bring up his earlier $6 million offer.

> AUSA: Now I'll turn your attention to December 6th. And you heard a call yesterday of this conversation between yourself and your brother on December 6th. Do you recall that?
>
> RB: No.
>
> AUSA: Would it help to see a transcript?
>
> RB: Yes.
>
> AUSA: So on the first page of the transcript on page 1, line 1, you say, "Here's one that's pending and possibly with Raghu."
>
> RB: Right; that was a part of a larger conversation.
>
> AUSA: And you were talking about the possibility of talking to Raghu Nayak at the fundraiser that night, correct?
>
> RB: Yes, because Rod and I had never finished talking as a follow-up on the conversation we had on the 4th, so that was still unresolved. So I was, once again, following up with him letting him know I would likely see Raghu.
>
> AUSA: And you say: "All I'm thinking about saying is, 'Your guy's meeting with Rod on Monday.'"
>
> RB: Yes.
>
> AUSA: That was in reference to the meeting that was going to be held in two days with your brother and Congressman Jackson, correct?
>
> RB: Yes.
>
> AUSA: That meeting wasn't secret was it?
>
> RB: I have no idea. I don't think it was secret, no.
>
> AUSA: It was a public event. There were newspaper stories about it, wasn't there?

RB: I don't know. I just know that Rod said that he was going to have a meeting with him in his office.

AUSA: And you were going to go to a fundraiser and pass on this political message, is that right?

RB: Yes.

AUSA: And in response you say: "That's all I'm going to say, I'll leave it at that based on what you told me, correct?" And your brother says: "Yeah, that's all. You know, if he says, 'I can do a lot more money.'" So your brother, in response to your suggestion that you would talk about Congressman Jackson, immediately goes to talking about Nayak offering to raise money, isn't that right?

RB: It would appear that way.

AUSA: That's what you understood him to mean when he said, "If he says, 'I can do a lot more money'"?

RB: Yes; could be.

We continued back and forth with similar foundational questions from Niewoehner which led to this exchange:

AUSA: Well, when your brother said, "I can do a lot more money," what other money did you understand your brother could be talking about?

RB: He could have been referring to additional fundraising.

AUSA: He could've been?

RB: Yes.

AUSA: But you didn't understand that in this conversation?

RB: I cut him off and I said, "One is not tied to the other. One is not tied to the other, and if you want"—I was referring to Nayak—"obviously, we want to help you do that." So we weren't shying away from doing more fundraising, but I just wanted to make it clear there was no condition—

AUSA: Well, actually—

RB: And he agreed to that.

AUSA: Actually, he says, "If he says I can do a lot more money." You didn't cut him off at that point, did you?

RB: You know, in the course of a personal conversation, it's sometimes hard to cut people off.

AUSA: Well, he continues and says: "That's, you know, you answered that, and just say, ah, look, you know, that, that's your decision."

RB: And then I cut him off. Then I cut him off and I said, "One is not tied to the other." So I let him run a little bit and I then cut him off. I mean, I just want to make it clear here, I was not going to cut a deal with Raghu Nayak whether it was December 4th, 6th, 31st, whatever; never.

AUSA: So I guess to be fair, you didn't—your testimony is, you didn't understand what you brother was saying when he said, "I can do a lot more money," you didn't understand what he meant?

RB: Not fully. Plus if you read further, I say down here: (referring to the written transcript) "All right, look, I'm freezing my ass off. I've gotta get in the shower." I'd just gotten through running, I'm talking to him, this conversation was longer than what it appears to on this page, and I wanted to get warm, and I was not going to cross any lines with regard to fundraising and the Senate seat.

AUSA: Well, if you didn't understand your brother was talking about raising contributions, why did you respond, "One is not tied to the other"? You said that because you recognized that he was talking about fundraising in the context of the Senate seat?

RB: He might have been, but I wasn't filtering it that way in terms of next steps, and I don't know how much clearer I can make it.

(Trial Transcript: pp. 56–60, July 20, 2010, vol. 27)

After several more questions on the same theme, Niewoehner told the judge he had nothing further. He was done with me.

Following two days on the stand, my testimony ended with a short redirect by Mike. He asked additional questions to clarify for the jury any accusations made by Niewoehner, direct or implied, that I was a willing participant to breaking the law.

After Mike told the judge that he was satisfied my answers cleared up the issues raised during cross by Niewoehner, he told the judge he rested. When Niewoehner had nothing further for recross, Judge Zagel told me I could step down.

When I got back to the defense table, Cheryl hugged me. "Where did that come from?" she asked. She was referring to the several times when my responses to Niewoehner's questions had visibly surprised him, forcing him to regroup before he would proceed with more questions.

Robyn hugged me as well and told me what a good job I had done defending myself. Then Mike came over. He whispered to me that Rod's legal team had decided not to have Rod testify and would rest their defense, believing the prosecutors had not made their case against him. This meant we were almost done. Rod's testimony could have taken weeks. We were going to resolve this thing before Labor Day.

As I sat at the defense table, lawyers for the defense and prosecution stood before the bench. Rod's team informed the prosecutors and Judge Zagel that they were resting their case. AUSA Schar stood there with arms crossed, his face and head turning bright red, visibly upset at what he was being told. Everyone was expecting Rod to take the stand right after I finished. Not so.

Before leaving the courtroom, I had to attend to a bit of unfinished business. I felt I needed to go over to Niewoehner and shake his hand. It just seemed like the right thing to do. He was gathering his stuff when I reached him. Not expecting to see me on his side of the room, he looked surprised as I came up to him and extended my right hand. I looked him in the eye and told him that he had done his job and I had done mine. I actually felt that I had done mine better. He smiled awkwardly and said, "Thanks." By his tentative reaction I could tell this didn't happen to him very often after cross-examining a criminal defendant.

As we made our way to the elevator, Mike informed me the media had gathered in the lobby and wanted me to make a statement. I had not anticipated saying anything and told Mike I was reluctant. Ignoring my protest, he said he thought I should say something to the press and answer a few questions. I frantically tried to compose my thoughts before we made it to the lobby. We exited the elevator to a wall of reporters with microphones and cameras waiting.

My comments were brief. After thanking my attorneys for their exceptional support, I told the press that I considered myself to be an innocent man and that the whole experience had been a test I hoped none of them would have to endure. A reporter asked me how I thought I did on the stand. I answered that I told the truth, and if the truth is good, I did well.

Day Twenty-six: Wednesday, July 21, 2010

Noted in my journal this day:

- ◆ "Today is the beginning of the rest of my life. At least that's how I feel after testifying for the last two days. By all accounts my testimony was well received by any constituency you can name. From the media to the lawyers to the court observers, my time on the stand was worth the risk. Phil Rodgers, NBC Chicago, told Cheryl that in all his years he's been covering the court he has never seen a witness more effectively testify than me. Unbelievable feedback from a credible source. Another reporter shook my hand and told me if he ever needed anyone to testify on his behalf he would want someone like me to do it. Yet another media person told Cheryl that if by some chance I was convicted, bar none, the media would cry fowl and help me with my appeal. Don't exactly know what that means, but how about that!"

- ◆ "I have no real idea why the reaction is so overwhelmingly positive other than as Cheryl kept saying, I was just being myself. I had the truth on my side, which allowed me to confidently tell my story just as anyone would in my situation. I managed to somehow effectively fend off the prosecutor's very dogged attempts to discredit me with trick questions."

- ◆ "Sam Adam Sr., one of Rod's attorneys, came to me before court, shook my hand and told me I was the best witness he ever saw. And that I substantially helped Rod's case and their strategic decision to rest the defense. It's quite a compliment that I didn't expect to hear from him."

- ◆ "Mike said a guy in the elevator told him he would vote for me even if I was a Republican. What a city!"

After the morning session concluded, the judge released us for a three-hour break. The team and I broke from our tradition of going to Marquette's everyday for lunch and instead treated ourselves to The Berghoff, an iconic German restaurant next door to the federal building. Our mood was almost festive in the aftermath of the feedback we had received about my testimony. By all objective measures, we knew it had gone well. During lunch we relived and dissected my testimony in a kind of nostalgic way. We did a play-by-play of my cross with AUSA Niewoehner. We enjoyed a peaceful time together much like good friends who had been through a life-altering trauma and lived to tell about it.

Noted in my journal this day:

- ◆ "Now 3:30, back from break, Zagel 40 minutes late."

- ◆ "We are currently waiting our turn to argue before the judge for acquittal. At this time the high that I was on is somewhat deflated because I'm listening to the arguments to Judge Zagel, and he has not relented in his unconditional support of the government. "Denied" was his judgment for our motion to acquit which would have freed me to go home. I am once again sobered by listening to the exchange and I have to keep focus on the remaining days of this trial and resist getting my hopes too high. This judge is ridiculously one-sided, and with that I can say that I can't stand him. His manner/demeanor is pompous and lacking humanity."

I really wasn't surprised by Judge Zagel's denial of our motion for acquittal. Over the past six weeks, he had sided with the government on every substantive issue. Before we left the courtroom, he told all the lawyers he wanted to see them the following day for any final motions and to discuss sequencing for closing arguments. Mike had already begun drafting his closing argument in anticipation of this day and, as promised, had been reviewing his progress with me. I trusted him to do his job, but I just wanted to make sure we were as thoroughly prepared as possible for this final shot to speak to the jury.

Day Twenty-seven: Monday, July 26, 2010

Noted in my journal this day:

- ◆ "Closing arguments today."

- ◆ "Cheryl just told me that one of the US marshals told her he and the other marshals thought I was innocent and were rooting for me."

In a surprise move, the government dropped one of the five charges against me—Count Twelve, one of the two original honest services wire fraud charges. We could never figure out why I got charged in the first place when I wasn't even on the call and had no knowledge it had occurred. We could only surmise the government dropped this charge to avoid confusing the jury.

Judge Zagel announced the order of closing arguments. As customary, the prosecution would go first, with two and a half hours allotted. Mike would go next with an hour and Sam Adam Jr. would finish up closing arguments, also getting two and a half hours. After all the closing arguments were given, the prosecution would get one more chance to make its case to the jury with an hour rebuttal. Again it seemed so unfair to me as a defendant that the government got the last word in to influence the jury.

Noted in my journal this day:

- ⬩ "Prosecution starts closing argument. Niewoehner referred to me as a crook because 'I agreed to do something.' He said it didn't have to be executed. He claims, 'talking is the crime here.' He said I was sent out by Rod to shake down people."

- ⬩ "Niewoehner also called me a liar when I testified last week. He said I lied numerous times on the stand. This is by far the toughest day of the trial, more so than when I testified primarily because I can't respond to him. He is twisting my words and misrepresenting what I had testified to, saying I danced and dodged during cross. I can only hope the jury members are good listeners and can distinguish between what I said and what the prosecutor is alleging. I have to just sit here and listen, and can't defend myself. I feel helpless to do anything to counter him, and have to rely on Mike to make my points to bring the truth home to the jury."

- ⬩ "Sitting here quietly is hard. I want to stand up and yell back at Niewoehner for lying about me, but I can't."

As I listened to Niewoehner's closing argument, I realized that the government's only recourse was to call me a liar. The prosecutors had nothing else, so they did all they could to discredit me. It seemed to me that they were not concerned about justice and were willing to say anything to win, true or false. Seeing how angered I was by Niewoehner's comment, Mike tried to calm and reassure me that we would get our chance when he did his close.

Mike's closing was excellent. The jury listened attentively as he reviewed the case against me, citing my words on the tapes and my testimony as proof that I was not guilty of the charges brought against me.

He went into detail to make his points, systematically leading them through the facts and even mixing in a little humor. He appealed to the jurors to let their consciences be their guide and to remember what I did and what I said, not what Rod said.

Mike emphasized that the tapes were void of any criminal intent and concluded that the jury should find me not guilty on all charges. When he got back to our table, I told him he did a great job defending me, and thanked him for following his well-prepared outline. Three days later, the twenty-ninth day of trial, the case was sent to the jury.

Day Twenty-nine: Thursday, July 29, 2010

During the trial, I marveled at how all the attorneys, defense and prosecution, interacted with each other when court wasn't in session. They chitchatted like they were longtime buddies hanging out together before an athletic competition. There seemed to exist a comfortable, informal back channel of communication where unofficial information was exchanged between them from time to time. I never knew, when Mike or Cheryl came back from talking with one of them, whether what they had been told was the truth. Now, minutes before jury instructions were read, Cheryl had some interesting information to pass on thanks to a conversation she had with the prosecutors.

Noted in my journal this day:

- ◆ "Cheryl just spoke with the prosecutors. They told her my handshake with Niewoehner was a class act and reflected on my character. Schar said he felt bad about me being in this and said if for some reason it went bad for me, they and Zagel know who I am. She also said it was clear from their comments to her that they were supportive of me and that they took their direction from a higher authority (Fitzgerald)."

Wow. After all we had been through, I didn't know what to think. Could Cheryl have misunderstood what she was told? The prosecutors were suddenly sympathetic toward me? They thought I was a class act? Out of nowhere they're showing their hand to us? It was hard to believe they had any goodwill toward me after what they'd put me through. They did their best to convince the jury I was guilty; that's what I knew. I couldn't make any sense of it and didn't try. I was tired of the games and just wanted it to be over.

A jury tries the facts. The judge applies the law. As the name suggests, jury instructions tell the jury what to do (or find) based on its decision about the facts of the case. Each side submits proposed instructions to the judge, who then makes the final decision on what to instruct the jury. As you might guess, each side proposes instructions most favorable to its case.

With multiple counts and multiple defendants, the jury instructions were, one juror later said, comparable to the manual for the space shuttle. In a word: complex. The government's proposed instructions alone were 123 pages.

After listening to Judge Zagel painstakingly read what looked like a three-inch stack of complicated instructions, I left the courtroom concerned. It seemed impossible to me that the jury would be able to understand and process everything from the trial and fit it to the instructions they'd just heard. I could only hope they would come to the right conclusion when they tried to put it all together in the jury room.

Consider this instruction:

To sustain the charge of wire fraud, as charged in Counts 1 through 10, the government must prove the following propositions beyond a reasonable doubt:

> First, that the defendant knowingly devised or participated in a scheme to defraud the public of its right to the honest services of Rod Blagojevich or John Harris by demanding, soliciting, seeking, asking for, or agreeing to accept, a bribe in the manner described in the particular Count you are considering; Second, that the defendant did so with the intent to defraud; Third, that the scheme to defraud involved a materially false and fraudulent pretense, representation, promise, or concealment; and Fourth, that for the purpose of carrying out the scheme or attempting to do so, the defendant used or caused the use of interstate wire communications to take place in the manner charged in the particular Count you are considering. (http://www.webcitation.org/6WSltNCyj)

Julie and I would spend the next several days waiting anxiously to learn my fate. Nothing we did felt normal as we tried not to think too much about the pending verdict. There was nothing else to say. It had all been said; we waited.

CHAPTER FOURTEEN

A Game of Chicken

A hidden drama played out every time the jury came in and left the courtroom when I testified. By design, the witness stand is located right next to the door the jury uses. The intimacy resulting from the close placement made it a little awkward for me and probably for the jurors as well as they came and went. I wasn't sure whether I should make eye contact with them or not; Mike and I had never talked about it.

Maybe overthinking it a bit, I decided I would make eye contact with any of the jurors who happened to gaze my way. I feared that if I didn't look at them, they might get the wrong impression and think I had something to hide. As I would make eye contact with them, I wondered what they thought, hoping in some weird way they liked me.

It was not possible to get my mind around the idea that those strangers would ultimately determine my fate. Three weeks later I would find out exactly what they thought about me behind those uncomfortable stares. After two false rumors of a verdict that caused us to rush downtown, the jury finally reached a decision on August 17 after deliberating for fourteen days. I hoped the third time would be the charm.

When we got the call from Mike, he was certain we had a verdict this time. Julie and I believed, whatever the outcome, our lives would change forever. She called Alex at work in his downtown office. He would meet us in the parking lot kitty-corner from the Dirksen Building. She and I somberly dressed for court, barely speaking a word to each other. What do you talk about at a time when twelve strangers are about announce their judgment of you? I was at a loss for words. The weight of the uncertainty that burdened us for nearly two years was about to be lifted, one way or the other. After we dressed, we hugged, got in the car, and silently drove to the federal building.

Due to the length of deliberations and the questions the jurors had asked Judge Zagel while deciding our fate, Mike speculated we were headed for a hung jury on some or all of the charges against Rod. He believed the government had presented such a complex, hard-to-follow case that jurors might be so confused they'd have a hard time reaching unanimity. At the same time, he was confident I would be acquitted on all counts. Julie and I had no clue what the potential verdict might be for me. By then we had been hardened by the roller-coaster ride of emotions that we had endured. Our strong belief in the American system of justice had been shaken beginning December 9, 2008, and was now virtually nonexistent.

As we waited for the jury, Julie and Alex sat right next to me in the spectator seats, close enough that we could talk. All I could think to say to them was to stay strong and to show no emotion when we heard the verdict, good or bad. We were braced for the worst but got something in between.

The jury was hung on all charges against me. Can you say "retrial"? I turned and looked at my family in bewilderment. By now I had become accustomed to disappointment. This was more of the same. The challenge of defending myself was about to go into overtime and I had to keep my game face on.

Rod was in the same boat. The jury was hung on twenty-three of the twenty-four counts against him. They did find him guilty of one count—making false statements to the FBI. His relief at escaping "guilty" on almost all of the charges was tempered by the fact that the single count carried a maximum sentence of five years.

The *New York Times* offered this postmortem:

> Prosecutors here once said that the conduct of Rod R. Blagojevich, the former governor of Illinois, was so despicable it would make Abraham Lincoln "roll over in his grave," but 12 jurors in the federal corruption case against him were apparently not all so certain. (http://www.nytimes.com/2010/08/18/us/18jury.html)

For many reasons I couldn't afford to let down. After the verdict I would have to meet the swarm of media waiting for everybody in the lobby. I felt impelled to counter any fallout resulting from a hung jury. I wasn't going to miss any opportunity to proclaim my innocence to the public, particularly the next jury.

After thanking my lawyers and the jury for their serious deliberation I said the following: "I have lived through the most surreal experience anyone could live through. This has been, from the beginning, a slow bleed both financially, emotionally, and otherwise. But I can tell you what, I feel confident, I feel strong, and I don't feel in any way deterred in my ability to articulate my innocence. I have ultimate confidence in my acquittal."

I then took a few questions. One reporter asked me what my thoughts were about the justice system. Smiling, I commented, "I would say the criminal justice system has flaws and I would like to speak out on those, but I don't think this is the proper time."

Another reporter asked if I would plead guilty to some charges rather than face a retrial. "I've done nothing wrong. Why would I plead? No!" I said emphatically.

I was then asked if I had any regrets about going to work for my brother. "I don't look back, I just look forward," I answered.

With that comment, the press conference ended. I left the federal building heeding the words I'd just spoken. My last conversation before heading home was with Mike about the next steps. I wanted us to objectively critique what went wrong and how we would fix it the next time around. He agreed that we should start immediately. We would talk in the morning.

That night we watched the local news for the first time since arriving in Chicago to find out what the media spin was on the verdict. We saw an interview of one of the jurors, a twenty-something young man, who said the jury voted 11–1 in favor of conviction. We were stunned by what we'd heard. We could make no sense of it. It sounded like I almost got convicted. How could we have been so off the mark in our strategy? My mind wouldn't stop racing as I tried to get some sleep. This was by far the worst night of my entire legal nightmare.

I called Mike first thing in the morning to tell him what the juror had said. I was anxious to find out what he thought went wrong with our defense. Maybe it's standard for every defense attorney to believe they're going to win and get an acquittal. With great confidence, he had believed I would be acquitted. As it turned out, we came up short.

I was not happy about the outcome and told him I wanted to meet to talk about what he would do differently in a second trial. He surmised from my tone and urgency that I might want another lawyer and asked me if I was considering a change. My answer was, "Of course not." I just wanted to know how we could fix it. He said he needed some time to talk with the jurors before he could give me his opinion. I told him I would stand by and wait for his call.

Mike called me a couple of hours later, with an unusually playful air. He opened up the conversation by asking me if I still planned to fire him. I reassured him that I wouldn't. Then he quickly went on to tell me he had some news he thought I would want to hear. He had spoken to a reliable source who had interviewed a number of the jurors. Contrary to what we'd heard on the news, the vote on each of my four counts was 9–3 in favor of acquittal.

The juror we saw on the news was talking about Rod's charges, not mine. It wasn't as bad as we had thought the night before. This was exceptionally good news for us, though not so for my brother. Everything had suddenly changed. This was an enormous relief to know all along we were on track with a strong defense. Now we only needed to tweak our trial strategy the next time around for an acquittal.

Mike and I also talked about doing a media blitz. He had numerous requests for interviews and thought we should consider doing some for the exposure. This was not our approach going into the first trial, but things were different now. We needed to consider adapting our strategy to the new landscape. The public still didn't know who I was, and we believed it was imperative to be proactive this time and reach out to the next jury.

Over the next two days, Mike, Cheryl, and I did seven interviews with all the major television, radio, and print media in Chicago. When the question of severance was brought up during an interview, I restated my desire for a trial separate from Rod's and explained my reasons.

A couple of days after the verdict, Julie and I were unexpectedly thrust onto the front page of the *Chicago Sun-Times*. The headline read: "Blago Juror: Rob Should Go Free." This headline seemed to sum up the public's opinion regarding me as we finished up our interviews. We had at last broken through the negative impact of Fitzgerald's press conference and the drag of being Rod's codefendant. I had finally managed to separate myself as a defendant, which was exactly what we needed to accomplish before going into a retrial. Our media blitz had paid off!

On the day of the verdict, the prosecutors had informed Judge Zagel they wanted a retrial as soon as possible. He accepted their request and scheduled August 26 for a hearing, at which a new trial date would be discussed. This was a procedural hearing and didn't require the defendants to appear, so Mike and Cheryl would go to represent me. If I didn't need to be there, I wasn't going. The last thing I wanted to do was hang around the federal building when I didn't have to. It's not like you get extra credit for making the effort.

The two weeks leading up to the hearing were eventful. Julie and I had several difficult discussions about how we would pay for another trial. The first trial, which cost us nearly a million dollars, was funded from our retirement savings and a second mortgage on our home. We decided we needed to get back to Nashville before the next trial to put our house up for sale. We could no longer afford to keep it. Also I needed to get back to begin the liquidation of my business in order to fund the upcoming retrial. As a consequence of this, my ability to continue to earn a living as an independent small business owner was put at risk by having to break it up and sell. Fair? You be the judge.

As we were trying to figure out our personal finances, I was also talking with Mike everyday about preparation for the next trial. He believed we needed to reset our strategy. The government had seen our defense and would be ready for it. Anticipating this possibility, we were seriously considering calling Congressman Jackson and Raghu Nayak as witnesses to testify about their activities. Their testimony at a retrial would have forced the government to rethink its strategy, which was exactly what we wanted.

The thought of waiting for a retrial was getting to me. I was anxious to get started as soon as it was practical because I wanted closure. I felt frozen in place. I wanted it over, one way or another, so I could get on with the next phase of my life, whatever it was. Mike was not as ready to get back at it as I was. He said he needed a break before the grind of another long trial and had to refocus on his legal practice. We agreed he would request a March/April retrial date at the upcoming hearing.

On the day before the hearing, Mike got an unexpected call from AUSA Reid Schar. Schar asked Mike if we intended to file a motion for severance. Mike told him that we had already filed one some time ago and reminded Schar the government had opposed it. Then Schar proposed that if we refiled for severance, the government would agree to it and give me what I always wanted—the opportunity to be tried separately from Rod. There was, however, a condition. I would have to wait until after Rod was retried before I got a separate trial. Though it seemed odd that at this late date they had a change of heart, their offer meant I could finally get what I had asked for eighteen months earlier.

Mike called me as soon as he got off the phone with Schar. Robyn was on the speaker with him. Initially he spoke in a normal, controlled fashion as he explained the government's offer. It was a development none of us had expected. I flippantly asked him why, all of a sudden, was the government being nice to me? As he had told me all along, the government didn't do anything to be nice to a defendant; it had an agenda.

Mike explained that if we took their offer I'd remain in legal limbo for up to another year before I was retried. He was concerned that if Rod didn't get acquitted the next time around, a bad result could negatively affect me when I stood trial alone. The longer we talked, the louder and more animated Mike became. I put him on the speaker so Julie could hear what he was telling me.

Without saying it, his raised, excited voice told me what he really thought of the government's deal. But just to make sure, I asked him point blank what he thought we should do. He didn't hesitate. Almost yelling by this time, he said, "Rob, we don't want what the government wants!" At the same time, in a strong, forceful tone Robyn encouraged me to take Mike's advice.

Simple as that, I knew exactly where he stood. By then Cheryl had joined us on the call and I could hear her and Robyn in the background shouting into the speaker for me to listen to Mike. We all knew a lot was at stake, and at times the call verged on chaos with all of us excitedly trying to talk at the same time.

Several times during the call Mike felt the need to forcefully remind me that we didn't want what the government wanted. My questions about what a shorter, separate trial would mean to me must have made him think I was leaning toward taking the feds' offer. He emphasized that I was better off being tried with Rod than separately because the prosecution's primary focus was Rod and the sharp contrast between us favored me in a joint trial. There were intangible but significant factors that Mike believed needed to be considered. He pressed me to give him the go-ahead to inform Schar that we rejected his offer for a severance.

I hesitated. We were all keyed up by the offer, and I thought we needed to slow it down some to evaluate further before we did anything. What had changed for them to offer us a deal they had opposed until now? Was Schar's offer a sign that the government had blinked? I asked Mike if he would mind calling his close friend, Ed Genson, a highly respected Chicago defense attorney, for his opinion. Being the consummate team player, Mike had no problem calling Genson to get his read on the offer.

After we hung up with Mike, Julie and I had a chance to talk about the surprising development. Since my indictment we knew the government didn't have a strong case against me. Did they telegraph a lack of confidence in their ability to convict Rod and me if we were tried together? We weren't sure and did our best to dispassionately assess what had been offered. I told her I didn't have enough experience to know what was really behind Schar's proposal, but that I thought Mike was right. She agreed. We would tell Mike to reject the government's offer no matter what he heard from Genson.

A few minutes later Mike called me back to tell me that Genson had said to take the offer. He thought the government was looking for a graceful way out and would drop my charges after Rod's trial. Mike told me he couldn't take the chance of trusting them to do the right thing by me at some point in the distant future. Again, he strongly recommended that we reject the government's offer. I agreed. Mike would inform Schar that we rejected the offer for severance and would propose a spring 2011 retrial date at the hearing in the morning.

The only reason we remained in Chicago after the verdict was to wait for the court hearing. Once we knew the retrial date, we planned to leave as soon as possible for Nashville. We had a lot to do back home and were anxious to get going. The hearing was scheduled for an eleven o'clock start. In Zagel's court, starting on time didn't mean much, so I didn't expect to hear from Mike until sometime in the early afternoon.

While I waited to hear from Mike, I decided to work on a long overdue plumbing project. Throughout our stay with Alex, the sink in our bathroom was slow to drain and annoyed me the entire time we were there. While I was laid out under the basin, the text message alert beeped on my cell phone. I got up off the floor to see who it was. I didn't expect it to be Mike.

The time displayed was 11:01 and the message read: "It's done, it's over, the government dropped all charges. You're a free man!"

I soon learned he had texted me as he was walking into the hearing. Schar had just informed him that the government had dismissed me from the case. This message had come out of nowhere. As the enormity of it was sinking in, my mind was racing, trying to make sense of it. Somehow lost in all the happiness was the fact that for once Judge Zagel had managed to start on time.

I called out to Julie, who was in the kitchen. She read the message and began to tear up. I cautioned her that we shouldn't get too excited until we officially heard from Mike. Yesterday they offered a severance, today they dismiss me? It seemed to be happening so fast that it was hard to comprehend. We waited for Mike to tell us that we hadn't misread his message.

He called shortly and told me it really was over. He explained that this was a highly unusual move for the government. In all his time trying federal cases, he had never been involved in a last-minute dismissal. The prosecutors explained that due to the disparity of our roles and in the interest of justice, they decided to let me go and retry Rod alone. They had dismissed my charges without prejudice, which meant I could still be retried if they chose.

After I finished with Mike I looked at Julie. She was standing in front of me in tears. We embraced and held each other for a long time while she sobbed in my arms. We barely had enough time to let the news settle in when the doorbell rang. I went downstairs to see who it was. This time it wasn't the FBI issuing a subpoena; it was a reporter asking for an interview.

That started a whirlwind afternoon of interviews with all the local news stations, the *New York Times*, *Time* magazine, and the AP. We were also flooded with calls from friends, family, and well-wishers who had heard the news. By the time we finished with all of them, we were hungry and ready to eat. Alex had arrived early from work and offered to treat us to a steak dinner downtown to mark the occasion. He took us to the Chicago Chop House where, as a family, we quietly celebrated our good fortune.

We could never have predicted when we woke up that morning the drama that awaited us. We believed the government acted not in the interest of justice, as stated, but out of necessity because I hurt the case against my brother. From the beginning I believed I was just a pawn to be used as long as I had value to them in their zealous pursuit of Rod.

The team and I believed the government, specifically Fitzgerald, recognized I couldn't help it in a second trial, and so it cynically offered us a severance deal. They chose to keep me in legal limbo so that I couldn't testify in a second trial with Rod. When we checkmated them by not accepting their severance offer, they were stuck and had no choice but to drop my charges. The government had grossly miscalculated, believing that we would be anxious to accept their deal and wait. We were not, and as a result they were forced to cut me loose. Instead of doing the right thing from the beginning by not charging me, the government chose to play chicken with my life, and in the end we beat them at their own game.

CHAPTER FIFTEEN

Unfinished Business

The morning after the prosecution abruptly dropped my charges, Julie and I took a carefree stroll to the neighborhood Starbucks down the street from Alex's place. When we walked in we were greeted by strangers who wished us well and who warmly congratulated us on our change in fortune. One man in particular stands out. He had purchased a copy of the *Chicago Sun-Times* to commemorate the birth of his daughter earlier that morning. Because I was on the front page of the paper he asked if I would autograph his copy. I happily signed it.

More than a year after the trial, I read that the Congressional House Ethics Committee was reopening its investigation of Congressman Jesse Jackson Jr. A House panel had found "probable cause" that Jackson had either directed someone to offer to raise funds in exchange for Barack Obama's Senate seat or knew of such an offer.

The investigation, which had been suspended at the request of the US attorney until Rod's trial was completed, was revived in October 2011. When I learned of this in April 2012, I immediately wrote letters to all ten representatives on the committee (five Democrats and five Republicans), offering to testify about the offers communicated to me by Jackson's emissaries.

Days after I sent the letters I received a call from the *Chicago Sun-Times* reporter Natasha Korecki, asking me if I was going to testify to Congress about Jackson. I confirmed that I had contacted the Ethics Committee and told her I believed I could help it in its investigation.

On April 13, 2012, the *Sun-Times* ran a front-page story with a headline reading: "Settling Scores? Blago's brother heads to D.C. with Jesse Jr. in his sights." The story featured a picture of me facing off against Jackson, and I was quoted by Korecki as saying, "Based on what I know, I believe Jesse Jackson Jr. has a lot of unanswered questions he needs to answer."

Korecki was the same reporter who had asked me in September 2009, months before the trial started, if I thought Jackson had gotten a pass on the Senate seat. I didn't have an answer for her then, but the time had come, almost three years later, for me to answer her question before a House Committee.

Five months after I sent the letters, the House Ethics Committee invited me to testify. I flew to Washington, DC, on April 24, 2012, to meet with its legal staff. We met in a conference room in the Longworth House Office Building, where I swore under oath that I would tell them the truth.

I answered many questions and testified for over three hours about the events surrounding Jackson's attempted bribe through Bedi and Nayak. I had no documents to present but suggested the committee contact the US attorney for the Northern District of Illinois to get copies of the FBI 302 interviews for John Wyma, Raghu Nayak, Rajindar Bedi, and, of course, Jesse Jackson Jr. I said that those documents would greatly assist them in getting to the bottom of Jackson's involvement.

I spoke to them from memory about what was in the 302s. I told the committee I had no doubt, after what I had experienced and what I had read in the interviews, that Congressman Jackson used Nayak and Bedi to attempt to buy the Senate seat.

I remembered from the 302s that Jackson, Nayak, and Bedi had met at the 312 Restaurant in Chicago on the morning of October 28, 2008. This was the same day Bedi had made his overture to me while we met to coordinate a fundraiser to be held later in the month. I also told them that I remembered reading that Bedi had gotten a call from Jackson less than two hours after we had met on the twenty-eighth. As I recalled from his 302, Bedi, recognizing that it was Jackson's cell number, didn't answer the call. Bedi told the FBI interviewer that he had bad news for the congressman and that he didn't want to tell him that I turned down the attempted bribe. I told the committee that Bedi did, however, return Jackson's call later that day and lied to him by saying that his meeting with me had been canceled.

I also recollected for the committee that Nayak said in his FBI interview that Jackson told him in November 2008 that he, Jackson, knew that Rod was being investigated by the feds for trying to sell the Senate seat. Jackson then asked Nayak if he had discussed money with anyone.

Nayak told him that he had, and Jackson then instructed him not to discuss money again. Jackson had been tipped off about the federal investigation, and, as of this writing, I am not aware of any follow-up by the FBI
to find out who leaked this information to him.

I recalled one other thing from reading Nayak's 302s that I shared with
the committee. Nayak told the FBI that Jackson had told him that he
could use his close relationship with Obama to secure a pardon for Rod
if Rod were charged and convicted of crimes. Neither Nayak nor Bedi
ever mentioned this to me in the conversations we had in October 2008.
Nevertheless, it was clear to me (and it would be to anyone else reading
the 302s) that Jackson was trying hard to entice my brother into accepting his bribe.

In summary, I did my best to tell the committee as accurately as my
memory would allow what I remembered reading in the 302s those many
months before as we prepared for trial. After I left the Longworth Building, I headed straight to the airport, satisfied that I had accomplished
what I had set out to do: telling the committee lawyers that I believed
that Jesse Jackson Jr. was the buyer in a failed attempt to purchase Barack
Obama's vacated Senate seat.

A month after I testified to the Ethics Committee, I spoke to the Chicago Bar Association at the Daley Center in downtown Chicago. I had
been invited to speak about my experience as a criminal defendant in
the most publicized federal case in the history of Illinois. The audience
was filled with a mix of municipal judges, attorneys, media, and staffers
working in the building.

After I finished my presentation, I was greeted by a gaggle of reporters
from local area news stations waiting for me in the lobby (WGN, CBS,
NBC, Fox, and ABC). The media's questions were welcome, as they gave
me a chance to speak about my lingering posttrial frustrations. Among
the questions: Did I visit Rod? How was I doing? And, most notably,
what did I think about Patrick Fitzgerald's resignation?

When I was asked this last question, I didn't hesitate. "I thought it was
a good day for civil liberties." I then spoke generally about the risk to
our liberty when we allow a public servant to hold a position as long
as Fitzgerald. I emphasized it can lead to abuse as it had my case—an
overreaching prosecution of an innocent man. I stated that I believed
Fitzgerald did anything he could to convict my brother, even if it meant
prosecuting me to win.

Coincidentally, as I was answering questions at the Daley Center, Fitzgerald was holding a press conference at the Dirksen Federal Building only a few blocks away to explain his resignation after eleven years as US attorney, and to talk about his time in that position. He had a reputation for being a hard-charging, organized crime–busting purifier of the corrupt Illinois political scene and probably figured that no one, particularly the media, would question his motives and tactics.

The media did, however, ask such questions. In particular, reporters wanted an explanation of Fitzgerald's behavior at the press conference the day of Rod's arrest in December 2008. At that time he had inappropriately announced that he had stopped "a political crime spree" that would "make Lincoln roll over in his grave."

I was glad the press finally brought this up. In my opinion these words, more than any others, undermined our chance to get an impartial jury. For Fitzgerald, though, the thought of having a brother under the threat of prosecution come in, flip on his brother, and give the prosecutors ammunition must have been titillating; he indicted me shortly after he uttered those words.

Fitzgerald's response to the criticism he received for those comments was flippant: "If you're asking if I regret that, it seemed like a good idea at the time, which tells you in all seriousness, I probably could have had a colder shower, a little more sleep, and some decaf."

That same day, Robert Grant, the head of the FBI field office in Chicago, was interviewed. He was asked about Fitzgerald's resignation and my comments to the media about the government's use of me as a pawn to get to my brother.

"This isn't powder-puff. This is about people's lives," said Grant. "This is about getting to the truth. And sometimes getting to the truth takes you through other individuals, and if those individuals are protecting bad public officials and bad characters, brother or not, I think it's fair" (http://abclocal.go.com/kabc/story?section=news/local&id=8675018).

In my case I wasn't protecting my brother—Grant knew that. And it certainly wasn't "powder-puff"; it was intimidation, pure and simple. In my opinion, Fitzgerald and Grant weren't concerned about what was in the interest of justice. They had an agenda to put another Illinois governor in prison. They instead zealously pursued a prosecution of Rod no matter whom they might destroy in the process, even if it was his innocent brother.

Respected and admired by many, Fitzgerald and Grant might represent to some what is best in public service. But if you read their words closely, these two men are the antithesis of good public servants. They are, in my opinion, the personification of a very real threat to our civil liberties. They were guardians of the public trust whom I believe arrogantly dismissed the rights of the people they were charged to serve and protect.

Epilogue

Who wouldn't feel good about resuming life after beating the odds, whatever the threat? I guess I should have, but I didn't. I was one of the rare 4 percent of people to walk away with my freedom after a federal prosecution. Yes, I had my day in court and "in the interest of justice" the prosecutor dropped all of the charges against me. And yes, I did reward my legal team with a "winners bonus." But, unfortunately, I haven't been able to move on as though nothing happened.

I remain frustrated and angry about how I was gratuitously used by my government to serve its agenda. This experience has forever changed my once unwavering, naïve belief that we live under a system of laws that serve the greater good.

Fighting through the ordeal took an enormous toll on my family and me. Someone close to my legal team said that Julie, Alex, and I probably each lost two years of our natural lives as a result of what we'd been through. My already tenuous relationship with my brother is now completely broken, with no immediate prospects for repair. My financial situation is slowly recovering from a hit that should never have been struck. My hard-earned reputation has been irreparably damaged. People have turned me down for loans and business deals because of what's happened to me. The briber, Jesse Jackson Jr., has not been held accountable in this matter. The US attorney and the FBI in Chicago knew that the now disgraced former Congressman Jackson tried to buy the US Senate seat, and they allowed him to get away with a federal crime. And most frustrating, I have no recourse against the US attorney or the FBI for what they needlessly put me through.

A day after the verdict, Mike told me his office got a call from one of the jurors. A young college student whose parents were both in law enforcement, she had said she'd like to speak with me and had left her number. Out of curiosity I called her back. Uncertain what to expect, I was surprised by her maturity and articulateness as she told me she took her civic responsibility seriously as a juror. She said that over the course of the trial, she became disillusioned by what she witnessed in the courtroom and during jury deliberations.

She told me that after I testified she was convinced I had not broken the law and that the government never made a case against me. It didn't make sense to her that an innocent man was on trial. She also stated that her interaction with some of the other jurors—particularly the men— contributed to her disillusionment with the whole experience. She believed they were condescending to the women, trying to intimidate them into changing their votes on verdicts that differed from theirs.

I told her I very much appreciated her reaching out to me with her observations and encouraged her to learn from her jury experience, just as I would try to learn from my experience being a defendant. Both disillusioned from different perspectives, I can only hope she has been able to move on happily with her life while I still try to constructively direct the anger that remains.

Being on trial in federal court is no fun. I've tried to recount many of the experiences with which I had to personally deal as a criminal defendant. However, there is another side to it all, the humanity and kindness extended to me and my family by people who didn't even know us, which helped to sustain us during a difficult time. Nearly every day during the trial strangers on the streets of Chicago, at the grocery, in the shops, at the federal courthouse, and in the neighborhood where we lived went out of their way to wish me well. A special thank you to the staff of the Uptown Starbucks on Wilson and Marigold for their warmth and hospitality each time we went in to escape the pressures of the trial. We were pleasantly surprised the morning we left Chicago to return home to find written on the sides of our coffee cups "Congratulations!" For all those many unexpected kindnesses I will be forever grateful to the people of Chicago.

In short, I wrote this book to record my experience as an innocent man facing the most powerful government in the world as a criminal defendant. I simply wanted to tell the story of how I went from ordinary citizen to citizen fighting for his freedom. I wanted to give the reader the opportunity to step into my shoes to know how I managed to get by and survive being wrongly prosecuted. Let's face it, if the government wants to come after you—whether you are innocent or not—it can do so. And in doing so, it can cost you a small fortune, your reputation, your health, your family, and in many instances your freedom.

RB

Where Are They Now?

Epilogues often include a "where are they now" section. If you've made it this far, you've lived with many of the people with whom I lived during my trip through the looking glass. So here's an update on the cast of characters:

Judge James B. Zagel: He remains a federal judge. He is also a FISA court judge. This court rules on warrants requested by the National Security Agency, FBI, and other federal law enforcement agencies desiring to conduct surveillance of enemies of the state in the USA.

Patrick Fitzgerald: In October 2012 he left his post as US attorney to go into practice at a well-respected national firm that represents high-powered individuals and corporations, some of whom may be defendants in criminal or civil matters. Like many from the US attorney's office, Fitzgerald has walked through the "revolving door," using his experience and reputation to earn a salary reputed to be significantly higher than what he earned as a public servant. It will be interesting to see if in private practice, he represents people and businesses similar to those whom he prosecuted.

Christopher Niewoehner: In July 2012 he, too walked through the revolving door, leaving the US attorney's office to join a large law firm based in Chicago. He is a partner in the White Collar Criminal Defense Practice and probably earning substantially more in private practice. I wonder what percentage of Niewoehner's clients will plead guilty to avoid the inconvenience of a trial.

John Harris: Rod's former chief-of-staff and friend, who made a deal with the government in return for his testimony, received a sentence of ten days for his part in the scheme for which Rod and I were charged.

Harris is currently working as an electrical contractor in the Chicago area. He is trying to get his law license reinstated.

John Wyma: Rod's former close friend and staffer, who cashed in on his relationship with Rod by earning more than a million dollars as a lobbyist, is now living in Washington, DC. He flipped on his friend to became a government informant and received immunity from prosecution in return for his testimony. Wyma was quoted by the All Michigan press while playing in a golf tournament at the Kalamazoo Country Club as saying, "I've actually moved on. I testified at the trial. I've gone forward with my life. I don't know any other way to say it. I'm having a blast." For all of us who were causalities of his treachery, I don't know how Wyma lives with himself.

Zachary Fardon: Wyma's attorney, succeeded Fitzgerald as US Attorney.

Lon Monk: Rod's former friend, law school roommate, and top aide, served a two-year prison sentence. I'm told he served his sentence at the US Penitentiary in Marion, Illinois, a medium-security prison for male inmates. At his sentencing hearing Monk said, "I'm prepared to serve my sentence. I look forward to coming back a better person, husband, father, and friend." He was released from prison in December 2013.

Jesse Jackson Jr.: The man responsible for sending emissaries to buy Obama's vacant Senate seat, resigned from Congress in November 2012 after seventeen years of service. His resignation letter explained that he was suffering from bipolar disorder and acknowledged he was the target of a federal investigation into the possible misuse of campaign funds. In August 2013 Jackson was sentenced to thirty months in federal prison for stealing $750,000 from his campaign fund, after pleading guilty to purchasing an array of personal items and memorabilia and using the money to support his lifestyle. Before climbing into a waiting vehicle after sentencing, Jackson said, "Today I manned up and tried to take responsibility for the error of my ways." I have repeatedly publicly asked Jackson to "man up" and take responsibility for trying to buy a US Senate seat, but he refuses to do so.

Raghu Nayak: In September 2013 Nayak pled guilty in a medical fraud case to charges of bribing doctors to refer patients to surgery centers that he owned and of filing false income tax returns. Standing somberly and speaking in an inaudible voice, Nayak told the judge he had become an alcoholic, stating, "I'm fighting for my life." In January 2014 he was sentenced to serve two years in federal prison.

Rajindar Bedi: In November 2010 Bedi was charged with one count of felony retail theft shoplifting, accused of stealing $166.00 in merchandise from a Home Depot in Chicago. Store security saw Bedi take items without paying. Bond was set at $10,000 at a hearing days after his arrest.

Michael Ettinger: Mike continues to practice criminal law from his Palos Heights office, arriving every day at 7:00 a.m. ready to face the day. We talk once a week and consider each other friends. In October 2014 Julie and I traveled to Marco Island to attend the beach wedding of Mike's daughter, Nicole.

Cheryl Schroeder: Cheryl became disillusioned with federal court and returned to the Cook County States Attorney's Office. She and four of her closet friends came to Nashville in July 2014. One of them was Cindy Rafter, our "jury of one" who asked after the mock trial, "Is that all there is?" We had a great time together touring Music City.

Robyn Molaro: Robyn continues to work for Mike part-time on federal cases, making time to raise her three young children. He tells me she is tough and tenacious as ever fighting on behalf of their clients.

Rod Blagojevich: When Rod was retried in 2011 he was found guilty of seventeen of twenty charges. Judge Zagel sentenced him to fourteen years in federal prison, a sentence that many found excessive. He is currently awaiting the outcome of an appeal submitted on his behalf by his attorneys. Rod and I are estranged and have no contact despite my repeated attempts to reach out to him. I love my brother and always will. It is my hope that with the passage of time we will once again be reunited as brothers. In October 2012 I traveled to Englewood Federal Correctional Institution, fifteen miles southwest of Denver, to visit him. I identified myself to the corrections officer at the front desk and asked to see Rod. He informed me that I would not be allowed to see my brother because Rod had not put me on the visitor list.